RESKILLING AMERICA

RESKILLING AMERICA

Learning to Labor
in the Twenty-First Century

Katherine S. Newman
Hella Winston

Metropolitan Books   Henry Holt and Company   New York

Metropolitan Books
Henry Holt and Company, LLC
Publishers since 1866
175 Fifth Avenue
New York, New York 10010
www.henryholt.com

Metropolitan Books® and ® are registered trademarks of
Henry Holt and Company, LLC.

Library of Congress Cataloging-in-Publication data

Names: Newman, Katherine S., 1953– author. | Winston, Hella, author.
Title: Reskilling America : learning to labor in the twenty-first century / Katherine S. Newman,
    Hella Winston.
Description: First edition. | New York : Metropolitan Books, 2016. | Includes index.
Identifiers: LCCN 2015048810| ISBN 9781627793285 (hardback) | ISBN 9781627793292
    (electronic book)
Subjects: LCSH: Vocational education—United States. | Skilled labor—United States. |
    Occupational training—United States. | Manpower policy—United States. | BISAC:
    SOCIAL SCIENCE / Sociology / General. | POLITICAL SCIENCE / Labor & Industrial
    Relations.
Classification: LCC LC1045 .N49 2016 | DDC 370.1130973—dc23
LC record available at http://lccn.loc.gov/2015048810

Our books may be purchased in bulk for promotional, educational, or business use.
Please contact your local bookseller or the Macmillan Corporate and Premium Sales
Department at (800) 221-7945, extension 5442, or by e-mail at
MacmillanSpecialMarkets@macmillan.com.

First Edition 2016

Designed by Meryl Sussman Levavi

Printed in the United States of America

1 3 5 7 9 10 8 6 4 2

For Jennifer Kalikapersaud—
Small-business wizard and master trainer of her coworkers

You know what's crazy? I got more than 400 people in vocational programs here. . . . I got people training as auto mechanics, in horticulture. This is a bigger vocational school than what we have on the outside. Why do we as a society wait until a guy ends up here before we give him a decent vocational education?

—Burl Cain,
warden of Louisiana's notorious Angola Penitentiary[1]

Contents

RESKILLING AMERICA

Introduction

After decades of off-shoring, downsizing, shuttered factories, and stranded blue-collar workers, the United States is in the midst of something of a manufacturing rebound. General Electric is now producing some appliances and water heaters domestically that were once manufactured overseas because, as their CEO Jeff Immelt explains, "The U.S., on a relative basis, has never been more competitive." GE is sensitive to the new requirements laid down by the retail giant Walmart, which announced that it would begin buying an additional $250 billion in US-made products over the decade that began in 2013.[1] Apple Inc. has promised to invest $100 million to build a Mac product line, also to be assembled in Texas, using components made in Illinois and Florida and equipment built in Kentucky and Michigan.

Energid Technologies Corporation, which moved its manufacturing facilities to India back in 2008, recently repatriated all of its production to Massachusetts after losing patience with tariffs on parts and an "unpredictable Indian bureaucracy." Energid's sales are rising and it needs to increase its production, but it is no longer searching overseas. Burlington, Vermont, looks much better.

"We can really do it from New England," said David Askey, one of the owners. "The thinking has flipped from being 'You must manufacture in China' to 'You have the right infrastructure in place here [at home].'"[2]

Foreign auto companies, from high-end luxury manufacturers like BMW and Mercedes to firms such as Volkswagen and Honda, which produce cars for the rest of us, have set up shop in the Sun Belt states of South Carolina, Alabama, and Tennessee. The old textile companies of the rural South have been replaced by high-tech, or "advanced," manufacturing firms that are attracted to the low-energy, real estate, and labor costs they can find in America's "right to work" states. Indeed, after decades of cheap labor in China replacing American workers, the "Chinese advantage"—China's labor-cost advantage over low-cost states in the United States—has shrunk to 39 percent, making it more cost effective to shorten the supply chain and produce manufactured goods close to the markets where they will be consumed.[3]

Although the number of manufacturing jobs has declined in the United States by about 35 percent since 1980, the expense involved in offshoring has led to something of an about-face. Production is coming back to US soil, where manufacturing is now number six in rank of growth industries. It has added nearly half a million jobs since 2010.[4] We will probably never see all the jobs we lost to cheaper, overseas labor return to our shores. Nonetheless, the manufacturing jobs that *are* growing—which include those for machinists, industrial machinery mechanics, electricians, and computer-controlled machine tool operators—demand more skill and, as a result, command higher pay.

So far, though, these positions have proven hard to fill, even when unemployment is high and millions are searching for work. Drew Greenblatt, a small-businessman interviewed by the *New York Times* in 2012, struggled to find the people he needed to keep his manufacturing business on a growth curve: "Over the past couple of years, we invested in robots to help us win back jobs from China," Greenblatt said. His company, Marlin Steel Wire Products, is based in Baltimore, where it manufactures high-quality sheet metal products for customers like Pfizer, Caterpillar, and Toyota. "Our big problem is that we don't have enough talent to run those machines at off hours," he notes, "which means they sit dormant 70 hours a week when they could be working."

Greenblatt explains that he has five openings for machine operators, positions that don't require college degrees but pay, on average, about $60,000 annually. What candidates do need are skills, like the ability to operate a computer, read a blueprint, and use a caliper.[5] Eighty-two percent of manufacturing companies report that they are in the same position. More than six hundred thousand jobs remain unfilled—a striking 5 percent of all US manufacturing positions.[6] Even jobs whose median wage is as high as $70,000 a year—like Web developers, engineering technicians, expert drafters, computer network support specialists, electrical and electronics engineering technicians, and respiratory therapists[7]—are "going begging." And that is before the graying of the manufacturing labor force creates another three million retirees.[8]

Other sectors of the US economy are gaining ground as well, many of them growing because our population is aging and the looming health care needs that follow are generating new labor demands. Indeed, according to projections from the Bureau of Labor Statistics, personal care and home health aides top the list of jobs with the fastest projected growth, expected to increase by 70 percent between 2010 and 2020. Also on that list are the skilled trades, such as for carpenters, brick masons, block masons, stonemasons, tile and marble setters (and their helpers), as well as for the pipe layers, plumbers, pipefitters, and steamfitters, who will all be needed when the current generation heads into retirement.[9]

Between now and 2018, the fastest-growing occupations will be jobs of this kind, which are considered "middle skill" because—in the American context at least—they require education or training beyond high school but not a four-year degree. Dental hygienists, construction managers, police officers, paralegals, and electricians are all required to have associate's degrees or occupational certificates but not a four-year college education. And from a wage standpoint, many of these jobs are far from second best. In fact, they can launch people into the middle class: According to a report of the Harvard Graduate School of Education entitled *Pathways to Prosperity*, 27 percent of workers with occupational licenses earn more than the average recipient of a bachelor's degree.[10]

To be sure, when it comes to the growth in manufacturing jobs, it's not your father's assembly line. What once required a strong work ethic and the willingness to withstand the heat of the furnace is now a highly mechanized, automated production process. Looking out over the vast expanse of a modern steel mill, there are hardly any people on the shop floor at all. Automation has replaced human workers with preprogrammed machines that can operate twenty-four hours a day without getting tired, at levels of precision that are far superior to what line workers once produced.

As a consequence, the re-shoring of manufacturing is not likely to produce millions of jobs. Ninety-four thousand people working in the steel industry in 2012 produced 14 percent more steel than nearly four hundred thousand workers did in 1980.[11] And as manufacturing comes back to the Rust Belt states, the employees it *does* need will be different from the ones it turfed out in the off-shoring era.

The workers who are finding their way back to America's car factories and steel mills spend their work hours in front of a computer screen. Some need to know how to do simple kinds of computer programming, while others must command aspects of electrical engineering and know how to spot a fault caused by a malfunctioning chip. Robotics is in demand, mechatronics is needed, and the focus on quality control is high on the list of talents that manufacturers are looking for.[12]

Universities are not the right proving ground for most of these workers, whether they are needed in manufacturing, the health care labor force, or skilled trades. The technical know-how and skills they require come out of two-year programs rather than four-year colleges, and the United States has a very weakly developed system for producing that kind of training.

There are robust alternatives in other countries that we can and should adapt to our purposes. We explore one model in depth in chapter 6, where we describe the German system of "dual education," which fuses the classroom experience with on-the-job training. It is enormously successful in "upskilling" that country's labor force. As a result, in a period when the United States faces catastrophically high unemployment rates for young people—verging on 50 percent among inner-city African American men—the Germans boast a youth unemployment rate of 7 percent.[13]

Lest we imagine that the United States is simply incapable of competing with the German human capital "machine," we should remember that we once had a very similar training system in this country. From Aviation High School in Queens, which contributed to the aircraft manufacturing and airline maintenance system of the wartime and postwar years, to Automotive High School (founded in 1923), which did the same for the car industry, our vocational high schools were integral to staffing American industry with the most skilled and productive workforce in the world. Moreover, although ours was a more informal system of workforce training than we find in other parts of the world today, apprenticeship—not classroom instruction—was the most common means of learning how to be a tailor, a hairdresser, and even a lawyer, if we go back far enough in our history.

Why did the United States abandon the kind of practical education that worked so well? We explore that question in chapter 2 with a look at the history of vocational education. We try to explain how and why "career education" faltered, despite dedicated teachers and motivated working-class students. Much of the problem lies at our own feet. The ambivalence that American parents, policy makers, and educational leaders display toward blue-collar life, and the high value they place on white-collar, professional work, have led to some poisonous debates about who is really keeping the best interests of our youth, especially those from low-income households, in mind.

From our perspective, two promises must be made to America's working-class and poor youth. First, we must dedicate ourselves to equality in educational access and to the goal of strengthening K–12 schools that are in trouble. Millions of students, especially in urban areas where poverty and racial segregation have grown, live in regions where the tax base to support quality primary and secondary education has shrunk, the wealthy have departed for the "safety" of the suburbs, and the most qualified teachers are often off-limits. No amount of testing is going to cure those gaps. Students in disadvantaged communities are just as deserving as anyone else of schools that will deepen their understanding of literature, math, science, and history, help to prepare them for the labor market, and provide the foundation for a good life. Policies that underwrite universal educational quality are imperatives we endorse.

But second, and here we depart from many progressives, we cannot ignore the profoundly uneven educational outcomes that are plain to see, and that presently offer few meaningful alternatives that will help today's youth become productive workers with decent jobs. Much as we wish for equal opportunity from pre-K through college, manifestly we are a million miles from that goal. Setting policy goals as if we were already there is a questionable route. Students from working-class and poor communities need options that traditional forms of higher education may not provide, and they need them now, not thirty or forty years hence, when their working lives are in the rearview mirror.

Yet when objections are raised to the most commonly articulated remedy—"college for all"—often a hailstorm of criticism bears down on those who advocate for the vocational alternative. And what is wrong with this approach? Apparently advocates for technical education "reinforce long-standing divisions by social class that funnel students from lower socioeconomic backgrounds disproportionately toward a vocational track, while affording those from higher socioeconomic backgrounds greater access to higher education and the higher incomes that come with it."[14]

Critics who agree with this perspective believe that vocational education will drive the poor into a backwater. News flash: They are already there and have been there since early childhood. Vocational education is not the reason they are boxed in. The legacies of racial segregation, local—and hence highly unequal—funding for schools, differentials in teacher pay, and class size mire them in educational disadvantage long before they enter the gates of their high schools. We urge them on to college, even though the likelihood that they will get there at all or prosper once they arrive is low. For all too many, the more likely outcome is persistent unemployment, low-wage jobs, high levels of incarceration, or enrollment in for-profit colleges that rip them off and leave them in debt up to their eyebrows.

They deserve better. If they could secure the kind of opportunity that vocational programs deliver to young people in other countries, demanding technical education and state-of-the-art training, they might instead be on their way to a reliable income and a stable future.

This does not mean that we should put roadblocks in the way of those who are properly prepared for higher education or that we should abandon the fundamental mission of educational equity that would ensure more students from poor households will be college-ready. On the contrary, we should put every resource we can muster in the hands of students who are likely to prosper in college and then redouble efforts to make sure there are millions more of them. From this perspective, policies put in motion by the Obama administration make good sense. In 2014, the White House issued a call to action on college opportunity[15] and joined with leaders of many institutions of higher education to expand access through increased investment in Pell Grants, college tax credits, and reformation of the student loan system. The University of Massachusetts, Amherst, inaugurated a special scholarship designed to ease the way for community college students who have excelled academically to finish their degrees at the state's flagship, Commonwealth Honors College.

This is all to the good. But it is not the right answer for everyone, as we show in chapter 2. If we limit ourselves to what the White House in 2014 has called "our North Star goal of leading the world in the share of college graduates by 2020," then many of the young people the president and First Lady were looking to help may not actually get ahead.[16] Their adult lives may be better served by robust technical training that will lead them to middle-skill jobs.

These occupations made up 54 percent of all jobs in 2012.[17] And looking ahead, they are expected to constitute 49 percent of all *new* jobs between 2012 and 2022.[18] Indeed, jobs requiring vocational training comprise eighteen of the top thirty jobs expected to grow the fastest between 2010 and 2020.[19]

Georgetown University's Center on Education and the Workforce has examined exactly what kind of middle-skill jobs will grow. Their study suggests that between 2008 and 2018 six career clusters will be especially robust: manufacturing (8 percent); marketing, sales, and service (9 percent); transportation, distribution, and logistics (9 percent); health science (10 percent); business, management, and administration (13 percent); and hospitality and tourism (16 percent).[20]

This job growth will not spread to all parts of the country equally but will vary from one region to another. For example, in San Antonio, Texas, there is a shortage of construction trade workers, due to both an increased emphasis on college attendance and the aging of the current workforce. Construction companies hold job fairs for high school students promoting the value of vocational training and the viability of these trades as a career.[21] High school graduates trained in vocational classes earn about $10 an hour as entry-level plumbers in San Antonio but can progress to running a crew and earning $40,000 to $60,000 a year after only four thousand hours of work. They have to pass a professional test and complete their high school diploma to qualify for an advanced license. But there is a modest pot of gold at the end of that rainbow.

Two other Texas cities—Dallas and Houston—are among the top ten expected to see the most substantial growth in middle-skill jobs by 2017, with Houston projected to add more than one hundred thousand of them, 40 percent of which will pay wages of $20 an hour. Driving that growth is an expected boom in the construction and petrochemical industries, which will call for machinists, pipefitters, and welders. Armed with a two-year degree from a technical college, petrochemical workers can make more than $100,000 a year.

Middle-skill jobs are also projected to boom in New York, Washington State, Los Angeles, Phoenix, Boston, Seattle, Atlanta, and Denver. They will lead the way in overall job growth—accounting for nearly half of all new jobs—in places like Augusta (Georgia), Salt Lake City, Knoxville, and Vallejo (California).[22] Among the states projecting the highest percentage of middle-skill jobs in 2018 are Indiana (54 percent), Arkansas (52 percent), Kentucky (52 percent), West Virginia (52 percent), South Carolina (51 percent), Mississippi (51 percent), and Pennsylvania (51 percent).[23]

In every one of these states but one—Washington—there are more jobs available than there are middle-skill workers to fill them.[24] Seven of the top ten US employers see middle-skill jobs as the most difficult to fill.[25]

To be sure, this "skills mismatch"—in which we have fewer workers than we need in fields that are growing and a glut of people in occupations that are stagnating—is not unique to middle-skill workers. Some states—most notably southern and traditional Rust Belt states—have substantially more low-skill workers than low-skill jobs, while others—particularly those in the Northeast—have more high-skill workers than high-skill jobs. And then there are those states, like California, that have both more low- and high-skill workers than the market demands.[26]

Workers qualified for middle-skill jobs will find thousands of them on offer in American firms, but many job hunters will seek their fortunes in foreign subsidiaries. Some of these foreign firms, having concluded that they cannot rely on the schools in the United States to train the labor force they need, are re-creating the apprenticeship programs familiar to them in their home countries. In chapter 6, we look closely at the German manufacturing companies that are setting up shop in Tennessee and South Carolina and are exporting the insights they have learned in the Southeast to Michigan, Kentucky, and the northern tier of New York.

To build these new training systems, foreign manufacturers have sought to form alliances with the part of the local education system that is best suited to this kind of collaboration: community and technical colleges. These institutions play a double role in the American system of higher education: They increase access to four-year degrees by lowering the cost of education for the first two of those years. Even more important, community and technical college vocational programs provide the foundational skills training that young people need to find their way into middle-skill jobs and mature workers seek when they need retraining to prepare for a career change. Overseas, this role is often fulfilled by high schools.

The United States is belatedly recognizing the importance of the community college system. In the recent past, it has actually been made harder for community colleges to fulfill this mission: Their funding has been cut drastically over the past ten years.[27] In Arizona, for example, the governor cut 100 percent of state funding to its two largest community colleges in 2015. Smaller state colleges in the Midwest, especially Wisconsin and Illinois, which provide vital training opportunities, have been cut off at the knees as their Republican governors seek to close budget deficits at the expense of higher education.

Those states will pay a high price for these shortsighted moves. Building a skilled workforce in the twenty-first century is going to require more, rather than less, targeted investment in training institutions. The National Skills Coalition points to more enlightened governors in states like Florida, Iowa, Missouri, and Pennsylvania, who know that a prosperous future depends on fostering human capital:

> These governors targeted middle-skill training for increased investments, including proposals to provide support for employer-led sector partnerships, to align the state's workforce system, to make technical and community college affordable, and to assist the long-term unemployed back to work.
>
> They are eager to see resources put into the hands of people who have suffered through the Great Recession.[28]

Parallel action is needed on the federal level, as President Obama was well aware. In July 2014, he signed into law the Workforce Innovation and Opportunity Act, "the first legislative reform in 15 years of the public workforce system." Its purpose was to "help job seekers access employment, education, training and support services to succeed in the labor market and to match employers with the skilled workers they need to compete in the global economy." But most of the WIOA was addressed to the needs of the nation's most disadvantaged workers and it did more to provide them with temporary support than equip them with the skills needed for the better jobs on offer. WIOA funded "one stop" career centers, youth programs, adult literacy programs, vocational rehabilitation for disabled adults, and programs for "vulnerable populations," from the Job Corps to migrant and seasonal farmworker programs.

This remedial approach certainly helps those most in need, but it will not provide for a competitive workforce.[29] The United States is "third from last" in its spending on labor market preparation compared to its European counterparts. What is worse, the funding provided is used to enroll people "in expensive training courses for careers with poor employment prospects or . . . low pay." This is why the *New York Times* concluded that "many graduates wind up significantly worse off than when they started—mired in unemployment and debt from training for positions that do not exist, and they end up working elsewhere for the minimum wage."[30]

We would do better to figure out how to avoid that abyss in the first place. To do so, we must take another look at the kind of educational system we once embraced when the United States was more committed to technical education. In the 1930s, we laid a foundation under this kind of training in the nation's high schools that enabled millions of Americans to find steady jobs and an ascent into the middle class. To get back to that point, parents and policy makers will need to understand that the traditional college route may not provide the job security that it once guaranteed the nation's youth.

Young people themselves will have to rediscover the respect we once accorded middle-skilled occupations. The family wage they provide is the answer to many of the problems of structural unemployment and high poverty that millions of inner-city residents have experienced for the past thirty years. They need bridges to somewhere, not bridges to nowhere. Rigorous, demanding vocational education, coupled with shop floor experience in the form of apprenticeship, fit that bill.

1

The Limits of the "College Solution"

Booker T. Washington, distinguished graduate of Hampton Normal and Agricultural Institute, founding president of the Tuskegee Institute, is remembered today as the man who lost a great debate with his arch-rival, W. E. B. Du Bois, champion of civil rights and advocate for the "talented tenth" among African Americans. In his well-known "Atlanta Address," Washington argued that black people less than one generation away from slavery would succeed in a racially polarized world only by pulling themselves up by their own bootstraps through "industry, thrift, intelligence and property." Always the great compromiser, Washington was willing to abandon the quest for the vote, tolerate segregation and discrimination, and refrain from campaigning against racist behavior in exchange for his highest priority: a free basic education for blacks. Training the hands, not the mind, was, he thought, the most expedient way to deliver African Americans from abject poverty. Accordingly, the "Atlanta compromise" proposed limiting blacks to vocational or industrial training, leaving the liberal arts off-limits.

Du Bois and his ally, William Monroe Trotter, utterly rejected Washington's stance, vigorously supported a crusade for civil rights, and insisted that African Americans should pursue a classical education so that they would be prepared to take their place among the nation's leaders.[1] Industrial training of the kind that Booker T. Washington urged would spell a lifetime of subordination. Instead, black elites needed to set their sights as high as possible, an aspiration Du Bois embraced as the first African American recipient of a Harvard doctorate. "Men, we shall have only as we make manhood the object of the work of the schools," Du Bois wrote.

> Intelligence, broad sympathy, knowledge of the world that was and is, and of the relation of men to it—this is the curriculum of that Higher Education which must underlie true life. On this foundation, we may build bread winning, skill of hand and quickness of brain, with never a fear lest the child and man mistake the means of living for the object of life.[2]

The dispute between Washington and Du Bois underlies the quandary we face today: Will the nation's "truly disadvantaged" prosper more if we insist that the right goal is to cultivate the mind through abstract ideas, through education for its own sake, and to secure access to the universal pursuit of the highest credentials? Or does it make more sense to dwell on the practical and ensure that at the end of the day there is a trade, a skill, a viable occupation to be had? When progressive critics in our own time attack vocational education for prematurely tracking the poor toward less prestigious jobs, while advocates for career and technical training push back in favor of pragmatism, we are replaying the debate that began with Washington and Du Bois.

In its own time, the "talented tenth" strategy was not directed toward the needs of the masses. As Henry Louis Gates Jr. reminds us, Du Bois was concerned above all with producing leadership for black America, with finding those "few gifted souls" who had the potential to become "an uncrowned king in his sphere."[3] This was not Booker T's issue. He was thinking about the economic fate of the other nine-tenths. As Washington put the matter, "The opportunity to earn a dollar in a factory just now is worth infinitely more than the opportunity to spend a dollar in an opera house."[4] He argued that industrial education would benefit his people, and he traded away almost everything else in favor of support for this ambition.

Du Bois carried the day. But his emphasis on the aspirations and cultivation of elites faded away in favor of a universal call to open the doors of educational institutions, provide employment opportunities, desegregate housing, and guarantee the right to vote. Everyone should be able to seek a spot among the ranks of the talented tenth. Accommodating to inequality—as Washington was prepared to do in the name of economic security—was unacceptable. Upward mobility into the professions was the path toward respect.

White America did not see the world so differently. Class intruded everywhere. Blue-collar work paid well, at least during the heyday of industrial unions, but it was not a source of pride. In David Halle's book on New Jersey chemical company employees, *America's Working Man*, a line worker instructs his eight-year-old kid to wave the father's paycheck in front of his second-grade teacher and ask whether she had anything to say for herself. On the defensive, the blue-collar dad argued that his money trumped her prestige. But it was a hollow stance since the status hierarchy was clear enough. Richard Sennett's landmark book, *The Hidden Injuries of Class*, draws a poignant portrait of working-class parents who watch with pride as their children go far enough in school to qualify for clean jobs, in banks or office buildings, but he records their private anguish when their offsprings' success stories leave the family behind. Parents imagine their children are ashamed of their roots, hence the upward mobility of the next generation translates into a rebuke and estrangement as much as it does a celebration of success.

On both sides of the race divide, the emphasis on upward mobility reserved self-respect to the white-collar world. That was the goal and it remains so today. The route to the American dream, then, runs right through the gates of the university and into entrepreneurship or the professions. There are few victories short of that end goal. And that helps to account for the trenchant attacks on vocational education as an alternative. To critics, it signals a capitulation to lower status and a denial of the chance for those born among the "truly disadvantaged" to surmount their origins and move up the ladder.

If we inhabited level playing fields, these universal aspirations would make sense and the critique would be warranted. If everyone had a fair shot at such a future, the talented tenth could indeed multiply. But the fields have never been level and have become less so every year since 1973, when economic inequality began to grow rapidly in the United States. As a result, what actually happens to young people coming out of weak schools in poor neighborhoods is that they struggle to reach even the most modest goals and end up unable to lay claim on economic stability at all.

The College Experience for the Poorly Prepared

The United States has made significant strides in stemming the tide of high school dropouts. As recently as 2000, the high school dropout rate for Hispanic students age eighteen to twenty-four was 33 percent. Today it is down to 14 percent. Black students have followed a similar trajectory as their dropout rates fell from 16 to 8 percent.[5] While these numbers are still too high, there is a lot to cheer about in the trends. Moreover, since college attendance is very high among high-school graduates—nearly 86 percent go on to some form of higher education—it would seem the message of "college for all" has reached the ears of the American youth of all colors.

College completion is an entirely different story. The higher education system in America is characterized by widespread access to college but a low rate of degree completion. After graduation, many high school students proceed immediately to college (68 percent in recent cohorts), but many of them do not complete their degree programs after they enter: Only 63 percent of entrants to four-year colleges complete a bachelor's degree in six years.[6] As a result, as of 2014, only 34 percent of twenty-five to twenty-nine-year-olds had at least a bachelor's degree; and 8 percent have an associate's degree.[7] Why do we lose so many along the way?

Inadequate preparation for the challenges of college is one of the most powerful reasons for attrition. Students coming out of weak high schools often lack the background to succeed in college, even when they have done everything their high schools asked of them. During the years when Katherine served as a dean at Johns Hopkins University, she occasionally heard from high school administrators in Baltimore who wanted her students to tutor promising public school students for advanced placement (AP) examinations. JHU undergraduates readily respond to these requests to help Baltimore teens prepare for the demanding exams, which are supposed to certify successful completion of college-level courses in everything from calculus to English literature. High school leaders noted with pride that the students enrolled in the tutoring program were receiving grades of 95 and above. Yet on the AP exams, these same kids would often receive the lowest possible scores. With marks of 1 or 2 (out of a possible 5), they could not signal to colleges that they were high-achieving. Locally, these students were high performers. When placed alongside their national peers, they were floundering. The preparation they received in the only high schools available to them simply was not strong enough even for the best of the students.

The Baltimore experience is repeated in many of the nation's urban centers. The City University of New York, the largest public university system in the United States, has grown increasingly concerned about the ability of students entering from New York public high schools to master its curriculum. Since 1999, students entering CUNY as first-time freshmen are required to take proficiency examinations before enrolling in any of the four-year colleges. There is good reason to worry: Nearly 50 percent fail at least one entrance exam and are required to take a remedial class. Indeed, it would appear that the entire city high-school system, which increased its graduation rates to an admirable 61 percent in 2010, is struggling to ensure its students are prepared for college-level work. Seventy public high schools earned the highest marks within the city's assessment system and a third of their graduates attend CUNY colleges. Yet well over half of these schools "posted remediation rates above 50 percent."[8]

CUNY's problems are repeated across the country. Sixty-eight percent of students beginning at public two-year colleges in 2003–2004 took one or more remedial courses in the six years after their initial entry.[9] Heroic and costly efforts are under way to make up for what these high school graduates lack, but remedial classes are often too little and too late to make a sufficient difference. So much of what college students need to master is cumulative: If their command of multiplication is shaky, algebra will be extremely difficult and calculus completely out of range. For those whose reading comprehension is weak or writing skills poorly developed, virtually everything they face in college—from passing exams to writing research papers—will be an uphill battle. The success rates of remedial education are low.[10]

As Nobel Prize–winning economist James Heckman has shown, we would do far better as a nation to invest heavily in first-rate, universal pre-school and K–3 to better ensure that children start out with solid fundamental skills. If we wait until students are in their late teens and early twenties, we are looking at significant deficits that are both difficult and costly to remedy. This translates directly into dropouts.

For the thousands of low-skilled students who determine it is worth it to try to get through college, the pain in the pocketbook is substantial, just to get to the starting point. They have to spend several semesters plowing through remedial courses that do not count toward degrees. Low-income students end up spending much of the financial aid they have been awarded to cover these "preclasses," which means they are paddling hard before they have even begun. Many run out of money long before their degrees are done.

As the advocacy group Complete College America has shown, less than 10 percent of the low-income students who start community college in remedial courses complete an AA degree in three years. Many don't even get to start a real college program: They get bogged down at the remedial end and exhaust their funding. Only 19 percent of students in the bottom quarter (measured by test scores in high school) will finish a college degree in six years. Most drop out, at least for a time.

The longer students take to complete a degree, the more likely it is that they face the need to balance the competing demands of parenthood and work alongside schooling. As Katherine discovered in her studies of fast-food workers in Harlem during the 1990s, many young adults stick to their educational ambitions against all odds. They juggle this load because they have imbibed the message that the key to a better life is a college degree. They work for periods, return to class, drop out to earn money again, pick up a class when they can. After all, they have to finance college out of modest earnings and take full financial responsibility for their children at the same time.

Paul Attewell and David Lavin followed a sample of women who entered New York City's public universities in the 1970s under their open admissions policy and showed that many of these low-performing students do eventually complete a degree, and it is worth their while to finish.[11] Their incomes exceed the pay of college dropouts and their children benefit from the educational investments of their parents.[12] But that time gap is long—often more than fifteen years—and that delay adds up to thousands of dollars in forgone wages.

The For-Profit Boondoggle

Student debt adds to the pressure to leave college. It has been mounting steadily among students in public and private universities. But nowhere is the student debt burden more troubling than that part of the higher education industry that is truly a business, one that is making a killing from federal government loan programs. The University of Phoenix, Kaplan University, Argosy University, and DeVry University, followed by a series of tuition-guzzling schools whose names were crafted to confuse: Brown College, Berkeley College, and Virginia College came into existence in the 1990s. They have been growing by leaps and bounds ever since. Subways, buses, and cable channels are plastered with ads from these schools, which charge thousands of dollars for an education that claims to prepare students for good careers but ends up—more often than not—leaving them with credentials that have little purchase in the job market and a legacy of sky-high debt. And this is the best case, when students actually complete their degrees. Thousands never do.

The for-profit colleges represent only 13 percent of the nation's college student population, but they constitute nearly one-third of the people who take out student loans and nearly half of those who ultimately default.[13] Sadly, it is precisely these students who can least afford the debt. "Low-income students—between the ages of 18 and 26 and whose total household income is near or below the poverty level—are more likely to be *overrepresented* at for-profit institutions and are *underrepresented* at public and private four-year institutions."[14] This problem is only getting worse. Between 2000 and 2008, the poorest students increased their presence in for-profit schools from 12 percent to 19 percent and they shied away from public four-year institutions in record numbers.[15]

In 2010, Katherine, along with Rourke O'Brien, authors of *Taxing the*

Poor, interviewed desperately poor residents of dilapidated trailers parked on scrubland in rural Alabama and ramshackle houses in crime-ridden neighborhoods of cities like Birmingham. In an effort to find a way out of this grinding poverty, several of the mothers they met had signed up with online colleges that advertise four-year degrees, in the hope of finding jobs as clerical workers that would be steady enough to improve their families' lot. One of them, Beatrice Coleman, had already taken out $40,000 in loans to finance a four-year degree in medical billing, believing that she would qualify someday for a job paying $15 an hour. Even if Bea were lucky enough to land the job of her dreams, it would be decades before she could pay off the loans. But to this disabled mother of two, the degree seemed to her to be the best option. And besides, her for-profit college was so "eager to help" that they processed her loans almost overnight and made sure Bea was always moving on to the next class, which, naturally, would cost her more in tuition (and loans).

Ninety percent of the funding that goes to support the for-profit education sector comes from federal government–backed student grants and loans. Clever and politically savvy manipulators of the Pell Grant system, which was created by Congress to support the educational needs of low-income students, the for-profits have become junkies for government spending.[16] In fact, half of for-profit college students receive government-funded Pell Grants, and those students make up 20 percent of Pell Grant recipients—despite the fact that the schools serve only 6 percent of the country's student population.[17] By law, this kind of debt cannot be discharged in bankruptcy proceedings and hence people like Bea who do not find jobs that enable them to pay these loans back will be hounded by collection agencies for the rest of their days.

It took Congress many years to catch on to the fact that these debt factories were soaking unsuspecting students as well as the American taxpayer by encouraging weak applicants to take out federal loans to finance for-profit degrees. As the Pew Charitable Trust has noted, "Student loan debt is now the largest form of consumer debt outside of mortgages."[18] "Nationwide, about 38 million people owe nearly $1.2 trillion in student loans, more than double from $550 billion in late 2007. Of those, 7 million borrowers are in default."[19]

This financial morass might be worth the cost if for-profit students could expect a payoff in the labor market. Unfortunately, the track record of this kind of higher education is problematic.[20] The Department of Education found that 72 percent of these programs[21] "produced graduates who earned less, on average, than high school dropouts, compared to 32 percent of graduates from public non-profit programs. Not only are these students sold a bill of goods, they are paying dearly. Those who take out federal loans have all the protections that the government has provided for; but millions of for-profit students are in debt to private lenders and they have none of those safeguards to rely on."[22]

Military veterans are also targeted by for-profits, a problem that came to the attention of Senator Tom Harkin's Committee on Health, Education, Labor and Pensions. In 2010 it released a devastating report on the voracious appetite of these institutions for GI bill funds.[23] By law, no one is allowed to receive more than 90 percent of their financial aid from the federal government, except military veterans. For-profit companies recognized a valuable loophole and went after the veteran market with a vengeance. The result, according to Senator Harkin's report, is that "between 2006 and 2010, combined VA and DoD (Department of Defense) benefits received by 20 for-profit education companies increased from $66.6 million . . . to a projected $521.2 million . . . an increase of 683 percent." The report concludes that "Congress may have unintentionally subjected this new generation of veterans to the worst excesses of the for-profit industry: manipulative and misleading marketing campaigns, educational programs far more expensive than comparable public or non-profit programs, and a lack of needed services."[24]

Superior marketing alone cannot explain the appeal of the for-profit sector. The industry attracts the attention of low-income students because they focus on something they want and need: practical degrees. For-profits are not trying to snag English majors or chemistry students. Instead, they advertise programs that seem to have direct application to jobs. When Bea was lured to Virginia University, it was for a program in medical billing. A decent community college or a technical program should not need more than six months to teach someone like Bea the ins and outs of billing. Yet four years later and thousands of dollars in debt, Bea was still laboring away online, hoping to complete a degree that would enable her to pull her family above the poverty line.

The very best of the for-profit colleges are actually expert at providing technical training and do quite well at placement. Sadly, there are far more fly-by-nights, from Corinthian College to Anthem Education to BioHealth College, many of which are now collapsing into bankruptcy, leaving their hapless students in the lurch. By the time their students realize they have been duped, it is too late: They will be paying off those huge loans, against which they cannot declare bankruptcy, until they are very old.

Who Sees a Payoff?

On average, a college graduate will earn $1 million more than a high school graduate over the course of a working life. The gap has been growing over time so that today the median earnings of workers with bachelor's degrees are 65 percent higher than those of high school graduates.[25] This is the reason why so many advocate for "college for all."

Yet underneath those numbers lies a long list of particulars that alter the picture: Earnings have skyrocketed for certain groups of college graduates, but not for all of them. Young people with credentials in computer programming and engineering are riding high. Their talents are sought after by many companies; they can expect multiple job offers and high salaries even as newly minted BSs. We seem never to have enough of them and hence, periodically, employers in Silicon Valley and Cambridge implore Congress to liberalize visa requirements so that more foreign workers with STEM credentials (that is, science, technology, engineering, and mathematics) can come to work in the United States.

Yet there are also degree holders working in retail, or as clerical staff, or even as teacher's aides, and these people are not earning enough to justify what they have spent on their education. Liberal arts or general studies majors can expect a starting salary of $36,988, but often not in the field of their choice. Their jobs may not lead to anything better. The Department of Education "calculated the percentage of students at each college who earned more than $25,000 per year, which is about what high school graduates earn" in an effort to provide consumers with an understanding of the value (or lack of value) of their expenditures on higher education. "At hundreds of colleges, less than half of students crossed this wage mark 10 years after enrolling."[26] According to one calculation by economists at Northeastern and Drexel Universities, in 2011 more than 50 percent of BA holders under twenty-five years of age were out of work or underemployed.

Diplomas pay off handsomely when they are in scarce supply relative to the demand for them. Once credentials become ubiquitous, the danger of oversupply looms. And that moment comes much sooner in periods of deep economic downturn like the Great Recession of 2008–10. When labor markets are "loose" and there are too many qualified people hunting for too few jobs, the result is underemployment and wage losses for many workers. Those who are at the top of the heap do better than those at the bottom, of course, but they can still suffer a significant degree of downward mobility.

Between 2000 and 2014, college-educated workers were increasingly likely to find jobs in low earning industries rather than high earning ones. This "filtering down" is more pronounced when we focus on college grads who moved into the labor market recently.[27] These unfortunate facts suggest that a college degree is less predictive of high earning employment than it once was in part because the labor market has been in such a weak recovery since the Great Recession and because BAs are becoming so common. The greatest wage gains in recent years have nearly all gone to those with more education than a BA, especially to those with master's degrees.

The Federal Reserve Bank of New York argues that we are in exactly that situation now: A large and increasing proportion of the nation's college graduates are working in jobs that "don't require their degree and pay less than $45,000 a year."[28] In 2010, the Bureau of Labor Statistics estimated that about 17,000,000 college graduates were working at jobs requiring less than the skill levels associated with a bachelor's degree. At the time, almost 320,000 waiters and waitresses had college degrees and more than 8,000 of them had postgraduate degrees. More than 80,000 bartenders and 18,000 parking lot attendants were also college graduates.[29]

Those overqualified grads are bumping down into occupations that used to be populated by people without degrees. The less credentialed could, no doubt, do the jobs since they are the people who used to have them. Some would argue that the well-educated workers will be more productive and hence employers are right to court them for jobs that used to require only a high school degree, especially if they can hire them for next to nothing. But a general deceleration of wages hurts everyone and big disparities between scarce fields and well-stocked ones create a two-tiered labor market in which graduates of elite institutions prosper and degree holders from more modest ones flounder.

Although a weakened economy has highlighted this problem, oversupply was in evidence some time ago, well before the Great Recession took its toll. College grads have seen only a 1 percent increase in their average hourly wages over the last decade. They appear to be much better off largely because workers without degrees have experienced a precipitous decline, seeing average hourly wages drop 5 percent. As Lawrence Michel, president of the Economic Policy Institute, told the *New York Times*, "Wage growth essentially stopped in 2002."[30] The relative position of college grads is higher, but in absolute terms they are finding this economy tough sledding.

Technical credentials often represent a better investment. As Anthony Carnevale, director of the Georgetown University Center on Education and the Workforce, has pointed out, they may be the "fastest, cheapest way to get a job that pays."[31] One million of these certificates were awarded in 2010 alone, 22 percent of all the higher education credentials given that year. Auto mechanics, drafting, electronics—these are the fields certified by community and technical colleges. Their prospects for strong earnings are often better than many college graduates'. For example, men who work in computer and information services earned about $72,500 in 2010, wages that are higher by 54 percent than the average of men who hold bachelor's degrees. Women in the same field earn less than their male counterparts, but at $56,500, they outearn 64 percent of women with BAs.[32]

One might imagine that with these examples of success before us, it would be easier to invest public resources in career and technical training. What stops us from doing so? One of the most trenchant critics of "college for all," Northwestern University sociologist Jim Rosenbaum, argues that one of the reasons we are falling behind on career education is that we just don't believe in it. We have put all of our eggs in a single, one-size-fits-all basket: We encourage all students to attend college rather than preparing any of them for work. We follow the example of W. E. B. Du Bois rather than the advice of Booker T. Washington.

Harvard's *Pathways to Prosperity* report argues that students need exposure to work opportunities and that the emphasis on placing everyone in college has been a failure. Coming from an indisputably authoritative source, the report provoked a furious response from advocates of college for all on the grounds that what was being proposed was nothing more than a dumping ground. Kati Haycock, president of the Washington, DC, think tank Education Trust, which focuses on closing achievement gaps, and a major player in the No Child Left Behind Act, was incandescent over the Harvard report. "Most schools still resist the idea that all kids can and should be college ready," she argued.

> By continuing long-standing, unfair practices of sorting and selecting, they create what is essentially an educational caste system—directing countless young people, especially low income and students of color, away from college-prep courses and from seeing themselves as college material.

Haycock seems to suggest that people who advocate for alternatives are prepared to sell children short because they are black or brown. Anything less than college for all, from her perspective, smacks of prejudice and a defense of educational inequality.

Because this criticism stings, particularly those on the left, it has diminished progressive support for alternatives that are desperately needed by those same countless American youth, who are indeed victims of an educational caste system and have been left without career prospects that could lift them and their future children out of poverty. The notion that we should turn away from the dire consequences of the educational disaster unfolding in inner-city America and trust in the power of the college ideal is an irresponsible position as long as the pathway to college is strewn with so many obstacles.

Moreover, it draws upon a different kind of prejudice: biases against careers that utilize the kind of intelligence and skill it takes to program a huge high-speed precision lathe, determine the cause of a plumbing problem, or spot a mistake in a drug dose in a hospital ward. This kind of talent built a booming nation and was once the bedrock of a proud blue-collar working class, whose unions organized for good wages. As a country, we stood in collective admiration of their achievements written in stone, glass, and metal. The United States was a mighty industrial power in the past and could be one again, but not until we find it in ourselves to respect what workers produce as much as we admire lawyers, doctors, or Silicon Valley computer wizards.

Modern manufacturers in the newly reindustrializing states are looking for people who can work with their hands and their heads, and they are having a hard time finding enough of them. In the meantime, thousands of young men and women are stuck in impoverished ghettos and rural backwaters where they cannot find jobs. Their families need them to earn a decent living. Why should they be left with no avenue to qualify for these opportunities when their counterparts in other countries—who want jobs in the trades and don't find college appealing—can choose from among multiple offers from companies prepared to pay them well? The answer is clear: Americans should be able to grab the same brass ring and compete for middle-skill jobs that do not require a four-year degree but do require advanced technical training.

Such a future will not unfold unless the country recognizes and then invests in the kind of schooling and advanced training necessary to make it a reality. And that, in turn, depends on recognizing that a four-year college is not the right goal for everyone.

2

A History of Ambivalence

Melissa Taylor[1] attended Sheepshead Bay High School in Brooklyn, graduating in 1997. The school had long had its share of problems. Across the street from a large, low-rise housing project, Sheepshead Bay had a reputation as "an unsafe dumping ground for troubled kids."[2] From 2000 to 2005, the school had a new principal every year. By 2004 the New York City Board of Education designated it an Impact School, which meant it was considered so dangerous that it needed special security. The most talented students in the neighborhood stayed well away, migrating to nearby Leon Goldstein High School for the Sciences, Midwood High in Flatbush, or Murrow in Midwood, known for its theater program. Ordinary Brooklyn kids, students like Melissa, were left behind at Sheepshead Bay.

Despite its discouraging history, the school managed to remain open through the 2000s by taking a comprehensive approach to the students' many social problems. There were 7 social workers; 10 guidance counselors, 5 police officers, 17 safety agents and 10 deans.[3] A peer mediation program (with a full-time mediator) handled 780 incidents of violence in

2010–11. (In 2013, the city began the process of "phasing out" Sheeps-head Bay. The process will be completed in 2016.) During the years that Melissa attended this school, the statistics were pretty much the same.

Melissa is an only child. Her parents are still married, but they have not lived under the same roof for years. Melissa's father owns his own limo business and her mother, now disabled, is retired. Melissa has lived alone with her mother since high school; she bears a heavy burden as the sole caregiver. As she has grown older, Melissa has experienced the desperation that many feel when tending the chronically ill. But she is a pragmatic person, not someone with a lot of grand dreams. She puts one foot in front of the next and always has.

When Melissa entered Sheepshead Bay, college was not on her mind. To the extent that she had ambitions, they revolved mostly around her social life. A popular girl in high school, she knew how to enjoy herself. Her memories of school are pleasant overall, but few of them have anything to do with schoolwork. She spent her time hanging out with friends and skipping class, though nothing Melissa did caught the attention of the principal's office. Her lack of focus was unremarkable at Sheepshead Bay, although her attitude wasn't universal. There were honors classes and students preparing for AP exams. Melissa just wasn't among them. They were the unusual ones, though. She was average.

Melissa can recall a couple of teachers she was fond of and one or two who offered her advice. But during most of her teenage years she was simply disengaged from the world of school and the studying it entailed. She didn't hate the place; she was just passing the time. In this, Melissa's experience was not unlike that of millions of American students for whom high school is an institution to endure rather than a proving ground.

It was not until her senior year that Melissa got involved in a few extra-curricular activities, like the yearbook and newspaper. At that late date, Melissa recalled, she suddenly realized that she might not have much to say for herself if a future employer asked her about her accomplishments or if she changed her mind about college. But her involvement was more of a hedge than a commitment.

What Melissa did care about was making some money, and she was motivated to do so. Like thousands of working-class young people, Melissa had a job throughout her high school years.[4] She started as a sales clerk in a jewelry store in the nearby mall. She was reliable, hardworking, and reveled in her adult responsibilities. This was her real calling, she reasoned. At the store, she mattered. Earning a living distracted her from schoolwork, but it seemed more real to Melissa. What's more, her earnings boosted her credibility among her friends. Melissa even had enough "juice" to work some magic for her buddies who wanted jobs as well. She maneuvered two of them into jobs in the jewelry store where they worked for her quite happily.

Being a store clerk was not a real career, though. There wasn't much Melissa could do to advance and after a while, especially after being promoted to manager soon after graduation, she started to chafe against the limits of her job. She tried looking for something better but floundered. For the next eight years, Melissa cycled into and out of various office manager jobs. She is good at running an office, but as a career path it feels like more of a default than a choice.

In the decade after she graduated from Sheepshead Bay High School, Melissa had had only one job that she genuinely felt was exciting. She started a side business during her jewelry store years promoting bands and concerts. It was a bit of a lark, helping out friends who had formed a band. But it was a reasonably successful enterprise that gave her experience with marketing companies and concert venues. Event advertising was something Melissa was good at, too, something she enjoyed that could be a career rather than just a job. Though she is not a big risk taker, Melissa decided to take the plunge. She left her office job and turned all of her attention to promoting. It worked for roughly three years, but then the work began to dry up. Reluctantly, Melissa backtracked to the mundane world of office management.

Melissa now feels trapped by not having gone to college, but she believes it is too late for her to change course. And school was never really her passion anyway. She liked working. Maybe if she had had more opportunities to develop practical, "real world" skills in high school, Melissa would have been able to set herself on a career path that played to her strengths, with much less likelihood of finding herself, at age twenty-seven, without of any sense of possibility, convinced that nothing in her life will change with time. There were no plausible options of that kind at Sheepshead Bay because its general high school curriculum just did not offer meaningful career training or technical options.

At fourteen, Wesley Buress ventured out of a rough neighborhood not unlike the one Melissa came from. The options for high school within his assigned zone were not appetizing. Assaults in the school hallways and on the streets were common. Intimidation was part of the landscape, since gangs were always in the mix. Fundamentally, when he started the search for a school, all Wesley wanted was a place where he would be safe.

Born in Jamaica, the eldest of three, Wesley moved to New York with his father. His mother and siblings stayed in Jamaica and remain there today. She works from home as a seamstress. Wesley's father works in the facilities department of a co-op management company in Queens.

Ever since he was a little kid, Wesley had been a "flying nut," crazy about airplanes. Sharing his passion with a junior-high guidance counselor led him to enroll at Aviation High School in Queens. Accredited by the Federal Aviation Administration (FAA), the school boasts the largest program of its kind in the United States. High school students train for FAA certification in either airframe or power plant maintenance while taking a full academic program.

Wesley was originally interested in being a pilot but when he got to Aviation High he found he had to abandon that plan. To pursue it would have required enrolling in an extra-credit after-school program that required an additional tuition payment he couldn't afford. The closest course of study he could find that didn't cost more was one that focused on airplane mechanics. Still, Wesley figured he could at least train for a job that would put him around airplanes all day long, and that was appealing.

Unlike the school Wesley would have attended in the Bronx, Aviation was a very safe environment, full of kids who took the program seriously. It was huge: twenty-five hundred students, about one hundred of whom were women. But the students were so focused and enthusiastic about what they were learning, Wesley felt energized. His classes ran him through math and science, history and literature—the Regents curriculum for New York State. But there was a sense of purpose in the air and an occupational destination to dream about, which cultivated a school culture that was enveloping in the most positive way. That climate made it easy for Wesley to make good friends while at Aviation; most of the people he is close to these days were kids he went to school with back then. His best buddies were Aviation students who lived in the Bronx and shared the two-hour trip to and from school every day.

After graduation, Wesley was somewhat at sea about what he should do next. But because his high school experience was focused rather than diffuse, and the advice he got from peers and teachers was specific rather than general, he was much better prepared to make a good choice than Melissa was. He enrolled in the College of Aeronautics in Queens, which had a partnership with Aviation High that enabled Wesley to transfer seventy-two of his credits toward his degree. That put him two years ahead, with only two more years necessary to earn a valuable certificate as a full-fledged aircraft mechanic. Like Melissa, Wesley had little interest in an academic track. But unlike Melissa, his high school experience had trained him in a set of specialized skills that both held his interest and cleared a pathway for him to a field that paid a good living.

Wesley has been working as a technician for what was Continental Airlines (which merged with United Airlines in 2010) at Kennedy International Airport for the past decade. When he began this job he was assigned the graveyard shift, but over the years, he has graduated to a day shift. When he gets to work at two p.m., he is assigned to cover a number of gates. He checks the aircraft logs of the planes that come in and talks with the pilots to figure out whether they experienced any mechanical problems with their planes. If they did, or if there are discrepancies between the log and what the pilots report, Wesley and his team do what it takes to remedy the situation.

Wesley's job is demanding and important; the detective work involved in diagnosing and repairing complex pieces of machinery taxes him mentally. Although his labor isn't visible to the public and is unsung, he knows that it has to be done right or a lot of people will pay the price. This responsibility makes Wesley proud of what he does with his head and his hands. And having the freedom and flexibility to manage the work on his own is also something he appreciates.

Wesley hadn't planned to remain a technician his whole life, but he got the job at Continental, worked his way up, and got paid well. He believes in stability more than he does upward mobility, and that counts for something in his family.

> Everybody, all my family and friends basically think—well know—that I got a good job. They all like the fact. . . . And, my father, especially . . . he's proud of what I did. Mom speaks about how I got a good job. I moved out, living on my own, I was very independent. My friends . . . are basically in the industry, too, so they think the same thing. Some of my friends that didn't finish high school, or who finished but didn't go into the field, are all wishing they would have gone into the field. Well, they see me going away every so often, and I'm making more than they are financially.

Wesley would have to become a supervisor to advance up the line at the airline, a move he feels is not worth the added responsibility. He already has the job he wanted. Wesley is an aircraft technician and that's fine.

The chances are that academically high-achieving students fare better in terms of employment and earnings over the course of their lives than either Melissa or Wesley. Certainly, kids who graduate from high-performing high schools and attend selective colleges are more likely to train for careers that garner more prestige and significantly higher salaries. But if the choice is between a general high school that provides little focus and one that is strongly directed toward the world of work, which is better for the average student?

Sociologist Nicole Deterding discovered how much career pathways can be shaped by the difference in high-school programs. She contrasted the outcomes for three groups of students: those enrolled in general high-school programs (like Melissa); those in work-oriented vocational programs (like Wesley); and students in between whom she termed Mid Mixers because they took some vocational courses in programs that were dominated by standard academic high-school subjects.[5] She compared how these three groups of students fared in terms of enrollment in post-secondary school or employment versus extended periods of unemployment. The data she turned to—the National Longitudinal Study of Youth (NLSY)—are particularly helpful in answering that question because they followed a large national sample of high-school graduates for many years and hence can tell us something about how their school careers shaped their adult lives.

Deterding found that vocational students like Wesley had better prospects than students like Melissa, who pursued a routine curriculum in a general high school. Students coming out of institutions like Aviation High School spent more of their time between the ages of eighteen and twenty-two in work or in school than those who lacked this direction; indeed, they worked or studied at rates comparable with students who pursued very academic programs in high school.[6] Work-oriented students were also less likely to drop out of the labor force later in life. Deterding concluded that "students with the strongest orientation toward the workforce in high school have better outcomes than their less-focused Mid-Mixing peers." It is the focus that counts because it improves the quality and meaning of the high-school experience itself and provides students with the tools and motivation to seek a defined path.

But beyond these benefits, research suggests that vocational programs have a positive impact on students' orientation to school overall. In 2007, New York City's Independent Budget Office found that vocational schools actually had higher graduation rates and lower dropout rates than the city's general public high schools. That finding was replicated in a 2014 report by the Community Service Society of New York, which also found that low-income and minority students stand to gain the most from career and technical education (CTE). While the graduation rates for both black and Latino boys at traditional public schools is just 52 percent, in CTE high schools they graduate at rates of 63 percent and 66 percent, respectively.

In the past few years, New York City has opened several smaller, mission-driven CTE schools, among them the Academy for Careers in Television and Film, the Bronx Academy for Software Engineering, and IBM-affiliated Pathways in Technology Early College High School (P-TECH), which boasts a six-year combined high school/early college program. The minority student graduation rates at these schools are even higher.[7] Most impressive, these positive outcomes hold even when taking into account differences in students' eighth grade test scores. In other words, students whose test scores suggest a problematic pathway to graduation do well when they have this alternative.

In the end, whether students at these schools go into the industry for which they have trained or not, they end up with a very positive experience of secondary education. They enjoy dedicated teachers, a serious and respectful atmosphere, and purposeful education that make them feel grown up. And that experience carries over, no matter what they do later on.

Indeed, the sense of direction that students like Wesley and his friends seem to possess is hard to come by among students in general high schools where the opportunity to try out different occupations is nonexistent. Highly motivated, academically inclined students are able to put those decisions off to the future and concentrate on school for its own sake. For the less academically engaged, the absence of an alternative focus leads to drift. Vocational students know they have had opportunities that general high school students lack.

The History of Ambivalence

Thousands of young people have benefited from robust vocational education and found their way to the middle class because of it. Why, then, has the United States struggled with vocational education and put our faith in general high school education of the kind Melissa endured? Over the years, we have invested more and more in educational institutions like Sheepshead Bay and let the Aviation High Schools wither on the vine.

Americans have waxed and waned—mainly waned—in their support for vocational education. As a consequence, the United States ranks only twenty-first out of twenty-nine developed nations in the amount we spend on vocational training. Even when we have invested in technical education, we often do so in ways that weaken its quality. We underfund the effort. We overtly or covertly link vocational education to stigmatized, remedial training. Either way, we virtually ensure that it will be seen as second best.

New York City has one of the largest vocational programs in the country, boasting thirty career and technical education–designated high schools and 125 CTE programs of study in regular high schools. Yet the money that is spent per student is significantly less at CTE schools than at general academic high schools (and is, in both cases, lower than at the prestigious "exam schools"—the nine highly selective public schools in New York City that in all but one case require an entrance examination). As of 2012, only 22 percent of the city's CTE programs were approved by the state, and less than half met federal No Child Left Behind[8] standards.[9] Indeed, despite periodic calls for reform, a 2012 report by then public advocate Bill de Blasio found that these schools continued to face daunting obstacles. They were saddled with negative public perception, uneven performance, disjointed management of industry engagement, and an inadequate share of the educational dollars. Students struggled with limited access and opportunity to enroll in innovative programs, insufficient preparation for postsecondary education, and an emphasis on "seat time" rather than competency-based pathways to graduation.

Despite pockets of genuine innovation and success, CTE programs throughout the country face similar challenges. A 2013 Georgetown report[10] found that "too many CTE programs in high schools . . . around the country still appear to fit the stereotype of having out-of-date practices that prepare students neither for college nor for well-paying careers." The report noted that in many cases—in part as a result of budgetary restrictions—teachers and equipment have not kept up with changes in the labor market and curricula have not been revised in ways that better integrate CTE with academics.

We need to understand the history of vocational education in the United States if we are ever to overcome it and evolve to the point where this pathway to skilled labor is accorded the respect it enjoys in other countries.

The Winding Roads Toward Vocational Education

Long before school systems considered entering into the vocational sphere at all, training for the work world was the responsibility of employers. Hence the first formalized system of vocational education in the United States developed outside of schools. In the colonial period, masters entered into legally binding, contractual relationships with apprentices whom they were obligated to groom. Apprentices of the eighteenth century agreed, among other things, to keep trade secrets and work without pay in exchange for basic education, training in the craft, room and board, and sometimes a set of tools or clothes upon completion of the apprenticeship.[11]

More often than not, apprenticeship was the destiny of poor orphans or delinquent children. The distressing origins of these programs may account for some of the stigma that attaches to apprenticeship even now. In the eighteenth century and beyond, as Charles Dickens's own life and novels attest, they were akin to indentured servitude, often thought of as a children's form of slavery.

With the advent of the Industrial Revolution, changes to the apprenticeship system emerged. No longer were young people dependent on a master for food, clothes, and shelter. Instead, companies began to pay wages to apprentices on a graduated scale. They tended to live with their families rather than board out. As new industries grew, apprenticeship systems developed within them, though the training was limited and not terribly systematic.

With factories replacing small workshops, the role of the one-on-one master-apprenticeship relationship began to wane and other institutions took over the care of indigent children. Indeed, the path to adulthood followed by poor youth increasingly ran through industrial education. The Carlisle Indian Industrial School in Pennsylvania, for example, was founded in 1879 to channel children of defeated Native Americans into jobs in industry.

From the mid-nineteenth century until the onset of World War I, the country underwent a period of rapid economic growth and prosperity that saw a decline in small-town life and culminated in early factory electrification and mass production, sometimes referred to as the Second Industrial or Technical Revolution. If the core industries of the First Industrial Revolution were textiles, iron, and steam engine technologies, the Second Revolution, which peaked between 1870 and 1914, was characterized by rapid industrial development and mechanization. Steel, railroads, petroleum and chemicals, and, ultimately, electricity were the central industries this time. The robber barons—from Frick to Mellon and Carnegie to Rockefeller—built unprecedented fortunes from the construction of the railroads, large-scale iron and steel production, widespread use of machinery, greatly increased use of steam power and oil, as well as the beginning of electricity and electrical communications.

This form of industrialization required a different kind of labor training system, and craft apprenticeship began to disappear. How to educate young workers so that they could take their places on the assembly lines became a policy preoccupation and a worry for America's social reformers. The Massachusetts textile towns of Waltham and Lowell were transformed in the 1810s and 1820s by the advent of the factory system. This process spread rapidly in the 1840s to the chemical and metallurgical industries and subsequently to virtually all market-based industries by the 1860s and 1870s.

The same period also saw the advent of the trade school movement in America. Trade schools were formed as a response to the need for specific training that could not be delivered adequately in the "largely bookish" evening schools or on the shop floor, where "master mechanics were not prepared to perform in an instructional situation."[12] Some of these schools were private, while others were free or were operated by individual companies.

The Hampton Institute in Virginia, among the first private trade schools, was organized by General Samuel Chapman Armstrong in 1868 to provide both liberal education and trade training to African Americans. Armstrong conceived of his mission as a fusion of the moral and the social: to improve "character" and social status. Eight hours a day were devoted to the study of a trade through organized courses, which lasted for three years, along with academic courses that required four. If students completed the entire four-year program, they earned a diploma.

Booker T. Washington was one of Hampton Institute's most famous graduates and he remained, throughout his life, a champion of this kind of practical education. For many decades after the Civil War, it was in fact Washington's perspective that most influenced educational policy. The first school to offer training with supplementary studies specific to each occupation was the New York Trade School, founded by Colonel Richard Tylden Auchmuty in 1881.[13] Auchmuty had studied labor problems and had developed a method of training designed to provide preemployment instruction as well as supplemental training for employed workers.[14] The New York Trade School offered bricklaying; plastering; plumbing; carpentry; house, sign, and fresco painting; stonecutting; blacksmithing; tailoring; and printing. Classes were offered both during the day and at night.

Auchmuty's model attracted attention across the United States and in international circles. An 1893 annual report of the Bureau of Industries for the Province of Ontario examined the accomplishments of the New York Trade School and reported back to Canadian authorities on the achievements of this new model of workforce preparation. It describes at length the kinds of skills young men were learning, noting, for example, that in the bricklaying course, students were instructed how to build eight-, twelve-, and sixteen-inch walls; how to turn corners and build walls intersecting at different angles; and how to build piers, arches, flues, and fireplaces. Instruction involved "lectures illustrated by experiments, and by carefully prepared manuals."[15] The tailoring department of the school received special mention because it was managed by the Merchant Tailors Society of New York. "The school is under the supervision of first-class teachers, who are practical tailors and understand every detail of the trade."[16]

Trade schools like these spread throughout the country in a limited fashion throughout the late 1800s. They were joined by endowed and proprietary vocational schools in agriculture, business, home economics, and trade, precursors of today's for-profit higher education sector and often with similar reputational problems. They were, in some ways, inspired by the birth of the land grant universities that were founded by Congress under the terms of the Morrill Act, passed in the midst of the Civil War. The land grant system looked to join the science of agriculture to its practice through agricultural extension systems, for the first time binding universities to the world of agrarian commerce on the theory that science could make farming more productive. Vocational schools also joined education to the market and hence bent the purpose of learning to the world of work.

It is possible that these private vocational schools would have proliferated more widely if it had not been for the wave of immigrants who flooded the cities of the Northeast in the late nineteenth century. Educational institutions began to wean themselves from the purpose of employment preparation to focus instead on the grand task of socializing these New Americans into their adopted country's mores and values.

At a time of such sweeping economic changes, vocational schooling also came to be seen not only as the best vehicle for preparing young people to work in the modern factory but also as the last best hope for preserving important Protestant values such as a strong work ethic.[17] These two competing needs—to shore up a fast-disappearing moral arrangement based on the dignity of work and to prepare young people for an economic system where craft apprenticeship no longer made sense—were central to the demand for public vocational education.

Thus beyond teaching practical new skills, these urban high schools served a symbolic and a practical function.[18] The prospect of socially and morally untethered immigrant youth roaming the streets had not been calmly received. An institution that would occupy the time and control the whereabouts of thousands of young people enabled city fathers to rest a little easier.

First, however, there were pedagogical shortcomings to address. Public education was not up to the task of training future workers because it was dominated by drill and repetition. Enlightened reformers of the 1880s and '90s advocated for a more active form of instruction, a manual training movement dedicated to the mastery of tools and machinery. "Training the mind by training the hand" was the new slogan. Young people were to be taken under the wings of instructors who would teach them how to link the two. An interesting illustration of this preoccupation can be seen in Charles Henry Ham's 1890 monograph[19] on manual training, which he deems "the solution of social and industrial problems." Ham was a member of the Board of General Appraisers, which later came to be known as the US Customs Court and then the Court of International Trade. A pillar of the community, Ham issued a paean to the virtuous nature of manual labor:

> This is a school; the school of the future; the school that is to dignify labor; the school that is to generate power; the school where every second contributes to the harmony of development, where the brain informs the muscle, where thought directs every blow, where the mind, the eye and the hand constitute an invincible triple alliance. This is the school that Locke dreamed of, that Bacon wished for, that Rousseau described . . .

From a chapter entitled "The Drawing-Room," Ham illustrates the approach by explaining how the school keeps students from becoming bored to distraction by linking the abstract and the concrete:

> The basis of the art of drawing is geometry, and its a, b, c consists in a knowledge of certain geometrical lines, curves and angles. This knowledge is gained from examples on the black-board which are reproduced on paper. But to relieve the student of this school from the tedium of reproducing, hundreds of times in succession, the same lines, angles, and curves, object-drawing is introduced very early in the course; and to render the exercise more attractive, as well as to impress it more firmly upon the mind, the objects drawn during the day are made features of the construction lesson in the carpenter's laboratory, the wood or iron turning laboratory, or the laboratory of founding on the following day.

And from "The Carpenter's Laboratory":

> The minutes having been consumed in the inquiry into the nature and value of the wood in which the lesson is to be wrought, the instructor makes working drawings of the lesson on the black-board . . .
>
> The instructor now quits the blackboard for the bench, where, in the presence of the whole class, he executes the difficult parts of the lesson, still propounding and answering questions.
>
> Now we stand in the presence of twenty-four boys, in twenty-four different attitudes of labor, making things. They are literally busy as bees, using the square, the saw, the plane and the chisel; they are, as the journeyman carpenter would say, "getting out stuff for a job." The course, bussing [sic] sound of the cross-cut saw resounds loudly through the room; above this bass note the sharp tenor tone of the rip-saw is heard, and the rasping sound of a half dozen planes throwing off a series of pine curling pine ribbons comes in as a rude refrain.

This pedagogical revolution was celebrated for helping to prepare youth for the workforce and reinvigorating learning, but its primary justification was moral. Honest labor of the hands was deemed virtuous, encouraging upright self-discipline, precision, and accuracy. Accordingly, the new vocational education was regarded as an especially appropriate form of discipline for those unfortunates most in need of social improvement: the poor, juvenile delinquents, immigrants, African Americans, and Native Americans.

By the first decades of the twentieth century, moral uplift began to wane as a goal and in its place grew a narrower view of vocational education, one that returned the enterprise back to its origins as an institution devoted to the pragmatic cultivation of skills. Young men needed training for jobs in business and agriculture, and young women for the "science" of home economics. Vocational schools were to supersede apprenticeship, which was viewed as unsuitable for modern industry both because they emanated from a craft tradition and because they were run by unions dominated by immigrants or foreigners.[20]

Having assigned vocational training to schools rather than to workplaces, the whole enterprise became entangled in messy arguments surrounding the spread of high school as an institution. Secondary school enrollments had increased dramatically, transforming the high school from an elite to a mass institution, one that served a more diverse population that included new immigrants and African Americans. Between 1910 and 1940, the high school population increased by over 50 percent. That spike came about for many reasons, including "changes in child labor laws and compulsory schooling laws motivated by Progressive Era campaigns to reduce child labor, eliminate youth idleness and delinquency, and expand schooling." But an even more important draw was the rise in wages for educated workers.[21]

Early on, some reformers had argued that vocational schools should be separate from academic schools, but the call for integration had been stronger and the comprehensive high school was born. Yet instead of offering a common curriculum to all students, which was the model used in the nineteenth century, schools increasingly offered divergent curricula based on a student's needs and future occupational trajectory.[22] Consequently, the rise of vocational education also led to testing and ability-grouping to sort students for different tracks.

This evolution was not without its critics. John Dewey, the University of Chicago philosopher and founder of its famous Laboratory School at the turn of the century, was one of the early dissenters. While Dewey was not opposed to including manual training in school curricula, he was against the dual-track system because he understood that it could be used to prevent working-class youth from rising above their original station, an outcome that he believed would undermine democracy. "Tracking" minority and low-income students into less rigorous, vocational pathways would later become a lightning rod for criticism voiced against vocational education. However, in Dewey's day, the majority of reformers argued against him that it was undemocratic to prepare all students with a common academic curriculum focused on foreign languages and ancient history when the majority would not continue on to college. What most students needed was a pathway that prepared them for a changing work world.

Apprenticeship and Vocational Education: The Second Act

For the most part, students would follow that path within the walls of the nation's schools. However, the state of Wisconsin attempted to blend the old and the new in 1911, by enacting the first law in the United States to promote an organized system of apprenticeships. Rather than have the private sector determine its structure, Wisconsin claimed a regulatory role for the state through an industrial commission created to oversee the training, and required apprentices to also attend school for five hours a week.

In 1917, with America's entry into the war on the horizon, the first federal legislation was passed to fund vocational education in secondary schools. The Smith-Hughes Act provided approximately $1.7 million to states to support programs in agriculture, trades, industry, and home economics for students fourteen and older. Funds could be used for full-time schools devoting half time to vocational training, part-time schools for young workers to receive additional training in their field, and evening schools to speak to the needs of adult workers.[23]

Momentum behind the apprenticeship program accelerated after World War I because the need for trained workers grew rapidly. A booming postwar economy and a shortage of skilled workers (exacerbated by immigration restrictions) lent further urgency to the training mission. The construction industry, which grew by leaps and bounds during this period, was particularly active in spurring a national commitment to apprenticeship.

In the 1930s, however, youth unemployment soared as the Great Depression took hold. Prompted by this catastrophe, President Roosevelt jumped on the apprenticeship bandwagon in 1934, forming the Federal Committee on Apprenticeship. Appointed by the secretary of labor and comprised of representatives from several government agencies, this group was charged with developing a national strategy for apprenticeship education to "safeguard the welfare of apprentices and assure their proper training and eventual absorption into the work force."[24] The "safeguards" were thought necessary because private firms had a habit of exploiting their youngest workers, underpaying them while they worked toward the status of journeymen. The Committee on Apprentice Training was empowered to formulate federal labor standards for the trainees that were enforced by parallel state agencies.

World War II strengthened the demand for vocational education as the war effort stimulated the need for skilled manufacturing workers. Between 1940 and 1945, the government spent an additional $389 million on special defense-oriented vocational programs. On October 25, 1940, the Engineering Defense Training Program was authorized under the Civil Functions Appropriations Act, which provided $9 million to be given to universities to help them deliver short-term engineering courses and training for industrial workers in defense-related industries. In 1941, the Labor-Federal Security Appropriation Act authorized chemistry, physics, managerial, and engineering courses to form an integrated Engineering, Science and Management Defense Training (ESMDT) program, the first class of which was offered at Rutgers University, New Jersey, in September 1941. By May 1942, over ten thousand people had passed through the Rutgers program.[25]

While most of these programs were dismantled after the Second World War, public opinion toward them was positive because they were so closely linked to a popular cause. That bedrock of public support was helpful as the next wave of technological panic swept over the country. Sputnik, the first Soviet satellite, spurred worries that the Russians were surpassing the United States in technology and space engineering. The silver lining to these Cold War obsessions was the National Defense

Education Act of 1958, which supported a massive investment in higher education through loan programs that fostered college enrollments, especially in defense-oriented fields, from foreign languages and area studies to engineering and mathematics. The vocational education section of the bill focused on training individuals for highly skilled technical occupations such as computer programming and aircraft mechanics, which were vital to national defense.

Vocational Education and the War on Poverty

The common purpose of the second wave of vocational education and its allied programs of apprenticeship had emphasized the needs of the labor market for skilled workers as well as the manpower requirements of war production. In the 1960s, a new mission emerged that had little to do with either of these goals. Instead, vocational training was deemed important as a weapon in the fight against poverty.

The Vocational Education Act of 1963 was the most significant legislation of this kind, providing states with appropriations of $60 million in 1964, increasing to $225.5 million in 1967. States were encouraged to spend federal funds on vocational education for students who had dropped out of college, workers who needed training or retraining, and individuals with academic, socioeconomic, or other handicaps.[26] It was this very association of vocational training with disadvantage, especially urban black and rural white poverty, that would saddle it with a remedial taint. That valence was reinforced by the association of practical training with blue-collar work in a country fixated on white-collar employment as a mark of upward mobility. While other countries linked skilled manufacturing to international trade dominance with almost nationalist zeal, Americans pushed the blue-collar training agenda into an educational corner and virtually ensured that anyone who ventured there would be tarred by stigma. The route to middle-class status ran through the managerial, white-collar, or professional world and getting a ticket was the ambition of the upwardly mobile.

As far back as the 1950s, the United States had developed a high-powered academic curriculum for elite students—the fledgling system of AP examinations was its national flag bearer. But this was the pathway of the few. Ordinary students were stuck with vocational or general education tracks that offered little more than watered-down versions of academic courses. Since manufacturing firms routinely drew their labor directly from high schools before World War II, whatever stigma this road entailed was largely canceled out by the stable jobs it led to.

The 1970s saw a push for broader and more relevant "career education," but the fate of vocational training in that era was all but sealed by the alarm generated by the publication of *A Nation at Risk* in 1983. This report charged that American students were receiving inadequate academic instruction and the country was losing ground to foreign rivals. "Secondary school curricula have been homogenized, diluted, and diffused to the point that they no longer have a central purpose," the authors declared. "In effect, we have a cafeteria style curriculum in which the appetizers and desserts can easily be mistaken for the main courses." The report condemned the American high school with this memorable conclusion: "If an unfriendly foreign power had attempted to impose on America the mediocre educational performance that exists today, we might well have viewed it as an act of war." President Ronald Reagan called for enhanced rigor in high-school education to ensure we could compete internationally.

The renewed focus on academic quality spurred by *A Nation at Risk* has perpetuated a nearly continuous and anxious drumbeat about the competitiveness of American education at the top of the academic spectrum. Workforce preparation was left to languish as we moved steadily toward a purely academic model of the American high school.

Ironically, the early '80s saw the first real spike in unemployment among exactly those workers who had graduated from purely academic programs: the highly skilled, white-collar labor force. Although the ranks of the jobless swelled across the board in the early years of the Reagan administration, for the first time since the expansion of the white-collar ranks began in the post–World War II period, executives and managers found themselves turfed out of their jobs. Unemployment rose to a forty-year high of nearly 11 percent. Shock and shame followed for middle-aged workers of all classes, but especially the highly skilled who had mistakenly thought themselves immune to this kind of tailspin.

The fallout from the powerful recession of the early '80s created yet another crisis of confidence in American institutions. In the realm of education, the United States was said to be stuck in a "rising tide of mediocrity." Educators and policy makers scrambled to rework the high school curriculum in order to meet rising economic competition from Japan, Germany, and other European countries. Reforms intended to increase academic standards and enroll students in four-year colleges chugged forward and the message became clear: We will win this race by increasing university enrollments.

At the same time, scholars of poverty and inequality were recycling the concerns first raised in the early 1960s about the fate of non-college-bound youth. *The Forgotten Half*, an influential report produced in 1988 by the William T. Grant Foundation, a leading research nonprofit focused on youth, was the catalyst this time. It raised an alarm over the 50 percent of the nation's youth who were heading directly into the labor market, bypassing higher education altogether. Other advanced industrialized nations were building training systems to acculturate young people to the world of work. The American high school avoided the question.

In days past, the non-college-bound would have found abundant opportunities in the blue-collar world. When unions were a powerful economic force, that end point would have guaranteed a family wage. But even as early as the mid-1980s this world was disappearing (the percentage of the workforce represented by unions declined from about 27 percent in 1973 to just around 20 percent in 1985; by 2011, the union coverage rate in the United States was 13 percent[27]). From 1980 to 1999, manufacturing jobs declined by an average of 0.5 percent per year. However, between 2000 and 2011, "the rate of loss dramatically accelerated, with manufacturing jobs shrinking at a rate nearly six times faster (3.1 percent per year) than the rate in the prior two decades."[28]

The options for the large proportion of Americans who were not university material were shrinking, wages were falling, and the specter of what sociologist William Julius Wilson termed the "urban underclass" of jobless, idle men loomed. A panoply of social problems that was said to follow—single parenthood, unstable households, children growing up in chaotic settings and then doomed to follow the increasingly poverty-stricken pathway of their parents—alarmed politicians, think tanks, and policy wonks.

For young men who did make it into the job market, instability seemed to be pronounced. In his classic article on youth labor markets, published in the early 1980s, MIT professor Paul Osterman pointed out that "churning" or job switching is not unusual among new entrants to the world of work. It is natural for them to "try on" different kinds of jobs early in their careers. This can be productive if it yields an effective match after a few years and young workers begin to move up career ladders. But Osterman's research showed that a sizable proportion of young people, especially low-skilled men of color, were unable to settle down into stable work. Their patterns of job hopping turned out not to be beneficial, but instead to signal to employers that these workers were unstable and hence bad bets.

Interest in how other countries solved this problem began to grow in the wake of the recession in the 1980s. Sociologists like Northwestern University's James Rosenbaum trained an eye on the Japanese school system, which seemed able to step into the breach and create a more effective matching system. In Japan, vocational teachers adopted the role of the trusted intermediary, creating connections between employers and graduates of vocational high schools. Employers routinely turned to teachers in these low-status high schools to find entry-level workers. Indeed, young people seeking employment could not approach firms on their own; no one would speak to them. It was the teacher who assumed the central position as the go-between linking would-be workers and the jobs they were after.

Instructors made it their business to know what a given industry was looking for and what kinds of skills were required of entry-level workers. Although vocational education was stigmatized in both countries, instructors shaped the Japanese vocational school curriculum so that students were trained in ways that made them more useful from the outset. The hand-in-glove transition from school to work ensured that Japanese youth at the bottom of the educational pyramid did not suffer the high levels of unemployment and job churning that their US counterparts routinely experienced.[29]

The American high-school system eschewed coordinated labor policies of the kind the Japanese (and the Germans) used to such advantage. Stoked by a hands-off view of the role of government, and a confidence in the power of the market to match people to the jobs they can handle, the kind of coordinated approach that was succeeding in other countries was a nonstarter in the United States.

The School-to-Work Movement

Instead of focusing on the special problems besetting poor and working-class students, a new emphasis in the late '80s and early '90s on integration of the vocational and the academic meant that a united approach would dominate, leading to a universal goal of preparing all students for college and work. The Carl D. Perkins Vocational and Applied Technology Education Act of 1990 required federally supported vocational education programs to integrate academic and work-related education through course programs that "articulated" or sequenced high school and community college study in specific occupational areas, such as engineering technology, agriculture, health, and business. Commonly referred to as "Tech Prep" or the "2+2 model"—because it connected two years of high school with two years of postsecondary education—the idea was to lead students to a two-year associate's degree or certificate or a two-year apprenticeship.

Perkins was the first of two federal efforts to integrate work-related education into the high-school curriculum. Robert Reich, President Clinton's secretary of labor, championed the second: the school-to-work (STW) movement.

Consistent with the thrust of the Perkins approach, Reich's policy encompassed all students, whether or not they were college bound. Career education could become less stigmatized, Reich reasoned, if it was something that all students pursued at least in modest doses, rather than reserving it for a minority. Thus by 1994, 97 percent of public high-school graduates took at least one vocational education course. But only 7 percent took it seriously enough to specialize in the vocational curriculum.[30]

What was lacking in both legislative provisions was anything approaching a national framework of youth apprenticeships that could convert vocational education into real-world work experience. This is surprising since only a few years earlier, then governor of Arkansas Bill

Clinton delivered a keynote address at a 1990 conference called Youth Apprenticeship, American Style. Going further, a 1992 White House Fact Sheet clearly underlined the disconnects in the American labor market and skill development system:

> Upwards of one-fifth of American students drop out of high school. Most experience difficulty in securing permanent employment. Few have the skills that will enable them to succeed in today's work force. The rapid pace of technical innovation demands not only higher skills but also higher levels of educational achievement.
>
> Many of those students who drop out view high school as primarily preparation for college. They do not consider high school relevant to what they intend to do in the future. Apprenticeship programs, which in many countries serve as a bridge between school and work, are not generally available as an option to U.S. high school students.

The School-to-Work Opportunities Act (STWOA), which was designed to attack the problem of disengaged and ill-prepared youth, allocated funds to states that were willing to reform their high-school programs, particularly those ready to align with the National Skills Standards Act, a voluntary national system of skills standards designed to give the STW programs, including youth apprenticeships, guidance and goals in terms of teaching.

As with most large-scale interventions, there were elements of the program that worked and some that didn't. One important contribution was to improve student engagement in school. For kids who were not excited by the traditional academic curriculum, STW programs provided the motivation to engage; they increased positive attitudes toward school, improved attendance, and decreased dropout rates. These payoffs alone would have made STW a worthwhile investment even if no job skills were cultivated. Unfortunately, what most of the program's advocates were hoping for, namely, improved labor market outcomes, did not come to pass.

It appears that American employers were not ready to think of internships as serious tryouts for permanent employment. In a US survey of roughly seven hundred employers, half of whom were part of an STW program, more than 50 percent cited philanthropic motivations, such as contributing to the community or improving public education, as the primary reason for their participation. Only a small percentage reported that the opportunity to test potential employees, access prescreened applicants, or address a local labor shortage had anything to do with why they chose to take part.[31]

Our ambivalence about work-oriented education was showing. The bill did little to engage existing vocational programs or help to reform or reshape them. The act ended up focusing less on youth apprenticeships in the working world and more on career majors in the school setting. It was a textbook case of ambivalence and conflicting interests.

The STWOA expired in 2001. Neither the president nor anyone in Congress proposed extending it. Interest groups in labor and education saw to that. Unions opposed government-sponsored youth apprenticeships, fearing they might lose control over available apprenticeships and the devaluation of the work status.[32] And, in turn, employers feared the potential opposition from unions. A historical account written in 1991 of the fate of one such program makes it clear that the very idea was an affront to organized labor in the United States:

> Within organized labor at the national level, there has been significant hostility to the concept of youth apprenticeship, which is seen as a threat to union influence in the nation's apprenticeship system. In Pennsylvania, PYAP [Pennsylvania Youth Apprenticeship Program] encountered some of that sentiment from the state AFL-CIO.
>
> More significant, though, was the resistance of local unions in large metalworking shops that might have become key program participants. For example, at Caterpillar in York, the Vice President of Human Relations was a member of the feasibility study team and an active supporter of the program. He knew, however, that his union was skeptical and that the firm's participation would have to be put on the bargaining table in the next contract negotiation. Caterpillar, therefore, could not promise participation. This was true of key union shops in other sites. As a result, the firms that could commit early were non-union and generally smaller firms, giving PYAP the appearance of being a non-union program, further fueling union skepticism.[33]

Progressive educators had their own reservations. They raised the traditional objections about tracking and questioned whether apprenticeship programs would be disruptive, forcing students to switch to the high schools that provided these opportunities. Other critics voiced concerns over the likelihood that the number of apprenticeships would be insufficient. "College for all" was invoked repeatedly, even by those whose livelihoods owe nothing to higher education. Parents also got into the act, complaining about a demonstration project mounted by Cornell University:

> The concern most frequently expressed by parents is that participation might jeopardize their child's chances of going to college. It is the rare parent of a high school sophomore who does not believe his or her child can and should go to college.[34]

Other parents also voiced suspicions that employers might be offering such opportunities merely to exploit the young people.

> A few parents expressed concern about the motivations of employers who were interested in participating in a youth apprenticeship. Some parents believed that employers would use the apprentice training positions to access "cheap, minimum-wage high school students" to displace adult workers.[35]

Perhaps parental fears influenced employers to be less than enthusiastic. Equally likely, the cost of providing this kind of training, alongside the fact that there was an abundance, at the time, of fully qualified adult workers, dampened employer enthusiasm.[36]

Finally, there were those who argued that market forces—rather than education and training-based programs—are sufficient to produce a skilled workforce. The *Economist* took this position:

> The training system which seems to be coping best with technological innovation and global competition is the most maligned of the lot, the American one. The standard criticisms of this system, about poaching, short-termism and amateurism, have always been overstated. Sensible

workers do not leave firms with good training records for fly-by-night operations just because they are offered a few dollars more. Successful firms take a long-term view of the skills of their workforces, even if they are subject to relentless hounding . . . to produce profits. Thanks to the pressure of competition, American plumbers, electricians and pest controllers are usually as competent as their certificate-toting counterparts in Germany.

Indeed, the American tradition of providing people with masses of general academic education, including a start at university for half the population and plenty of second chances for everyone, and leaving specific training to the market, is becoming more, rather than less, relevant. Economists have long argued that the returns on general education are higher than those on specific training, because education is transferable whereas many skills tend to be job-specific. . . . The most urgent task facing the United States is to reform its highly uneven school system (perhaps through rigorous national exams) rather than to re-invent an apprenticeship system.[37]

This position did not carry the day in regions faced with skills shortages, which is why, despite all the ambivalence and conflicting interests, some states (e.g., Wisconsin, Georgia, and Maine) did develop viable and sustained youth apprenticeship programs specifically modeled on Germany's dual system. In 1991–92, Wisconsin's top elected officials from both political parties, as well as its Republican governor, Tommy Thompson, and Democratic state school superintendent, Herbert Grover, traveled to Germany with the aim of modeling a high school youth program after its apprenticeship system. The following year, the first Wisconsin youth apprentice (YA) students were enrolled in a program focused on printing. Within two years, eight more YA programs were introduced in automotive technology, biotechnology, drafting and design, finance, health, lodging, insurance, and machining, with 348 students enrolled in YA programs involving 200 employers. Ultimately, state agencies, working together with industry and labor groups, developed twenty-three skill standards in different fields. By 2008,[38] enrollment was at 1,791 students and there were 1,307 participating employers and 247 schools. They are still flourishing.

The Lessons of History

What can we cull from this account of the country's journey through the thicket of vocational and general education? Early histories of American vocational education were written by advocates of the movement, emphasizing its democratizing power. Critical histories followed, arguing that this kind of education was an antidemocratic force, a means of tracking students. Others criticized it as a tool deployed by business and efficiency-minded educators bent on using schools to socialize young people for "the unjust nature of the corporate-industrial society" emerging at the turn of the twentieth century.[39] These tensions still plague public discussion about the desirability and proper place of career and technical education.

Lurking in the background of this debate is a more fundamental divide over the relationship between education and what we might call "skill regimes." Economies and firms require different kinds of skills in a workforce, ranging from the more general (the ability to read, write, calculate, or locate information) to the very specific (how to operate a particular lathe or use a computer program designed for one bank). Arguably, the roots of our ambivalence can be traced to the American affinity for education as a route to mastering general skills rather than specific occupational training.

Harvard economists Claudia Goldin and Lawrence Katz, authors of the often-cited volume *The Race Between Education and Technology*, argue that the strength of the US economy throughout the twentieth century followed from the fact that American workers had better general skills. They credit this to geographic mobility in the United States in the early 1900s, since people who move around have to be able to transfer their general training and be prepared to adapt it to new markets with firm-specific training.

The dynamism of the American labor market adds to this high level of mobility. American workers face higher rates of job loss and reemployment than Europeans do in comparable jobs. (The European labor market also features much higher structural unemployment, meaning there are more people who want work but never gain a foothold.) The failure of American business to support training for the labor force has been attributed to the reluctance of employers to equip their workers with transferrable skills, lest they leave and deploy that investment to the benefit of others. Yet workers also hang back from investing in specific skills. If they perceive the risk of losing their jobs to be high, why bother? As a result, certain skills will be in high demand and low supply unless institutions, like firms and/or the government, step in to protect this investment.

Indeed, political scientists[40] interested in the intersection between the economy and public policy argue that three types of institutions are necessary to ensure such protection: *employment protection* (legislation that mandates protection from layoffs in an economic downturn), *unemployment protection* (protection from wage reduction as a result of unemployment), and *wage protection* (a mechanism that helps protect wage levels from market fluctuations).

For workers to invest in firm-specific skills, they need a high level of employment protection because these skills are likely to be of little value outside that particular company. For those who invest in industry-specific skills, this kind of protection matters much less since their skills are portable; nonetheless, these workers can benefit from unemployment protection, which would enable them to turn down lower-wage jobs outside their field in periods where their specific skills are in oversupply. (Clearly, the greater the insecurity in a given field, the more workers are incentivized to master transferrable, general skills.) Wage protection is important because it enables workers to calculate a lifelong return on their investment in certain skills and thus gives them more of an incentive to acquire that training if the return is high.

Wage inequality and labor-market stratification have increased everywhere since the early 1980s. Economists argue that the widening of these gaps is best understood as related—at least in part—to the growth of what they call "skill-biased technological change." Wages are growing fastest for people with technical skills that are not in sufficient supply. The counterargument is that it is not that demand for skilled labor has increased but that we have seen a slowdown in its supply. The problem, then, lies in the "political economy of skill formation," the delicate balance between what we incentivize workers to learn and how we protect them from the loss of their investment when jobs disappear.[41]

The US training system is fragmented and privatized. As a result, job seekers absorb much of the cost of acquiring human capital. Without assurances from companies that their jobs will be protected, potential trainees may underinvest in themselves. Meanwhile, firms face a potential "free rider" problem: the people they train may jump ship and sign on with firms that have not born this burden. These conditions pose a significant challenge to the development of apprenticeship programs or any other costly investment in skill training. Employers look over their shoulder, wondering who is going to rob them of their skilled workers and complain about not being able to find skilled labor rather than paying for the training that will guarantee that supply.

As we will see in chapter 6, these problems don't plague the German model, in part because a goodly proportion of the training expense is supported by the government and hence by taxpayers as a whole. Moreover, within a relatively short time, a very high-powered apprentice starts to cover the costs by generating the same goods and services that the rest of the workers produce (at more modest wages).

The advantages of a well-organized system of skill production are becoming clearer as the United States faces another round of shortages, this time compounded by the retirement of the boomer generation. Prosperity will flow to the countries that figure out how to replace them with a twenty-first-century workforce up to the challenge of the modern, technically sophisticated economy.

3

The New Vocational Turn in American High Schools

"I've hated school my entire life," Fred Holmes says with a smile, as he pushes a few strands of his chin-length sandy blond hair behind his ear. We are sitting in a small conference room at Tri-County Regional Vocational Technical High School in Franklin, Massachusetts, where Fred is a senior concentrating in welding—although, given his quietly confident demeanor and outlook on life, he could easily pass for someone at least a decade older.

"College wasn't for me. I had known that for a while. My dad owns a machine shop and I've always liked to use my hands more than anything," Fred adds by way of explaining his decision to attend Tri-County, one of thirty-nine vocational technical (VT) schools in the Commonwealth of Massachusetts.

Fred's antipathy toward traditional schooling doesn't mean that Tri-County is a place for kids who don't like to learn. Indeed, while the school offers three curricular paths—college prep (the lowest level), honors (the middle level), and AP (the highest level)—all VT students must pass the state's assessment tests, known as MCAS (Massachusetts

Comprehensive Assessment System), with a score in the "proficient" range or higher in math, English language arts, and science. In 2013, 39 percent of Tri-County's graduating seniors went on to a four-year college and another 28 percent to either a two-year college or technical school. A third went directly into the labor market.

By law, students in Massachusetts are eligible for trade certificates only if they also qualify for a high school diploma. These "certificates of occupational proficiency," granted to students who successfully complete a comprehensive education and training program in a particular trade or professional skill area, are the end goal of most vocational students.

Fred is not college-bound—he plans to move to Texas after graduation, where he says opportunities for welders are plentiful—but he has a 99 average in math and loves trigonometry, which often figures into his welding work. "I use a lot of trig. For structural iron working, triangles are the strongest thing," Fred explains.

> We do a lot of measuring of course to cut metal, and everything's got to be very precise because you can throw things off balance. In my job we build a lot of spiral staircases, so the metal has to be bent in two different directions and everything's got very precise math equations that go along with it.

This year, Fred has a paid job as a welder. He's taken advantage of what is known as "co-op"—the opportunity for seniors in good standing in Massachusetts VT schools to spend every other week out of school, working and being paid. In the week before we met, Fred worked a total of forty-one hours. "I do like six hours Saturdays, $16.50 an hour. In high school," he adds with a sly smile.

One of his projects this year was fashioning stair treads for a staircase for the Kennedy Memorial Library. He also worked on the gates at Harvard. "I've always dreaded going to school," he says without hesitation. But not work:

> I have to be there about six a.m. for work. I have to wake up at four forty-five and leave my house by five. I feel like a working-class American.

I don't feel like a leech, I don't feel like a bum. I like to feel like I'm
contributing to society and the future of America.

Over the past decade or so vocational education has been rebranded as
career and technical education (CTE) to avoid the stigma that has long
dogged vocational schools as dumping grounds for students who couldn't
cut it in college prep. It has experienced a modest revival in the US high
school, where students like Fred are receiving serious training to prepare
them for well-paid, middle-skill jobs. This training is delivered in a variety of models, including vocational and technical high schools that offer
preparation for multiple careers, like Tri-County, and those—typically in
large, urban areas—that specialize in a single career area or a few related
areas. There are also CTE programs within larger comprehensive high
schools.[1] In some regions of the country, like South Carolina, students
can spend half the day at a regular high school and the other half at what
is known as a career and technology center—a building that is set up like
a vocational high school but without any academic subjects—being
trained for a particular occupation.

The trend in all of these programs is toward career and college prep
at the same time. All of the vocational schools we visited had academic
tracks into which all students were placed, regardless of their vocational
major, and required the passage of statewide academic tests for a diploma,
even where the majority of students will not attend a four-year college.
Several national organizations have fostered new STEM (science, technology, engineering, mathematics) curricula. For example, Project Lead the
Way, which was launched in 1997 in New York high schools, has become
the largest national provider of K–12 STEM curricula. Another program,
High Schools That Work, started in the South and has become the
biggest program in the country—with over one thousand schools in more
than thirty states participating as of 2011—to integrate rigorous academics with CTE.

The particulars of these programs vary a good deal. For example,
while students at Tri-County in Massachusetts alternate between one full
week in shop class and one full week in academic classes, vocational
schools in other northern states, such as New York and New Jersey (and
also in the South), typically block out what amounts to one double period

a day for shop, making it more like an elective. These programs also vary in the extent to which they facilitate meaningful internship and/or work experiences, which is related to the way these programs are structured and supported, as well as to the actual employment opportunities in their regions. Hence, while seniors in good standing at Tri-County can go out on co-op placements, students in New York and New Jersey vocational schools have no such formal option.

All of these programs confront the stigma that attaches to vocational education, which is being addressed by insisting on the simultaneous focus on college preparation rather than by making a concerted effort to alter perceptions about the value of middle-skill work. This approach supports the continuing emphasis on standardized testing, which vocational teachers and administrators see as a mixed bag: A strong performance on standardized test scores can demonstrate to the world that vocational education is neither inferior nor meant for students who can't cut it academically. At the same time, the mania for testing that has swept the nation not only fails to capture much of what vocational students learn and know—and, in so doing, devalues that learning—but also takes time away from the training itself.

Writing in *EdWeek* in 2013 about the impact on vocational education of the Common Core standards—national standards introduced in 2010 that are aligned with a testing regime that has come under fire from educators and parents alike—Paul Barnwell, a high school English and digital media teacher in Kentucky, articulates this concern powerfully:

> The Common Core State Standards are ostensibly all about college and career "readiness," but I'm worried that the pressure for schools and students to achieve high scores on standardized exams will have adverse effects on the number of students who are truly ready for the next steps of their academic or vocational journey. . . .
>
> Instead of taking two years of foreign language to meet college "readiness" requirements as a junior or senior, why can't more students take core classes for half the day, then leave school to intern or train as carpenters, electricians, auto technicians, dental assistants, or fitness trainers?
>
> Instead of being pressured into a college track for the sake of

improving accountability numbers, why can't teachers and administrators honestly assess students' college potential—or lack thereof—and help place students in programs that give them the best shot of having a productive life? It's one thing for a student to be in a remedial rut, it's another to compound the problem by not considering other program options.

This is where a lot of tension lies: The skills learned in technical classes or work-study programs don't necessarily translate to standardized tests and the common standards, nor do they [jibe] with the national push for college readiness. The common standards might look good on paper, but implementation based on standardized-test preparation doesn't seem conducive to creating more pathways for students to thrive.[2]

Academic requirements are also state-driven in some cases. All Massachusetts students have to pass the demanding MCAS assessment test, which has made it impossible for even a superstar in a technical field to be certified unless she has also cleared that bar. The MCAS is considered one of the toughest tests in the country, and the state is proud of its strict standards. Of course, approval of these exams is far from universal. Dissenters have argued that it leads to "teaching to the test," and when MCAS was originally instituted, teachers feared that poor and immigrant kids, who initially scored dismally, would be deprived of diplomas.

Indeed, according to a 2008 Pioneer Institute White Paper, MCAS was resisted by the administrators of most vocational-technical schools when it was instituted in 1998. Many changed their tunes later as CTE students began to perform well on this demanding test. The White Paper notes that "an early acceptance of the inevitability and usefulness of MCAS made Blackstone Valley Regional Vocational Technical High School the first vocational school where 100 percent of its students passed MCAS to graduate." A Blue Hills Regional VT principal noted in that same report that "MCAS really did us a favor, because now every high school in the Commonwealth is on a level playing field."

A 2003 article on the website of the *Boston Globe* reported that Whittier Regional Vocational Technical High School in Haverhill "saw its passing rate for math jump from 43 to 51 percent, while its English rate rose from 69 to 81 percent. Northeastern Metropolitan Regional Vocational Technical High School in Wakefield saw its math passing rate increase from 26 percent in 2002 to 74 percent this year. Students at Lynn Vocational Technical Institute saw similar improvements."[3]

In a state that boasts among the best-educated citizens in the country, the prestige associated with university-level education and markers of intellectual prowess like standardized tests is a given. After a school or an individual can clear that hurdle, pursuing a vocational path is fine, even admirable. Without that credential, the enterprise is forever open to the charge that vocational education is a dumping ground for those who cannot compete.

The principal of Lynn Vocational, Bart Conlon, believes that improved MCAS scores "definitely . . . changed some of our minds" about the abilities of vocational students. Conlon attributed the higher scores to increased coordination between the academic and technical teachers and attempts by the latter to incorporate reading, writing, and math into the shop classes. "They might write about building a handicapped ramp," he told the paper. "The crossover between the two sides has been excellent."[4] Even though some students need to take the MCAS multiple times before they pass—vocational schools are particularly committed to offering help and remediation for students who fail—only three seniors did not receive diplomas in 2002.

Moreover, Massachusetts vocational schools do far better than comprehensive high schools on crucial performance metrics.[5] The statewide dropout rate at regular/comprehensive high schools averaged 2.8 percent in 2011 but was only 1.6 percent among the thirty-nine vocational technical schools and averaged 0.9 percent among regional vocational technical schools. (Massachusetts requires every school district to offer students a career vocational technical education option, either by providing it themselves—common among the larger districts—or as part of a regional career vocational technical high school system.)

These encouraging test results are only part of the reason we should be optimistic about the value and importance of CTE in the United States. We visited CTE schools and programs in Massachusetts, New Jersey, New York City, and South Carolina. Everywhere, we found students who were deeply engaged in the work they were doing, enthusiastic about high school, and close to their teachers. Within the confines of their vocational schools, they developed a strong sense of respect for themselves and their peers and see themselves as engaged in meaningful work.

Tri-County, with an enrollment of 950 students and programs in seventeen trades, is considered midsize by Massachusetts standards. The student body is 93 percent white and 22 percent of the students are eligible for free or reduced lunch. The school is housed in a 285,000-square-foot building. The culinary, cosmetology, early childhood education, computer systems, and graphic communications programs are all located in the center core of the building. All of these "shops" serve the public, and their location makes for easy and efficient access.

Cosmetology students work in the salon, which offers haircuts and blow-dries for $8 and hair coloring for $30 or more. There is also a restaurant in the school, run by the culinary students, that is open four days a week for lunch and also sells baked goods. The culinary program does the catering for school and private functions. Tri-County also houses a day care center that is staffed by the early childhood education students. There is a three-day program for kids between nine months of age and three and four years, and a one-day program for eighteen-month to two-and-a-half-year-olds. These programs provide students with an opportunity to practice their trades within the school. Of course, students also get experience working in commercial firms through internships and co-op arrangements.[6]

The medical careers, dental assistance, engineering, legal, and protective services programs are also located in the building's center core. The construction trades (HVAC [heating, ventilation, and air-conditioning], electrical, carpentry, and plumbing) are all together in one wing, while the heavy and loud work and the trades that produce odor and residue (metal fabrication, auto collision, auto tech, and construction) are in a separate wing. The auto body shop is available to local residents who need a front-end alignment or an oil change at very reasonable rates.

Academic classes are held on the second floor of the building, purposefully housed away from excessive noise, odors, vibrations, and any other distractions that come along with learning these trades.

In the past several years, about 35 percent of Tri-County graduates have entered the workforce within six months of receiving their diplomas. In 2013, ten students graduated from the auto collision program. Of those, one went on to a two-year degree program and three to a technical school, while two went directly into the trade. (Two others took jobs not in the trade, while two more were undecided at the time of graduation.) The field with the most graduates that year—twenty-four—was cosmetology. Of those, seven students went on to four-year college and ten went directly into the trade. Culinary arts was similarly popular, with twenty-two graduates, eleven of whom went on to four-year colleges. Four went on to two-year programs and four went into the trade, while two went into the military.

Aside from the obvious fact that a serious and rigorous vocational education prepares students for a specific career path, there is a lot more about the process itself that, when done well, is beneficial for young people. For one, vocational students get to engage with adults who actually have ties to the industry they are pursuing and who, most report, treat them with respect—something that often is not the case in a regular high school.

Take Fred, the welding student from Tri-County:

My [shop] teacher is probably a top-notch guy, top of the list. He taught me everything I know. I've never had a problem with him. He is very understanding. He knows how to explain things. If you don't get it he'll take the time to elaborate. And he's had a bunch of years in the field. He welded on the Alaskan Pipeline so he knew his stuff.

These programs also have the ability to create community, often out of a very diverse student body. For example, the students at Aviation—whose families hail from the Dominican Republic and Puerto Rico, Morocco and Nigeria, the Bronx and Staten Island—reflect the immigrant composition of New York City's youth population. Sixty-seven percent of the school's population is of Hispanic origin; those of Middle Eastern descent come next. A small fraction are African American and white. But to hear the kids tell it, their origins don't matter very much. They are bound together by their common fascination with flying, so much so that the traditional masculine culture now embraces girls who are just as interested in the world of airplanes.

Most important, though, the students in vocational programs respond well to school itself. We heard over and over from students and teachers that in vocational classes, concepts come to life in a way they often do not in regular, academic classes. "When you're in a classroom, who cares if the radius is half the diameter? But in [the HVAC shop] you need to know the difference between radius and diameter because you need to know what size pipe to use, you pay attention," an HVAC teacher at Tri-County explains.

Indeed, Cody, the senior in the HVAC shop who currently has a co-op placement working for an HVAC company, said he learned a lot of environmental science in shop. "We have a thing called EPA," he explains, "which is the certification you need within HVAC just to buy the materials you need."

> Certain things, the unit for inside your house, because it uses a refrigerant, you can buy a dry one that doesn't have the refrigerant in it, but you can't buy the refrigerant to finish off the job without the license because if that stuff is let off into the air enough over time, it ruins the ozone. Now they have like a set regulation on how you're supposed to do it.

For Cody, who is in the middle (honors) academic track, being able to learn in this kind of environment has been a blessing.

> I can't, like, read from a book and learn. I have to do something hands-on. So it was good here because we have the classroom time to learn what we're going to go put our hands on. But then they also show us how to use our hands. And I've grown up around tools my entire life. I've grown up in a garage or job site state of mind.

Fred, the welding major, feels the same way. "I've always been a hands-on person. I don't like to be sitting in a little office," he explains.

> I learned most of my math in math [class]. In shop, we learned mostly like technical names for the trades, different things that we would come across in the field like different types of metal, different terms for

metal, different types of rods, all different equipment, we learned about voltage for the welding machines, we learned about all the different machines, how to use them.

Contending with Stigma

These reactions—likely fostered at least in part by the flexibility implied in the mix of college and work-bound students—suggested that some of the stigma that for decades has attached to the very idea of vocational education among young people has begun to erode, at least among students. Their parents may take more convincing, according to Mary-Ellen MacLeod, Tri-County's director of cooperative education.

> It's that problem child, high-school dropout, grease monkey model. It's a hard, hard one to get rid of because even in this enlightened age we still have those formally educated, academic parents who are afraid that if their children come to a vocational school it puts them off the map for college. And these parents, because of the young age of their kids, haven't actually walked into a trade school and seen what they have to offer lately. They don't understand that we have engineering technology, computer information systems, medical and health careers.

When those parents do walk in the door, according to MacLeod, "it's a done deal."

> The whole emphasis on STEM, which is now becoming STEAM—the "A" is the arts—means you're seeing more of these trades, like engineering, CIS [Computer Information Systems], graphic communications. Those presses are not dirty things anymore. Everything is automated. With the advent of STEM we're seeing more kids going to college because we're offering those kinds of trades.

Tri-County students are not entirely immune to these crosswinds. Strength of character is needed to stick with a vocational program in a state where college is one of the leading industries. "There are a lot of kids who say we're stupid," says Sam Maigret, a Tri-County student majoring in pre-engineering with plans to attend a four-year engineering college. "And that's why we came to the vocational school."

> They were raised around the stigma that vocational schools are for people who are too stupid to get an academic career. . . . I find that completely untrue, I don't know why people have that stigma, considering the fact that there's lots of high-level classes and a lot of capable teachers and it's a good learning structure.

Indeed, while helping a friend from Rhode Island with AP calculus, Sam discovered that "she was doing on Monday what we are doing today, Wednesday, so we are right up here with what everyone else is doing." The emphasis on college prep is a direct result of changes in federal funding that have forced vocational schools to focus not only on career but college readiness. And a nursing teacher at Tri-County backs Sam up: "Voc Ed once was for the people who didn't have academic skills. Where are [those low-performing students] now, because clearly they are not here. What crack did they fall through?"

Academic stature is particularly important to vocational students who concentrate in engineering, which is a college preparatory program. For the eight years that Tri-County has hosted this program, all of its students—who study civil engineering, architecture, aerospace engineering, and digital electronics and get to make use of computers, a 3-D printer, and a CNC (computer numerical control) machine in the process—have gone on to college, most of them to four-year degree programs.

In many ways, Cape May County Technical High School, located in the southernmost county of New Jersey, has a lot in common with Tri-County. Physically, it looks similar—long, wide hallways, spacious shops, and a student body apparently free of the kind of cliquishness that abounds in most high schools. With an enrollment of 591 students, the school offers twenty-one different trades along with three academic tracks. Located on an eighty-four-acre campus, the high school is housed in three main buildings and a greenhouse, an administration building, and a beachfront facility on the Cape May Sound. Like Tri-County, it is also overwhelmingly white (89 percent), with a small Latino (5 percent), black (4 percent), and Asian (2 percent) population, generally reflecting the racial demographics of the area. Boys slightly outnumber girls.

Cape Tech, as it is known, first opened as Cape May County Vocational in 1915, offering agriculture and domestic science, or what its current principal, Mike Adams, described as "chicken farming and housekeeping." Raising poultry and cultivating lima beans were the main industries in the area at the turn of the twentieth century, a period when Cape May was largely a subsistence economy. Over time, the need to prepare young people for work in more viable fields led the school to expand its offerings, and in the 1960s the campus moved to its current location, functioning as a "shared time" vocational school. This model, which is still common today throughout the state, requires kids to take academic classes at their local high school for half the day and then get on a bus to a "voc" school to attend technical classes, ultimately graduating from their local high school with a certificate of completion (or in some cases, such as cosmetology, a state license).

According to Adams, starting in the '60s, the school was for many years geared mainly toward providing low-skill training for minimum-wage jobs to "disaffected" or learning-disabled students. It offered subjects like upholstery—there were a couple of major clothing manufacturers in the area, all of whom left about forty years ago—low-level food occupations (e.g., line and short-order cook), and trained young men to run gas stations. Courses in mechanical electrical repair, says Adams, started attracting a "slightly different" disaffected student—one who didn't fit the mold of the standard comprehensive high school—and the school's menu evolved even more throughout the 1980s.

Then, in 1993, the school moved from a shared-time vocational school to a full-time high school with a technical focus. "What drove the change, which is the same thing driving it in every other state, was the testing," according to Adams. New state requirements mandated that every student be tested and those who were attending Cape May Tech "were losing two periods going back and forth on the bus." As a result, the high schools stopped sending students to Cape May Tech and the school declined rapidly.

"So, the decision was made to become a full-time comprehensive and career and technical school," Adams explains. "The school board at that time was not interested in capturing just the disaffected population and decided to put in some programs that are challenging academically and that lead to more high-level employment."

This full-time vocational model in New Jersey had actually been introduced about a decade earlier, with the opening of the Marine Academy of Science and Technology in Sandy Hook in the early 1980s. The school was the brainchild of a group of parents and teachers who were, according to a recent article in *New Jersey Monthly*, "concerned that New Jersey was the only East Coast state without a high school devoted to the marine sciences."[7]

In its early years, the school offered courses in marine sciences and related trades and today students can take classes in oceanography and environmental science, as well as marine biology, chemistry, and physics. Its popularity soared and that success led ultimately to the creation of other career-focused high schools in the state, including Monmouth's High Technology High School, focusing on engineering and the other STEM disciplines, in 1991; County Prep High School in Jersey City in 1993, offering ten specialized majors, including business, graphic technology design, culinary arts, and medical science; Academy of Allied Health and Science in Neptune, specializing in the medical sciences, in 1996; and Biotechnology High School in Freehold, integrating life science, technology, and engineering, in 2005.

Some of these schools, also known as career academies, have impressive track records of getting their students into top colleges. In 2011, students at High Technology High "racked up an average combined SAT score of 2,145—the highest in the country." Its 2014 senior class saw students accepted to MIT, Princeton, the University of Pennsylvania, Yale, the University of Chicago, Cornell, Notre Dame, Duke, and the University of California at Berkeley.

Cape Tech does not have that kind of a college admissions record, but Adams says that no student of his has failed the state high-school proficiency assessment. And even as the school acknowledges that college may not be for everyone, it also emphasizes the importance of acquiring a strong academic base. "For the electrical union, you need to pass an algebra test," Adams offers, adding that students are encouraged, if not mandated, to take a fourth year of math.

The growing emphasis on academic achievement has clearly rubbed off on its students: 29 percent of the class of 2013 planned to attend a four-year college/university and another 44 percent were headed for two-year colleges. Three percent of the class set its sights on attending a vocational/technical school, while 6 percent planned to enroll in the armed forces. Another 3 percent were slated to enroll in apprenticeship programs while 7 percent were headed into full-time employment.

Whether aware of this history or not, students at Cape Tech don't seem to feel there is any stigma attached to their school or the education they are receiving. Take Eleanor Nuss, a shy senior concentrating in pre-engineering, whose mother is a florist in Cape May and whose father is a pharmacist at a nearby hospital. To Eleanor, attending Cape Tech feels like "definitely a privilege."

> I've made a lot of great friends here. Just the environment here I feel is a lot better than in regular public school. Everyone is just so friendly with each other. There's no real cliques, like in other schools. . . . The teachers work with you. I e-mail teachers and they get back to me within the same day. They're very helpful to me. They're all supportive.

Eleanor was accepted to Rutgers and planned to enroll the following fall. She did not detect any stigma associated with attending a CTE school and in fact believed that the kids at Cape Tech were the envy of kids who didn't go the vocational route.

Jess McNulty, a feisty brunette who is concentrating in law enforcement, chose Cape Tech because she knew she wanted to work for the Federal Bureau of Investigation and believed the school's concentration in law and public safety would give her a leg up. Jess also felt no stigma about going to a vocational school. Now a senior, Jess has taken courses in the basics of criminal justice, including the study of seminal court cases defining the scope of law enforcement power, as well as forensics. In her senior year she attended the local police academy one day a week. By the spring of 2015 she will graduate from the academy as a class 1 police officer. She will also get her certification in 911 dispatching. Jess has already been accepted to a five-year BA/MBA program at Stockton, a nearby state college.

Morgan Teller, who is concentrating in welding and wants to use her skills to work in underwater welding for the Navy, chose Cape Tech because she knew she wanted something different. "I wanted to do something that girls don't do. I was interested in masonry, too. I did welding and I was like, I like that. So I chose that one." Morgan credits her mother with shaping her interests in unconventional directions. "My mom does a lot of stuff with cars. She likes manlier roles, I guess. She built my barn for us, where our horse is. She fixes all of our cars whenever they need to be fixed."

Cape May opened those doors to her and nurtured an environment that made it relatively easy to defy gender stereotypes. Morgan appreciates the role her teachers have played in normalizing her interests, and, like the faculty at Tri-Country, they are eager to help students who are less academically inclined get where they need to be.

This openness to alternative approaches doesn't mean that students who tilt toward the academic side feel the school isn't for them. Mara Veltri, who is concentrating in graphic arts and hopes to major in art history in college, ended up at Cape Tech after her mother "saw how many technical classes it had. And it could help you get right into college with credits and everything that it offered."

Indeed, rather than feel stigmatized for being low achieving or unable to hack academics, Mara believes that kids outside Cape Tech think it's a school full of "weirdos and nerds. I don't think anyone realizes that this is just a regular school with classes that help you with college, basically." That's a far cry from the traditional reputation of vocational education.[8]

Stigma does not seem to be a problem for the teaching staff at the High School for Construction Trades, Engineering and Architecture (CTEA), in Ozone Park, Queens. The school's visually striking, state-of-the-art building was designed to serve as both a teaching tool and a showcase for the career options available in the architectural and engineering industries. Divided into sections to serve different activities, the building features distinct, multicolored, and multitextured areas: The L-shaped brick section contains classrooms and offices; the gray corrugated-metal section houses computer-aided design (CAD) and mechanical drafting labs; a gray-striped concrete section contains the auditorium; and a yellow metal panel encloses the library.

A light, airy lobby gives the school the ambience of a contemporary urban art space rather than a New York City public high school. Scanners and metal detectors are nowhere to be found. Students dressed in the school's uniform—a red or black top with the school's coat of arms and black pants or khakis—mill around in this pleasant setting. It is a multiracial crowd. CTEA's student body is 42 percent Hispanic and 31 percent Asian. Fifteen percent of the students are white, 11 percent are black, and 1 percent is Native American.

CTEA—which opened in 2006—is open to all New York City students. The school received a grade of A on its most recent 2013 progress report. That is excellent news for its 924 students, one of the smallest of student bodies in New York City.

Admission is screened and students applying to the school must attend an open house in order to be considered for admission (tickets are distributed at a citywide high school fair). Students with standardized test scores level 2 or above (level 1 is the lowest score)[9] and grades of 75 or better in core academic subjects may apply. However, the administration encourages students with fairly low middle-school test scores to give the school a try.

The school makes a point of communicating to potential students and parents, however, that CTEA is not a school for people who want to slack off or kids who don't want to work. According to Mitchell Almonte, a carpentry teacher and the school's work-based learning coordinator, "We make it clear to everyone entering our programs not to expect to come here to have an easier time. You are going to come here to meet your graduation requirements and work harder than everybody else in normal high schools."

Some students graduate and go on to get unionized apprenticeships in the construction trades while others, after obtaining a strong background in engineering or architecture, go on to four-year colleges. In fact, 82 percent of the class of 2012–13 enrolled in college or career programs after graduation. A majority of the kids who go to college enroll in the City and State University systems. CTEA fosters the pursuit of a college degree through an articulation agreement with City Tech, a four-year technical college in Brooklyn that is part of the City University of New York system. Students who pursue a City Tech degree are able to waive introductory course requirements on the basis of the courses they have completed in high school.

Likely as a result of its A score and high college enrollment rate, CTEA does not feel like an institution battling stigma. Indeed, one young man we spoke with in an architecture class explained that because he was interested in getting a college degree in engineering, he and his parents had picked CTEA over his zoned school—much closer to his home—because it was in good academic standing and had a reputation for being safe. Even though he had to get up earlier than he would like in order to get to school on time, he was certain he'd made the right choice.

A young woman in the same class whose parents are Southeast Asian planned to go to college for computer engineering. She also reported having had a very happy experience at the school and felt she had been well prepared for a college computer engineering program. She was proud to put CTEA on her résumé and would not hesitate to recommend the school to others.

Struggling Schools

No doubt the elegant architecture and the modern occupational specialties on offer have helped CTEA avoid the vocational education stigma. Automotive High School in Greenpoint, Brooklyn, has not been so fortunate. Its motto, "Manhood, Service, Labor, Citizenship," captures its upstanding, historical origins. A child of the New Deal and the industrial power that attended gearing up for the Second World War, Automotive High was a statement in its own time about the close integration of education and economic prowess. The mighty industry of automobile manufacture was one of America's signature strengths and the East Coast was a central node, along with Detroit, of its production hub. Up until the mid-1980s prospective students were required to pass an entrance examination for admission to Automotive High and its alumni went on to well-paid, rewarding careers in the industry.

But ambivalence toward vocational education took its toll on the school and created a downdraft that left Automotive High School "a dumping ground for students judged unable to handle college-track work," as one former city official put it. In 2011, it was deemed a "Transformation School"—a designation that requires the replacement of the principal and allows for the implementation of approved annual professional performance review (APPR) plans to serve as the basis for rewarding effective teachers and removing ineffective teachers—thus making it eligible for hundreds of thousands of federal dollars. Nonetheless, the New York City Department of Education slated Automotive for closure the following year. A court order prevented that from happening and the school remained open, but in 2012–13 it received an overall grade of F on its progress report and a C for student performance. Its highest grade, a B, was in the area of college and career readiness. That same year, the four-year graduation rate was 45 percent, its six-year rate 64 percent, and the school scored lower than the citywide average—though pretty much in line with peer school averages—on measures of safety.

In 2015, Automotive was placed on the New York State Department of Education's "out of time list," indicating it had failed to substantively improve after three or more years of intensive support. The school had earlier been designated for the city's Renewal Schools program, which aims to improve struggling schools with social services and academic supports. As a result, the principal was forced to reinterview for her job (which she did, successfully). Even though New York's mayor de Blasio and the school's principal say the school is improving, the city's Department of Education was forced to submit improvement plans for the school in the summer of 2015. At that time, a key element of the Renewal Schools program had not yet been implemented at Automotive: the social services—delivered by the likes of substance abuse counselors, mental health experts, and medical professionals—that are supposed to help to transform every struggling school into a community school.[10]

Automotive is located right in the middle of a gentrifying urban neighborhood. Its student body is 66 percent black, 33 percent Latino, and 96 percent male. Seventy-eight percent of students are eligible for free lunch. Founded in 1937, Automotive is no match in its physical appearance for schools like Tri-County or Cape Tech, let alone some of the new vocational high schools popping up in New York City. Its hallways and classrooms are dingy and antiquated. Students enter through a back entrance abutting the school's parking lot, passing through metal detectors and scanners on their way in. Over the security desk hang posters urging the importance of "showing respect" and "obeying the rules." The wide hallways, which were built to accommodate car parts and mechanical equipment, are uniformly drab, with little decoration, save for some notices and trophy cases that house awards from automotive contests. A large elevator built to transport cars goes unused by students who instead travel between floors using the stairs.

According to the school's principal, Caterina Lafergola, the decision to do away with the entrance exam brought more kids into the school who were looking for an easy ride, a place to coast for four years. They weren't particularly interested in getting into the automotive industry or doing the hard work that was at one time expected of all Automotive students.

> There's this misconception that CTE high schools, or what were known as vocational high schools, are for students that don't have academic aptitude. The reality is that nothing could be further from the truth because students in our program require very strong mathematics and numeracy skills and very strong literacy skills.

Unfortunately, this misconception is embraced by many middle-school guidance counselors. They compound the reputation problem for CTE schools. Typically, the counselors do not recommend vocational education to their strongest students. Lafergola explains:

> Students meet with their guidance counselors in eighth grade. There's not a whole lot of articulation, we don't have a specific feeder school because our school is a commuter school. None of the students in this school actually live in the vicinity.
>
> Some students are picking us because there's a misconception on the part of the guidance department that they don't have to meet the same requirements because it's a CTE school. So we have been doing a lot of outreach, specifically this year, in changing that by going to the middle schools. . . . So, in theory the students should pick us as one of their top three choices but sometimes they pick us as a twelfth choice or they don't pick us at all and they are placed here by the enrollment

office, which again mitigates outcomes. We would like to see the [entrance] exam come back.

Automotive's limbo status and its failing grade have resulted in a student body—about 420 in number—that is at less than half capacity. "Two years ago, parents didn't even know the school existed because they were told it was closing," explains Don Morisette, a teacher at Automotive.

> Kids who were here when that happened had a chance to opt out. Not only did that deprive us of a group of kids that we would have had coming in, but it took the group that we did have and dropped them down. A lot of good kids left.

The metrics that are employed to compute grades for schools measure some things that we might agree are important, but they do not tell us whether students—especially vocational students—have passed national certification exams or been employed. When low grades are issued to a vocational school—or it delivers low standardized test scores—parents are discouraged from giving vocational education a chance and that, in turn, endangers these programs.

Automotive stands as an example of the negative impact of the testing craze. Teacher Don Morisette captures the problem well:

> The focus has shifted over the last fifteen, twenty years—the standardized tests, the graduation requirements jumping up, up, up, up. Everybody's focused on outcomes, which is not a problem. But I think they neglected this pathway that didn't become any less relevant. It got harder, it got more technical. The demand if anything is probably increasing because our lives are mechanized and electronically controlled and everybody carries around a computer on their hip nowadays.

Absent a different kind of evaluation system, principals like Lafergola end up having to focus on raising test scores to ensure their survival. And while higher standardized test scores will no doubt increase the prestige of and options for both the school and its students, what it takes to achieve them can also hinder what the school is trying to accomplish in vocational training.

In recent years, New York State has required all high school students to pass five Regents exams in order to graduate. Those tests cover coursework in English, math, science, US history, and world history. It is not easy to integrate coursework that is supposed to prepare students for such tests and also teach certain industry or field-specific ways of thinking, skills, and competencies. Indeed, some teachers feel that the need to do this—and the fact that students in New York City can graduate from a CTE school with a Regents diploma even if they fail their vocational courses—actually downgrades CTE. Since the demonstration of technical mastery is not required for vocational students to receive a Regents diploma, in effect their CTE classes are treated as if they were electives.

According to Said Youssef, who teaches engineering at CTEA in Queens, this may also discourage kids in CTEA programs because they are not sufficiently acknowledged for the extra work they do, particularly since not all programs lead to an industry-recognized license. Instead, he believes they should be given additional recognition, a special diploma:

> Whether you take it in the ghetto sense, or in the Wall Street sense, or in the highest academic sense, this is disrespectful. Because you take a student who has spent four years studying social studies, language, science, and math. But add a fifth element, which is CTE, which also requires some intellect, discipline, some work, and you don't reward the students after four years for that? . . . We should also have a certificate or a second diploma, to qualify you as a person who can work in this field as a trainee.

As a way of acknowledging their seriousness, Youssef favors making the passage of CTE mandatory in order to obtain a Regents diploma. Indeed, Youssef wants to push for legislation to this effect, and to see the Department of Education institute a system of two diplomas—one academic and one CTE. He also laments the fact that the Common Core standards have replaced older ones that he believes more accurately assessed the accomplishments of vocational students:

So as an engineer, you go to a job and the first question they ask you is going to be, when did Napoleon Bonaparte invade Russia? We need [a different kind of assessment] for us as engineers and technicians. We have to write a manual, read a manual, interpret a manual.

I love what I do. I love to be with my students. I know my job as a teacher is to produce good citizens. More than just teach you how to wire, I teach you how to be disciplined, think straight, make right decisions as much as you can, use your resources to make decisions. That's what we need for the next twenty years in this country. But now we have a politician sitting in Albany and his job is to produce numbers. . . .

We, the foot soldiers in the school, should have a voice, to make decisions that affect 2.2 million students in the state of New York. We should have people from industry, from the schools, from CTE, talk with the people from Albany. Because I am disgusted by what I'm seeing now.

Youssef cited one of his former students who is working on submarines and making $90,000 a year. Another student who graduated with training in air-conditioning and refrigeration was in charge of servicing a truck. At nineteen or twenty, he could make $75,000 a year.

Examples like these have convinced Youssef that the current obsession with college is deeply misguided. His students are equipped to be successful and those trajectories are helping them write a ticket to the good life. He doubts a college education could do more for them. Although the common belief is that college graduates earn more, Youssef compares one hypothetical student four years out of high school with an HVAC license making $70,000 annually, to another, just graduated from college with $70,000 in debt. He also cites poor recruitment efforts. He was asked, as a Muslim, to go to his mosque and bring in students, and to do this on his own time.

From Youssef's perspective, the lack of confidence in the entire enterprise that is career and technical education is reflected in the backgrounds of school principals, who are selected by district superintendents. If the city—via its superintendents—really believed in the mission of vocational education, it would hire principals who exemplify it, Youssef believes. Instead, more traditional principals with backgrounds in academic subjects are put in charge, and they have neither the appropriate backgrounds nor the right values to lead schools with a different mission. Youssef explained:

> When a teacher has a background in English or a history teacher becomes the principal of a school that does CTE, it is doomed to fail. If you're an English teacher, a history teacher, you don't have it in your heart. So, the last one was an electrician and it was good. The CTE principals should come from the field. But nobody wants to be a CTE principal. It's just too much responsibility and little reward. Nobody wants to be a CTE principal.

Steve Flynn teaches at CTEA in Queens. He is a journeyman electrician and well equipped to take students through the process of qualifying for a good, blue-collar career. Respect for his own trade propels him to work every day. But given the rigid emphasis on the Common Core, he cannot rest until his students have enough knowledge of pure math to pass those tests. It takes time to meld those two worlds and he is not sure it's the best way for him to invest it.

Flynn knows how to prepare students for their chosen field of work. He doesn't dumb their curriculum down. On the contrary, he is training them in the high art of deductive reasoning and problem solving, and also teaching them to regard their work as the foundation of a career. From his perspective, that is more valuable than mastering a theorem. It is what will make them worthy of a living wage and the status of a professional.

> We need to stay competitive here in New York City or these industries are going to be broken down. The salaries, the benefit packages are going to be broken down. Every day, so many people depend on the employment from the industry that they are in to raise their family. So they want to hold on to that through skills and ability and training. This is how we feed our families. This is a career.

There is no doubt that Automotive High School has the ability to train students for jobs that will enable them to live productive lives, if it overcomes its current difficulties. And it may help that the New York State

Board of Regents, which has been wrestling for several years with the issue of alternative pathways to graduation, in January 2015 voted unanimously to approve a change in high school requirements that would allow students who want to graduate with a CTE concentration to obtain a waiver from the need to pass one of their Regents history exams. (These new requirements still mandate that all high school students will have to complete courses in both US history and government as well as global history; however, they will no longer have to pass Regents exams in both.) Marking the biggest change in New York's diploma requirements in two decades, the new rules were slated to take effect with the 2015 graduating class.

While some groups representing teachers, including the Long Island Council for the Social Studies, disapproved of granting exam waivers, other leaders in both business and education, including Robert Lowry, the deputy director of the New York State Council of School Superintendents, supported the change. After the vote, Lowry was quoted in *Newsday* saying, "There are lots of ways to be successful in adult life. There ought to be more than one way to pursue a diploma, which is a passport to adult life." The assistant state commissioner for school operations, Chuck Szuberla, also endorsed the newly approved requirements, noting their potential positive effect on graduation rates: "This allows kids to pursue their passion—something that leads to greater participation and graduation results."[11]

Vocational education has begun to shed its long-lived stigma in American high schools in some states. Ironically, this has come about in part because of federal requirements that CTE prepare young people for both work and college. This is a laudable goal, particularly as proponents of this type of education have long understood that training the hand is not distinct from, but in fact inextricably linked to, training the mind. Yet the emphasis on college, and the near obsession with standardized testing, have also hampered efforts to deliver CTE that succeeds in meeting this goal.

Truly effective CTE requires close coordination between the education system and industry, well-trained teachers with experience in their technical fields, the integration of what we think of as academic subjects with skills training, and the use of methods of evaluation that capture and can communicate what students are learning and achieving. Much of this, of course, is beyond the control of the very institutions that are currently tasked with providing this type of education.

Leaders in CTE schools know how to get this job done, but they have to watch out for other audiences, particularly those who are sensitive about tracking, to be sure they are not defaulting on a competing promise to push their students over the testing hurdles. Vocational educational has long been conceived of as a solution to a problem: the integration of immigrants, a remedy for poverty, a way of dealing with disaffected kids, or a fix for a skills gap. It has just begun to climb out of the shadow cast by this kind of social remediation. In the countries where it has been most successful, CTE is respected in its own right and understood as a legitimate, worthy form of education that demands a great deal of its students and teachers, while benefiting society as a whole. It is unlikely that we will get past the on-again, off-again attitudes we have toward vocational education until we can come around to thinking about technical education as a valuable end in and of itself.

4

What Industry Needs

Vocational programs aim to equip their graduates with skills that are in demand. Staying up to date with what that requires is not a simple proposition in a country where industry and school are intended to be separate institutions. Vocational schools have to break that paradigm and to court firms that help them stay up to date on industry needs. A welcome side benefit of that alignment can emerge when companies provide financial support or in-kind contributions (especially equipment), as well as internships for students and job opportunities for graduates. Schools that are too distant from the industries their students hope to join will be poorly informed and their graduates penalized for it.

As scholars of labor markets have learned, the matching process that links job seekers and hiring managers depends on the flow of information and the nature of preferences. In a society dominated by various preconceptions about what—or who—makes for a good employee, connections are crucial for overcoming inequality and prejudice. When labor markets are tight, hiring managers may have to descend far down the hierarchy of their desires because otherwise they will not be able to find enough workers. When the economy tanks and the lines of the unemployed stretch outside the door of every firm, hiring managers can be very choosy. And skill is not the only thing they are looking for.

Sociologist Devah Pager mounted some clever field experiments that bring the point home. She sent "testers," young men of different races, with fake résumés to firms that advertised entry-level openings, having coached them extensively in how to comport themselves so that they were as alike as possible, right down to the clothing they wore to interviews. The black and Hispanic testers offered identical biographies: high-school graduates with some work experience. Because Pager was particularly interested in racial differences in job hiring, she introduced one distinction: the white tester's résumé listed a felony conviction. This should have made him far less employable. But Pager's data show that employers were more likely to offer a job to the white felon than to take a chance on minority men who had no criminal records of any kind.

Disturbing as Pager's finding is, we should not be surprised since other sociologists have told us about the biases at work among employers in urban centers. In an important study in the early '90s, two graduate students at the University of Chicago, Joleen Kirschenman and Kathryn Neckerman, ventured out of Hyde Park to interview employers in the region about how they saw the reliability, skills, and temperament of different kinds of people in the labor market. They were trying to understand the statistics on racial differences in hiring, to figure out why black men in particular faced such difficulties. Their landmark paper, "We'd Love to Hire them, But . . ." made it clear that minorities—especially men—faced an extraordinary uphill climb.[1]

Chicago employers started from the view that black men would not work hard, tell the truth, or behave in a cooperative fashion on the job. They could point to individual black workers and say just the opposite: great employees, totally reliable. But these workers were thought of as exceptions that proved the rule. Employers assumed that since black men are disproportionately behind bars, black applicants were more likely to have criminal records; that since education levels in inner-city communities are, on average, low, applicants who were black were less likely to be competent. Hence the form of discrimination faced by applicants was not the old-fashioned kind of explicit skin color bigotry we classically label racist. It was, instead, a kind of statistical prejudice. Rising above these assumptions is a tall order, particularly when the labor market is crowded. Employers don't have to settle for anyone they have suspicions about. Black teenagers coming out of poor neighborhoods are left on the sidelines regardless of their personal qualities.

New York University sociologist Deirdre Royster showed in her book *Race and the Invisible Hand*[2] that equally qualified black and white students who completed the same blue-collar training programs end up in very different jobs because of these background factors, which have nothing to do with their individual abilities and everything to do with differences they cannot change.

Connections are important to all job seekers because they confer advantages over competitors who cannot bring the same influence to bear. Those who are on the receiving end of bias are most in need of that helping hand. Even a superior high school performance may not do much to reverse the bias. A Census Bureau study of four thousand employers found that they considered grades, teachers' recommendations, and the prestige of an applicant's school the three *least* important factors when hiring.[3] Talking with employers, Northwestern University sociologist James Rosenbaum found that employers don't trust teachers they don't already know. Instead, they rely on their own judgment of interviews and lean heavily on social networks for recruiting.[4]

These networks, which can help a student get over the hurdle of getting that first job, are not cultivated in general high schools, especially the ones that are located in poorer neighborhoods. Vocational education can help to solve the skills gap, but unless it is accompanied by a strong emphasis on labor market connections, these job seekers will likely hit the walls that these sociologists have identified.[5]

American high schools that do invest in cultivating ties with employers actually show some fairly impressive results. Students who graduated from high schools with school-business partnerships had significantly less unemployment, higher annual earnings, and higher wages than students who graduated from high schools without these partnerships.[6] Indeed, building networks with local employers may be the most important mechanism by which these students get jobs.

Unfortunately, such partnerships are relatively rare. Instead, connections between school and work are usually left to individual teachers who take it upon themselves, often as a kind of personal crusade, to make a difference for their charges. Rosenbaum interviewed 110 vocational teachers in twelve high schools (including four labeled as vocational) and discovered that 95 percent of them had previously had a career in the industry in which they were now teaching. Eighty-six percent made special efforts to learn the specific needs of local employers. Though the school systems that employed them neither asked them to make these efforts to place their students with firms nor rewarded them for doing so, they often harvested from their personal experience to create the kind of ties, introductions, and pipelines that Japanese teachers routinely develop precisely because it *is* written into their job descriptions.

American schools that work hard to match kids to jobs may find a willing ear among local businessmen, but other than self-satisfaction they see few rewards for their efforts. Teachers' salaries do not rise if they have a good track record of connecting their graduates to jobs. Schools that have been successful in finding kids jobs will not be singled out, as they would be if their test scores improved. Individual teachers and principals may decide that freeing their students from poverty traps by helping them find employment is a worthy use of their time. But this is their choice on their own time, even in periods where the whole country is wringing its hands over youth unemployment rates.

The Challenge of Aligning with Workforce Needs: A Case Study of Aviation High School

Poor alignment with workforce needs has long plagued vocational education. New York City's vocational programs offer a case in point. In 2008, the city's Department of Education issued a report by a mayoral task force noting that the fields offered in CTE school programs and schools were not well matched with the job market.[7] Many CTE programs focused on training in the arts, AV (audiovisual) technology, and communications (18 percent), and business management and administration (14 percent), while the areas in which job growth was projected by 2018 are human services and health sciences. A handful of CTE schools, like Aviation

High School in Queens and Ralph R. McKee CTE High School in Staten Island, are notable exceptions, consistently turning out graduates who are able to compete for coveted jobs in industries, even those where jobs are scarce, and/or pursue higher education or training. But their experience has not been the norm, though attempts are under way to make it so.

Aviation High School's history is visible all over its campus. A New Deal–era insignia, flight chevrons with a globe in the middle, adorns the front door. Photos of decorated military veterans in full-dress uniform standing proudly next to students twenty years younger line the walls. A fully overhauled and restored Cessna 150—a senior project—was featured in a celebratory picture denoted proudly as the best work of the year. "Mothballed" on an airfield in upstate New York for over eight years, the plane was subsequently donated to the school for this project. Senior teachers in Aviation Maintenance taught the students how to strip its old paint, overhaul the engine, repair the fuel lines, and ready the little blue propeller plane to present to the school principal and JetBlue's chief executive officer during the graduation ceremony.

Respect for the role of aviation in the country's war effort comes through not only in the history classes the students take but in the daily interaction in the hallways with military officers who recruit actively among the fifth-year students. Yet the atmosphere is less military and more a fraternity/sorority of young people who understand that they are part of an honored culture with a storied past. Founded in 1925 as the Central Building Trades School, the forerunner of Aviation High School opened on East Twenty-First Street in Manhattan. Three teachers and a handful of students attended classes four hours a day, which, in those days, were designed to train young men in woodworking, plumbing, plastering, sheet metal, and electrical installation. The New York City Fire Department condemned the building only five years later, sending teachers and students to what is today one of the richest zip codes in the United States: East Sixty-third Street.

The program evolved into a full-time high school and, as the Second World War edged closer, added aviation training to the curriculum. Its popularity rose as the flying bug caught on and, courtesy of philanthropist Baron Maurice de Hirsch, the Central Building Trades School moved again to a building it rented from him for $1 a year. He also changed its name to the Manhattan School of Aviation Trades. By 1949, it had become the largest aviation high school in the United States and the source of thousands of mechanics.

Over the next several decades, the school developed training programs that qualified students for airframe and power plant certifications, and then, in 1993, added an elective—and selective—fifth-year program that enables them to receive both Federal Aviation Administration certificates and meet the state Regents exams required for graduation in New York State. This is an extraordinary opportunity to train and certify in a field where job opportunities are not as plentiful as they once were but still exist for those who are well qualified. Students who enter the field when they are older go to community colleges and trade schools to qualify for FAA certification. The training and certification will cost them north of $30,000, a daunting sum for young people who come from households of limited means. The value of the opportunity at Aviation High is not lost on eighth-grade students in New York City: 3,600 vied for the 480 seats in the school's freshman class in 2013.

Students now train at a purpose-built campus in Queens that houses an aircraft hangar with twenty planes and a helicopter. Thirty-five shops provide "aircraft engineers, landing gears, and propellers, hydraulic systems, welding booths, air-conditioning, and complete avionics laboratories." An annex at Kennedy International Airport is reserved for the select fifth-year students who will have the chance to work on the school's only jet plane.

On the day we arrived, students in Rick Browne's class were working on eddy current. "What is the eddy current inspection method?" they were asked, and "In what situation would [it] be preferable over the magnetic particle or dye penetrant inspection methods?" "Why are crack and conductivity standards used?" "Explain the absolute and comparison method." Organized into crews, with chiefs who take responsibility for orchestrating the work flow, the students were trying to answer these technical questions on a job sheet that mimics what they would use in the workplace. Each person in the crew was expected to contribute to the work, and they were reminded that the unit required them to know and understand principles, theories, and concepts of aviation.

The curriculum at Aviation proceeds methodically through a series of technical domains after the freshman year. It begins with aircraft sheet metal and composites so that students become familiar with the materials that are used in the manufacture of planes. In their junior year, students take courses in "basic airframe" (the study of the structure of the aircraft and all of its systems) and "basic power plant" (the study of aircraft engines and related systems), and then go on to the advanced versions of each subject. Students qualify for a license in one field at the end of four years and, if they are selected, they have the optional fifth year for further specialization.

Their "shop classes" represent the culmination of several years of study in classrooms where they learned to test for fractures in aluminum or leaks in fuel lines. Outside on the tarmac beyond the annex, they can see the modern version of the planes they are learning to repair lifting off into the clouds from the runways at Kennedy International Airport. Framed against a bright blue sky, those jet trails represent their dreams of good jobs in a high-technology industry.

The students benefit by having passionate teachers, some of whom moonlight at JFK or across two rivers at Newark Liberty International Airport in New Jersey. They are all flying nuts, who would rather work on planes than breathe. Some are military veterans who learned their craft in Afghanistan or Iraq, on the decks of aircraft carriers. Others are themselves graduates of Aviation High, which has trained thousands of (almost entirely) men for the civilian aviation industry, aircraft manufacturing firms, cargo transport, and even private jet transport for the rich and famous.

In addition to the vocational training, students at Aviation take a full New York State Regents program, including honors and AP classes. As well as airframe and power plant shops, they are required to master English, math, social studies, science, health education, a foreign language, music, and drawing for trades. Those who are on the high end can also take AP physics, chemistry, biology, English, calculus, European history, and global history.

Few outside the school seem to recognize that this aspect of Aviation's offerings is part of the school's tradition. Like most vocational schools, Aviation has a hard time rising above the skepticism that middle-class parents have about this kind of education. This is a sore subject with teachers and the principal. For at least four years running, Aviation was recognized as one of the best high schools in the nation by *US News & World Report*. Between 2007 and 2011, the school earned four years of straight A grades from the New York City Department of Education. Even so, parents who think their children should head for college often believe that a school like Aviation High would put that future at risk. If only they knew: 80 percent of its graduates go on to two- and four-year colleges, as well as trade academies. Students who go on to programs in aerospace technology are often able to claim college credits for the courses on aviation maintenance they completed in high school. If they complete the FAA certification, they can receive up to two years of advanced standing, which is a huge financial advantage.

Despite this admirable track record, for most of its recent history, Aviation High School has been hampered by a budget so constrained that it cannot cover the cost of modern equipment. Forty-five students in one class share an instrument that tests for aluminum fractures. They have to be content with worksheets until their turn at the machine comes around. The engines they work on in another practicum were extracted from planes that flew in the 1950s. They have been fortunate to receive one or two modern planes as donations, but the classroom work is hobbled by out-of-date equipment. "We could use ten times the budget we have," Principal Deno Charalambous says.

This is an Achilles' heel for vocational education in the United States. Few high school budgets can withstand the expense of modernizing equipment for welders, mechanics, computer technicians, and the like. Yet if the students cannot train on state-of-the-art instruments, they will have a harder time competing for the jobs they hope to land. Both aircraft manufacturing and the airline industry maintenance business have become ferociously competitive. The companies work overtime to drive costs down and that means looking worldwide for less expensive sources of skilled labor. Flying an empty plane to China or Costa Rica for servicing can still be significantly less costly—because of wage differentials—than parking it in an American hangar and letting a domestic crew take care of the work. These pressures have shrunk this workforce and narrowed the bottleneck through which Aviation High School students must pass on the way to classic aviation jobs.

At the same time, new fields—like the overnight delivery industry represented by FedEx or United Parcel Service and the behemoth Amazon—have emerged that make use of airplanes. These companies have entire fleets of cargo planes that need all of the services the airlines offer, save the passengers. Moreover, the hydraulics that students learn at Aviation High applies to subway systems and even the rides at Disneyland. This provides some options for students who don't fit through the eye of the needle at JetBlue or United Airlines.

Despite these new opportunities, overall the students emerging from Aviation High School face a competitive landscape in their search for work. That puts a premium on the skills they can boast, the work experience they can pile up while still in school, and the connections they can lean on.

Connecting to Firms

Because of the financial constraints that hamper schools like Aviation, students look to gain exposure to up-to-date equipment and current methods by landing internships. (Aviation's industry partners include Delta Airlines, JetBlue, and British Airways, and they accept students as interns.) Firms have the latest equipment or they cannot compete and hence they become the locus of training for those students lucky enough to find a placement. They also can become sources of permanent employment for students. Paid internships are, of course, the most desirable option and, for students from low-income backgrounds, often the only feasible pathway to the experience they need. Not all companies are that generous; they know that the opportunity they offer is valuable and they don't have to pay to find talented interns. But the absence of that support often means that a student whose family circumstances dictate the need for a salary will have to bypass the chance.

Among the schools we visited, Tri-County in Massachusetts was the only one that offered the senior year co-op placement in which students spend alternating weeks away from school and on a full-day, paying job (in some cases with opportunities for overtime or weekend work). This is a way for students not only to gain valuable work experience on up-to-date equipment but to connect with employers who could—and often do—offer them full-time work upon graduation.

Mary-Ellen MacLeod, the director of cooperative education at Tri-County, works very hard to ensure that students have these opportunities and she spends much of her time working her contacts, nurtured over many years of working in vocational education; she also advises students on how to turn summer jobs into yearlong placements. But this means that generating and maintaining industry contacts largely depends on relationships she has built rather than a formal system of linkages that can be sustained even as individuals come and go. And this can make keeping up these industry contacts—and the work opportunities they generate—challenging.

It certainly helps when the teachers themselves come out of the industry their students are trying to break into. At Aviation, many of the shop teachers are alumni of the school and have come back to teach after retiring from careers in aviation because they love planes and the maverick culture that comes with the flying bug. The connections they develop out of their career experience facilitates the placement of their high school advisees. Wesley, the Aviation High graduate, benefited from these informal ties and the willingness of his teachers to go the extra mile. Most of them either had worked in the industry at one time or were working there still when he was a student. These teachers could rely on real experience in crafting their classes and were very useful in linking students to work opportunities in the airline business. Wesley remembers two such teachers, one who worked for American Airlines and another who worked for the now defunct Tower Air, because they constantly informed students about work opportunities and helped students land jobs. Wesley got his first job at Tower Air this way.

Mario Cotumaccio is a full-time teacher, a 1990s graduate of Aviation High, and president of its alumni association. At the end of his teaching day he drives forty minutes to Newark Liberty International Airport, where he begins his second job with one of the airlines. As an employee, Cotumaccio is completely up to date with the latest aircraft technology, and he has the connections to place students in internships because his networks are robust. He uses those bonds to create a pipeline between his day job at Aviation High and his evening job.

Employing teachers with ties to industry would seem important enough to make it an essential qualification. In some states, a certain number of years of industry experience is a requirement for employment in CTE schools,[8] but this is not the case everywhere. In New York City a shortage of trained CTE teachers prompted the creation of an alternative route to the teaching certification called Success Via Apprenticeship (SVA). SVA is a five-year joint program between the Department of Education and the New York City College of Technology that aspiring CTE teachers can enter right out of high school. While in this program, they take college-level coursework, are employed in high school teaching internships, and get industrial work experience required for a New York State initial teaching certificate.

In practice, this means that potential CTE teachers may have little or no industry experience and lack the ties that are vital to the success of these schools, let alone the skills they would have developed had they had that experience. This has been an issue at Automotive, where the time commitment and responsibilities of teaching don't allow for many of the school's teachers to easily maintain industry contacts, let alone acquire skills on the latest equipment, unless they want or are able to hold down two jobs—a tall order. But Automotive's difficulties in securing industry ties have other causes as well.

Automotive sustains strong relationships with city agencies, like the New York Sanitation, Transportation, Fire, and Police Departments, all of which own large fleets of cars that need constant maintenance. Indeed, an organization called NYC Fleet has partnered with the Department of Education to expand Automotive's internship program, providing students with hands-on experience maintaining high-profile city vehicles. Student interns, who are paid for their work, learn from experts and professionals who service what is the largest municipal fleet in the United States.

But Automotive High School's relations with the car industry more broadly are fractured. The school once had strong partnerships with Toyota and Mercedes-Benz, but those fizzled out as the school's reputation began to slide (the school also has private-sector partnerships with local car dealerships). Dedicated faculty and administrators are doing their best to change that, but it is a tall order.

"If I could say there's a guiding vision right now," explains teacher Don Morisette, "it's that in our field we need to distinguish ourselves by becoming the hub of all things automotive."

Because the automotive community, the industry people, and the kids coming up through the pipeline, they all depend on each other. The kids are going to depend on industry for jobs and industry depends on the kids for their next wave of workers. There should be an investment there between the two sides.

Morisette believes that if his students have a place in the industry community, a role that matters, their motivation will rise accordingly: "Kids need to see all of this. That's what makes them invested, when they feel like [they are] part of something that's bigger than this room. Our push has been to get more industry contact. The Riding With Us Foundation is one aspect of it." The foundation donates cars that students restore. They recently gave the school a 1968 Chevrolet pickup truck, which the students are repairing and will then auction off to benefit the school. Working on projects like this helps motivate the students. Getting car clubs—nonprofit groups of auto enthusiasts often organized around a particular type of vehicle—involved would help, too:

> We're going to host a meeting here of all the car club representatives from the area and ask them to help us plan our next car show, let's get a bigger venue, get more people in. When those people come, we have conversations. The kids are able to market themselves, they can approach people. We look for the internship sites, we look for the donations.

It makes a difference when external eyes are watching Don's program and see what he is trying to accomplish. His school's advisory council meets twice a year to advise Don on how to improve the quality of instruction, to point out gaps in the curriculum and changes they should consider. Among other things, they serve as an accrediting body for the National Automotive Technicians Education Foundation. Its members include a local union president, a representative from an NYPD garage, and a representative from Snap-on Tools, as well as someone from the Universal Technical Institute's postsecondary partner. Automotive is always looking to expand the group and widen the school's support base. As Don Morisette says:

This is community involvement. Within the automotive community, if we get the people in there and make them feel invested, we could really have something here. We invite groups to use our facilities. General Motors did Chevy Volt training for some of the NYC agencies here this last summer. Their mechanics are now inside the building. Some graduated twenty years ago.

I think if we can tap into that and get them involved, it's all part of building a community that centers around this program.

Despite this activity, which Morisette and his colleagues have worked very hard to generate, he feels that the city itself is only slowly coming around to playing a central role in helping these schools foster meaningful, sustainable industry connections. While the NYC DOE does have a small work-based learning branch that provides networking and professional development opportunities for its schools, its ability to actually secure and sustain industry partnerships and involvement is limited. "It's not like the mayor's office said, 'let's support let's connect everything, let's help build what it is we actually need help with.'"

New York City's High School for Construction Trades, Engineering and Architecture (CTEA) is trying to avoid the difficulties that Morisette describes for Automotive, and it helps that the school is relatively new and lacks the baggage of a school that has been publicly deemed "in trouble." CTEA has worked closely with the city and industry partners to develop its curriculum and, as part of the state approval process, to take care that everything they do is up to industry standards. Those partners—which include the Cooper Hewitt, Smithsonian Design Museum; the National Action Council for Minorities in Engineering; Turner Construction; the New York City Department of Design and Construction; and the Building Trades Employers' Association—continue to play a role in the school as members of an advisory board that meets four or five times a year. The board provides input into the curriculum, keeping the school abreast of changing demands of consumers, weighing in on equipment, and, whenever possible, helping students obtain meaningful work experience. Industry partners also provide training in occupational safety and health for CTEA teachers.

Mitch Almonte is a teacher and the learning coordinator at CTEA, which means he is responsible for connecting industry partners with the students so that they are exposed to real-world experience, particularly since the school has neither the space nor the funds for some of the equipment students will use in the field. To that end, he does a lot of networking and "job site visitations to make sure that the kids are satisfied, the employers are satisfied with the quality of the students, and also just continue to network. Because one employer can lead [him] to another, or to someone who wants to be involved in another capacity."

Keeping those connections takes work. "As a fairly new school," Almonte recalls, "we had a lot of partners who started to work together with the city when the whole concept of the school was being put together." He continued:

> Then as my role in the school developed, it was my job to keep them engaged, have them somehow find a connection to the learning that's happening in the school so that they could find their role as to how they can assist in that process. So some of the partners have been able to provide internships and others have been able to provide other kinds of activities—field trips, job shadowing, career fairs, summer internships, which can be paid or unpaid. It really depends on the needs of the student and the availability by the employers.

Almonte tries to convey the rules—and the possibilities—to the employers he works with:

> Yes, some internships can be paid, some are unpaid. Some of it is supported by the DOE funding, they get paid from the city. Some employers pay from their own budget. They have no problem paying minimum wage. I have one partner who is a cabinet-making shop, and he paid the kid fully out of his budget. And I sat down and educated him on the whole liability issue and he was cool as long as the kid was eighteen. So I then had to limit which kids I could send there.

But leaving so much up to one person's labors seems risky. What if, despite Almonte's best efforts, the internships don't materialize? That is what has Automotive's Morisette worried, wishing for more sustained, institutional support. "It's interesting that such a big component of education in this system doesn't have these things worked out already."

Almonte's task would be made easier if the DOE could take responsibility for counseling employers on tricky matters like liability insurance, since few understand that they are covered for students as long as they are supervised. Confusion on the part of employers about what can and cannot be done when taking teenagers into their firms inhibits more robust connections. Then Almonte could concentrate on streaming the right students to the right firms and build up the alliance so that it is closer to automatic:

> Once I have an employer like that who's already been educated and sat-isfied, I've got to make sure I keep him and keep sending him kids so he'll be motivated to continue bringing more kids. For most of our construction kids, I've been able to send them to construction management companies, where danger is not so much of an issue, they are working at estimating, working on contracts.

Almonte also gets industry support through Skills USA, an organization that sponsors student competitions and provides opportunities for industry to connect with the instructors. The organization facilitates industry education, including new certification programs, to keep teachers up to date with the standards and labor market needs in their fields.

For CTEA students who want to enter the construction field and the labor unions, the school works with the Edward J. Malloy Initiative for Construction Skills, which offers preapprenticeship training in the construction trades to graduating New York City public high school seniors. The initiative provides classroom and hands-on training, the successful completion of which results in referrals to union apprenticeship programs through what is known as a "direct entry track" that allows students to bypass the public recruitment process.

According to Almonte, the students "just have to work with us in workshop training during their senior year," and that puts them at the front of the list when the unions take in enrollment.

> Union apprenticeship is just a different type of college education. We do make sure that the kids understand that when they're pursuing this

route, but we definitely encourage college education because it is going to make them more competitive when they enter the workforce. With the apprenticeship, the difference is that they are getting paid instead of paying the college.

Tri-County in Massachusetts also has articulation agreements with several unions that agree to accept into training programs graduates who meet certain admission standards and to offer advice, assistance, and support to CTE programs. According to Mary-Ellen MacLeod:

> Our plumbers, our electricians, and our carpenters, those are all apprentice programs. But when they graduate, we have an articulation with those trades that they get their apprentice card, so the thousand hours of vocational training counts [toward their union card]. . . . [The masonry and construction shops also have an articulation agreement with the unions, which] have no problem taking on sheet metal and welding kids.

The unions "want trained workers," she continues, noting that because the students have already had these hours, "they are going to be certified and out in the labor force quicker."

The Massachusetts Department of Transportation is one agency that has been somewhat resistant to taking students from the construction and craft labor unions because, according to MacLeod, they incorrectly believe that the students don't have enough training. She feels this erroneous perception is fueled by a lack of information about what the school actually equips students to do, about how much they know.

As a result, MacLeod is convinced that educating the unions should be higher up on the school's to-do list, she explains, noting that some enlightened unions that have embraced vocational graduates as apprentices understand that "they get huge bang for the buck. The beauty of a voc high school kid, particularly in the heavy trades," she explains, "is that not only have they been trained here in Massachusetts, supervised with state-of-the-art equipment with teachers who have been certified, they learn the right way."

Because they're young they don't have any shortcuts yet. They are still young enough to be in awe and a little afraid of the heavy equipment, of the electricity or those blowtorches, that they're not going to be taking foolish shortcuts. You think oh, kids, they're crazy, their brains aren't developed yet. They're not. You don't have to untrain them. They don't have any bad habits.

This hesitancy is actually a big advantage, MacLeod notes.

I tell my kids, when you're sitting there and feeling all meek and small in these interviews with these companies, whether it's a trucking company or a high-tech company like EMC, and they say, tell me about yourself, you look them right in the eye and say, "I'm a big bang for the buck." And then go on, "I have been certified on state-of-the-art equipment and my teachers have been certified by the state of Massachusetts and they have many, many years in their field." Some of the kids get squeamish about that, isn't that conceited, isn't that bragging. No, it's confidence. And it's factual.

New Jersey's Cape Tech High School in Cape May has had to scramble harder for industry engagements, and success has been elusive, largely because the economy in the region has been on a downward trajectory. The school offers twenty-one CTE programs, all of which are fully integrated with academic subjects including advertising, design, and commercial art; culinary arts; HVAC and sustainable energy; agro-science and horticulture; diesel mechanics; entertainment production; law enforcement and public safety; travel and tourism; natural science; and welding. In 2011, the school's agriculture program was selected as the 2011 New Jersey Outstanding Middle/Secondary School Agricultural Education Program.

Cape Tech typically receives 500 applications for 120 slots, and that demand has made it easier to garner support from its school board, which recently put together about $14 million to build labs and auxiliary gyms to accommodate more students. This raised the school's capacity to 150 students, though it still cannot accommodate everyone who wants to attend.

Like Tri-County, Cape Tech has developed a number of ways to provide its students with experience that will facilitate their entry into the labor market. It has a number of mini-businesses that serve the public directly: a restaurant, a hair salon, an early childhood center, and a television production studio. Cape Tech channels graduates directly into the police force via a program for "summer cops," who can start at the age of eighteen, having finished the school's law and public safety program. These are seasonal jobs; the officers are empowered to issue summonses for motor vehicle violations, city ordinance violations, and disorderly persons violations. One of their primary duties is crowd control, and for that they are assigned to the bicycle patrol units, the boardwalk beat, or the beach area. These officers receive two weeks of formal training at the Cape May County Police Academy that includes classes on criminal law, report writing, motor vehicle law, use of force, responsibility to the community, CPR (cardiopulmonary resuscitation) and first aid, handcuffing, baton, and self-defense techniques. For this work, students receive New Jersey State certification as Class One Special Law Enforcement Officers. With this background, most go on to get the college degree that is required to join the state police, military police, and the FBI—all popular career choices for these students.

Cape Tech's experience bears out the importance of coordinating with industry. For example, students who have taken classes in HVAC, which in the 1990s expanded to include heating, cooling, plumbing, and electrical, eventually found it impossible to find plumbing or electrical jobs; heating technology changed dramatically, rendering the school's equipment and training obsolete. As a result, the school was forced to revolutionize the program, which involved purchasing state-of-the-art equipment and hiring a teacher who had taught college students at Drexel University. Principal Mike Adams explains:

> We had a dead program. Nobody hired a kid [for a plumbing job] from this school from 2001 on. By 2004, we had three students, four students who would choose it because you couldn't get a job. One kid who works in plumbing took the welding class and business at night. Not plumbing.

The 2008 recession made the situation even worse, further highlighting how critical it is for CTE schools and programs to be closely aligned with the job market and flexible enough to jettison obsolete programs and create new ones. "When 2008 hit, we were rock bottom in this county," Adams says.

> In 2009 there were two residential building permits in the county and three commercial. We had twenty-five plumbing firms in this county vying for that work. And other companies coming down from other counties. How does a kid coming out of high school get a job? Vocational education is absolutely employment driven.

Masonry—which used to be folded into construction technology and then construction occupations—has been a popular pursuit for kids who are not inclined toward further education, but graduates of that program must now compete with highly skilled immigrants from South and Central America whom locals believe undercut the prevailing wage just to get into the workforce. That said, Cape Tech has sent three kids on full scholarships to a major industrial building school whose graduates qualify for the union and for management, something Adams sees as critical.

Today, the school no longer has a plumbing shop, but it does feature a shop for heating, ventilation, and sustainable energy (geothermal, solar, and wind). "It's green engineering," says Adams, and it's a growing field. "Every kid wants to be in there. It's hard to get ahead of the curve in terms of investment. We're doing everything."

The carpentry shop was also discontinued for lack of job prospects, although the school recently appealed to its county legislators to rehabilitate it. The aim is to turn it into a property management shop. Hopefully, students will learn how to maintain summer properties for their wealthy owners during the off-season and make a go of it as entrepreneurs.

Some programs cannot be sustained despite labor market demand. For example, environmental regulations made it cost-prohibitive for Cape Tech to continue to teach auto body repair and hence that shop was recently eliminated. They would have had to spend $3.5 million to recapture and store the waste produced by the shop, as there are no recycling facilities nearby.

Something similar happened in Massachusetts, where Tri-County no longer has a concentration in machine technology. In the 1990s, when the field started to computerize, companies retrofitted older machines with digital capabilities. For Tri-County to have done this, however, would have cost almost as much as buying new technology, which was not manageable within the school's budget. Rather than teach students outdated skills on obsolete equipment, a lot of the vocational schools began substituting other offerings for the machining trades.

Tri-County is also wary of depending too much on industry to remedy the problem. MacLeod notes, "The state of Massachusetts is very careful with any kind of an articulation with outside industry because we still want to remain autonomous." Indeed, even donations of needed equipment can create problems. "Our priority is the kids. If we end up with a shop with all this grand and glorious equipment and the kids don't want to do it, or it's not their forte, we don't want to be pushing kids into it. Plus, there's the whole indebtedness," MacLeod continues.

> What do we have to promise them in order to get that equipment? And what happens when that company goes down, the students are totally groomed for that industry and whatever they learned, and the applications that company used don't transfer to other companies? Now that person is really stuck.

As a result, Tri-County prefers to rely on government funding rather than industry gifts to purchase its equipment.

> We want to think of things on a more global level. So if we can access federal funding like Perkins funding, our Chapter 74 federal funding, to get this equipment, it allows us to train the student on a more global level as opposed to what this particular company wants and needs because they gave us the equipment. And that's pervasive throughout the vocational system throughout Massachusetts. The state is very careful about what they accept and who they partner with.

Funding has been a factor in the elimination of some of the other Cape Tech shops, according to Adams, who claims that Perkins dollars are not only drying up but increasingly flowing away from high schools to community colleges. This might seem a trivial adjustment—moving vocational programs from one educational venue to another—but in a country where 80 percent graduate from high school,[9] the disappearance of vocational programs from high schools makes it hard for the 20 percent who do not graduate from high school to access this kind of training. They are often the students most likely to need the options that vocational schools can foster.

According to Adams, Cape Tech's success stories end up leaving the state after they graduate because work is hard to come by not only in the Cape May area but in the Northeast more generally. Adams believes that the heavy regulations and the general lack of new industries in the Northeast make it much more attractive for businesses to move elsewhere. "If I moved my school five hundred miles south, I could get a lot more cooperation," Adams says wistfully.

> I would love to lure manufacturing, but in New Jersey there are tons of environmental regulations and the price of real estate and taxes are high. In the South, they are far more nimble, have far less state regulation. These companies will go south and train a population to work for them.

He recognizes the need to be nimble so that Cape Tech does not end up training kids for opportunities "that do not exist in our county."[10] Administrators have to remain on the lookout for opportunities and be willing to change. Says Adams, "If something's not working, we move on."

Southern Strategies

About seven hundred miles to the south, things do look much brighter for students in vocational schools. And a big reason for that is the concerted effort being made by South Carolina to lure companies to the region and facilitate cooperation and collaboration between industry and the educational sector. Manufacturing companies from Europe and from other parts of the United States are headed to this region, attracted by its right-to-work laws, the absence of labor unions, and—accordingly—the lower prevailing wage. From a social policy perspective, that is a problem because it contributes to persistent inequality. For young people looking for a leg up into manufacturing industries, the motivations of the firms locating in states like South Carolina are less important than the opportunities they can look forward to.

On any given day, visitors to the Pickens County Career and Technology Center in Liberty, South Carolina, encounter a lot of creativity. In the machine technology shop, they may find students programming CNC (computer numerical control) machines to make plastic worm molds, while in another part of the U-shaped building, in a state-of-the-art kitchen, aspiring chefs might be planning or preparing a multicourse catered meal. These are just two of nineteen different programs offered at the career center, which also offers training in auto technology, health sciences, mechatronics, machine tools, masonry, electricity, carpentry, graphic communications, computer networking, and mechanical design.

The center serves thirteen hundred high school students, who are bused there daily from four district feeder high schools. These students spend half their day at their regular high school and half the day at the career center. This setup enabled the center to receive $300,000 in federal Perkins funding in 2014—the lion's share of the county's Perkins funds and the funding is based on a formula that considers the number of "completers," or graduates, the center has—but that money has to cover all nineteen programs plus the business programs in the feeder high schools.

According to the career center's director, Ken Hitchcock:

> Many of the students come from relatively low-income families in which neither parent has a college degree. About 18 percent of the county, which is overwhelmingly white, lives below the poverty level. Its economy, historically rural agrarian and textile-based, took a hit as those industries died out.

Nonetheless, the career center has been making a name for itself in STEM activities, bringing home top awards at robotics competitions in the state and the nation. "We're kind of the cash cow for the district," notes Hitchcock with pride.

> The high schools would get a bigger piece of the pie if they would adjust their curriculum to have the completers in business. So we're bringing

in the Perkins money but having to share it with the high schools. And some middle schools are adding Project Lead the Way[11] classes now, which you can fund with Perkins funds, too. At the local level, before the 2008 budget crunch, with the recession, prior to that, the supply budget was about $70,000 and was cut to $30,000 after that. You're trying to do welding programs and machining programs on a $30,000 budget and that money is supposed to be for consumables, like lumber or steel or wire for the electricity class.

Hitchcock says that the center does additional fund-raising by applying for grants from local companies like Duke Energy. The need to chase donations troubles him, as "we spend so much time fund-raising when we need to be doing instruction."

One of the center's big success stories is a young man named John Hayes, who grew up in a very depressed rural area where neither of his parents graduated from high school. Hayes became interested in mechatronics at the center because a friend's older brother had taken classes in it. The program includes instruction in mechanical technology, pneumatic and hydraulic actuation, electronic control theory, and computer programming, and students learn to design, program, and build robotic controls and high-tech gadgets. "It's like maintenance on steroids," Hayes explains, "with a dose of math. Kind of basic trig, your main algebra, math that everyone needs to learn. It comes into play huge, especially with the machining side. And even with the pneumatic side. You have to do your formulas."

John loved attending the career center. "It's not like regular school, you're not just sitting there bored, 'I wonder if I can squeeze in a nap.' You get a lot of hands on. You have a lot of fun. You're learning useful skills for your future."

In June 2013, John and a classmate won the bronze medal at the Skills-USA's Forty-eighth Annual National Leadership and Skills Conference in Kansas City. Both were also on a team of county students who successfully programmed a robot to build a prototype capacitor for the electronics company Cornell Dubilier, which is headquartered in Liberty. The collaboration with CD was the brainchild of Patrick Lark, an R&D engineer at the company. A few years earlier, Lark approached Hank

Hutto, the head of the career center's mechatronics program for the past thirteen years, with a problem its engineers did not have the time to devote to solving: an old robot that they needed programmed to weld a new capacitor. They were hoping the students could help.

According to Lark, Hutto presented the challenge to the students, "like, here's the problem, here's what we think we want to do with it. They did some Internet research, read up on tig [tungsten inert gas] welding, we said yes, no, maybe along the way to keep them on the right track." A lot of brainstorming was involved.

The work was done at the school by seniors in the mechatronics and machining shops. Employees of CD checked in with students once or twice a week to see what they needed in terms of materials and resources, which CD provided.

The result? The students, all seniors, had the robot welding in three weeks. "The students did all the research to figure out how to do it," says Lark, who says he was surprised—and gratified—that the students actually made it work. "It was the coolest thing to watch them motivated, all that drive." In fact, after being a part of the robotics project with the career center, Lark wishes he could have had "some other type of education than sitting through AP English."

The robot works with a welder and a PLC (programmable logic controller) "to weld the capacitor and spit it out. It's fully automated. They did this with twenty-year-old technology that hadn't been used in a long time." The students had the computer and programming skills many of the older engineers lacked—engineers who will soon retire. Indeed, Lack says this was the impetus for CD's decision to take on two apprentices, one of whom was John Hayes. Subsequently, Hayes worked at CD during the second half of his senior year and after graduation. He continues to work at CD while he attends a technical college.

The career center's curriculum is set by state CTE standards, but an advisory board gives input into the kinds of skills and equipment the students need in order to be competitive in the job market. Indeed, Alliance Pickens, the area's local economic development group that recruits industries to the county, is always clamoring for more machinists. According to Ken Hitchcock:

In the manufacturing sector, maybe we are graduating about fifteen kids in mechatronics, twenty kids in machining, another twenty in welding. If I was God, those are the first three programs I would expand. Manufacturing is the backbone. Once you built that up, all the other fields will benefit. You'll need more firefighters, more cosmetologists. It's all based on that.

The center has also formed a partnership with an informal group of local industry leaders, known as Manufacturers Caring for Pickens County. The group is starting to collaborate with the career center's guidance counselors, giving them tours of plants and other local facilities. For example, through this group, the counselors plan to tour a local concrete plant in order to learn what that industry needs so as to better advise their students, making it clear that "you don't need a four-year degree; you can get a two-year degree and earn money."

Local firms help the school in other ways, too, with supplies, for example.

> One of our welding programs has a program with a steel company that has given them scrap steel, but we need to get some quality stuff. Cornell Dubilier has been great, BMW has donated robots that they have phased out, but it would be good to get some cutting-edge stuff that the industry is using.

About 60 percent of the career center's graduates go on to Tri-County Technical College or Greenville Technical College. In fact, the career center has what is known as a dual-credit program with Tri-County, in which students can take some classes at Tri-County while they're still in high school.

> It's a win-win for everybody. Kids have a foot in the door with college. Our kids are scared to deal with college. A lot of their parents didn't go. They are already in the door. They can see, hey, I can do this. They have committed. Tech will get their money and their butts in the seats.

The career center is also trying to establish a dual-credit program for machine tool and welding so the seniors can apply their high school credit to an associate of arts degree, but that has proven trickier. "It's a territorial thing," Hitchcock explains. "And there's a teacher certification issue. The teachers would need state certification as a high school teacher and also something that they can be employable as an adjunct. There are turf issues, but the kids could knock out four classes."

According to Hitchcock, about 15 percent of the career center's graduates head off to four-year colleges, mostly in the health sciences (almost all of the center's Project Lead the Way students go to four-year programs in engineering). The rest go on mostly to get industry jobs. A number of industry certifications are available to students, among them one for computer hardware repair and, for those in the agricultural mechanics program, certification in small-engine repair. Students are also to get their Occupational Safety and Health Administration (OSHA) safety cards, something that normally requires a $500 class, for free.

Placement Practices

One of the most important things a vocational school can offer its students is access to internships and jobs. Schools and programs vary in terms of how institutionalized these placement practices are. For example, at Tri-County all students who qualify (close to 70 percent) can participate in the co-op program, which enables them to spend every other week out of school at a job. Even so, they have to exercise a degree of quality control if they want firms to continue to receive their students. This is why an important criterion for senior-year co-op placement at Tri-County is attendance rather than academic performance; if a student has more than three unexcused absences in a term, he or she is blocked from participating. Students who have been suspended from school are also ineligible. And while seniors must also have a C− average or better in their academic classes to be able to go on co-op, those who feel their grades don't reflect their effort can appeal to the principal.

"I have access to every single grade," MacLeod notes.

I can see why they got the D or the F and if I see that the student got every single assignment done, and took every test and quiz, they're just really lousy at it, then we can [make an appeal]. History is not their forte. We get it. You did everything you possibly could but it just wasn't clicking for you. But when I go into the grades and I see a bunch of zeros because they neglected to do their homework . . . that puts them off the radar.

MacLeod's dedication to helping even struggling students get co-op placements reflects her school's commitment to training, as well as the more general conviction among many we encountered in this field that academic achievement, while important, is not always the best measure of a student's abilities. Perseverance is, however, nonnegotiable. People who don't turn up when they are supposed to are going to be a disappointment to the firms that accept them into co-ops.

While MacLeod has the ultimate responsibility for co-op placements, shop teachers are also instrumental in helping students find them, as well as internships and even postgraduation jobs. According to Cody Rose, a student majoring in HVAC, the shop teacher contacts every business within a half hour or forty-five minutes from the high school when he knows students are looking for opportunities.

So if we approach him and say, we want to go on co-op next year, we want a job for the summer, he has the numbers to give us. I went to one guy and he took me on for two weekends. That was the end of last year. He loved me. He was like, "I'll hire you full-time for the summer and then I'll take you on for co-op." Once I graduate he's going to take me full-time.

Work-Based Learning

Like other CTE schools in New York City, CTEA does have a work-based learning component. Students are not required to undertake an internship or job outside of school, but according to Mitch Almonte, "It's required that we offer the opportunity to them." Indeed, at the moment, CTEA does not offer internships during the school day; however, there is a program that upperclassmen are involved in called Scholars at Work, a partnership among the Department of Education, the New York City Department of Small Business Services, and the New York City Workforce Investment Board that tries to provide work options for young New Yorkers graduating from the city's CTE high schools. The internships—which are for the most part in the transportation and manufacturing industries, start before school lets out, so students often need to leave school early in order to get there on time. The school is usually able to juggle their schedule so they don't miss classes.

Automotive also offers work-based learning. Luis Alvarez[12] is one of the beneficiaries of this program. When Luis was a freshman, he approached one of his teachers to find out whether he could get an internship. While students don't typically get to work as interns until their junior year, Luis was determined and persistent, and his teacher arranged for him to work part of the day at the Sanitation Department, which has an enormous fleet of trucks that are in constant need of repair. Having already worked as an intern for Sanitation during the summer, Luis wanted to pile up more experience before graduating and enhance his value to this city agency. He understands how to corner an opportunity, since by the time Luis graduates with his Regents diploma, he will be fully certified as a mechanic with several years of hands-on experience under his belt. He hopes to have his own shop one day.

In addition to this, along with a dozen or so of his classmates, Luis spends a considerable amount of time working in Automotive's service shop, diagnosing and repairing customer cars. The supervising teachers, both certified mechanics, give relevant instruction in a section of the shop set up like a classroom where a large computer screen mounted on the wall shows the status of the various repair jobs, logged and tracked using special software. According to Principal Caterina Lafergola,

> We've tried to create an experience, where students are also learning about the customer service component. What does it take to create quotes, to build a business, and market a business? We've integrated that into our senior service shop. The students are doing a little bit of everything there. It's purely run by the students. . . . They do the billing, they do the outreach, and the teachers are just supervising. And they do the work. So if you bring your car in and you need new brakes,

the kids are taking it in, logging it, telling you here's your estimate, they are explaining, troubleshooting, what you need done. And they'll say come back tomorrow morning at ten o'clock and your car will be ready.

The shop's two large rooms can accommodate about four cars each. There is also a tool room and lockers for the students. Teachers bustle around the shop floor, which is run as a real business. Students in overalls punch a time clock, having been admonished by their instructors that failing to do so in a business outside the school would result in docked pay. They write up service orders and reports, communicate with customers, and, of course, repair cars. Customers are charged a $5 donation, which is a great deal in a city where fixing a car can be an expensive proposition.

Luis loves this part of the school day. "When you're here in the shop," he says, "you're always moving around fixing things, taking customer phone calls." The day we observed, one group of students was inspecting and reinstalling the brakes on an old Plymouth while, in another area of the shop, a teacher and student were conferring about an ignition issue in front of an old maroon-colored Ford with its hood open.

"This is a complex problem composed of many smaller problems," the teacher was saying. "You have to remember resistance/voltage, electronics class from last year. We need to deconstruct the circuit in our heads." The student listened intently and began puzzling over the problem, looking at the engine and then running his thoughts by the teacher, who prodded him further without guidance.

Kids like these learn in service shop class that what they are doing on the academic side has an application, and that if they have trouble there are people there to help them. Despite all this, Luis almost never gets to work on newer cars with complex electrical systems. However, Automotive has shifted its curriculum to keep up with these changes in the industry, putting more "emphasis on the electrical components and the computer components." The students have yet to have broad access to these newer vehicles.

"As a matter of fact," notes Lafergola, "we are now training our teachers in hybrids. As they are being trained, they will in turn train students."

But for now, Luis must content himself with learning about hybrids during his internship with the Sanitation Department, where he got to watch and learn from Toyota-trained mechanics who are his mentors.

Earning Industry Credentials

One of the biggest benefits of a vocational education is the opportunity for students to earn national, industry certifications. CTE schools and programs are increasingly aware of the need and are working to tailor their programs to offer these certifications, which are ever more meaningful to employers and are portable.

Despite its academic struggles, one of Automotive's big advantages is how well it prepares its students in terms of certification. According to Principal Lafergola,

> Automotive is one of five schools in the country that offer five or six of the eight NATEF [National Automotive Technicians and Education Foundation] endorsements. Our students are assessed using NATEF standards after each module of study. Those assessments are industry assessments. NATEF requires two years of practical experience before they get their Automotive Service Excellence certification. Our students, if they're successful in our CTE course of study, get one year of credit just for being in the program. And they have all of their safety tests. They come out of this building and they are recognized in the field.

Students in the nursing program at Tri-County can graduate as certified nurses, home health aides, CPR attendants, and Alzheimer's and EpiPen certified care workers. They are also certified in mobility training and feeding people with throat disorders. Seniors who elect not to go out on a co-op placement can train to become emergency medical technicians (EMTs) in their senior year. They spend time working at health care sites, including acute-care facilities and hospitals where they can get experience inserting Foley catheters or assisting Alzheimer's patients.

Vocational teachers in American high schools are a dedicated lot. They often labor without recognition, putting in hours to smooth the path to jobs for their students, even when their formal job descriptions do not require that commitment and the thanks is confined to the appreciation individual students have for that special teacher who helped them along the way. The "system"—such as it is—is often cobbled together rather than intentionally organized to produce the outcomes the economy needs and students are yearning for. Vocational schools, in turn, need to devote themselves to alignment with industry, which means staying abreast of what employers are looking for in the ways of skills and gaining access to equipment—whether in schools themselves, in regional training centers that pool students from across a district, or on the shop floor of firms that accept co-op placements, interns, and other forms of student engagement. The training-to-job pipeline is an essential part of the picture and it is massively more effective when on-the-job experience is built in.

Since workers don't always stay in the regions where those connections can be built and may have to move from an aviation program to a subway system where the same training in hydraulics can be put to use, a credential system that makes clear the skills that a vocational student has mastered is essential. Certificates, special diplomas, short courses that indicate additional specializations on top of generic courses in, for example, plumbing or electrical repair, can make a difference as well.

On all of these counts, the American vocational education lags behind those of our counterparts in other countries. Though the teachers we employ are dedicated to the cause, they are often stripped of the means. This is not uniformly true, as we have seen in special programs in Massachusetts, New Jersey, and South Carolina. But it is not comprehensively the case either.

5

The Community College Connection

The high schools we have profiled thus far are, in many ways, unusual. They represent a commitment to a mission that many educators had given up on. But decades of poor outcomes for general high schools, and deepening poverty in the inner city, have spurred the search for alternatives, and the concept of high school vocational education seems to be gaining more traction of late. Yet given the uneasiness that many feel in coaxing students toward vocational education in a "college for all" culture, the notion that technical education is best delivered to postsecondary students has prevailed. Accordingly, much of the action is found in community colleges. This evolution makes sense even for those who believe high-school students should be provided with the vocational alternative. The investment necessary to mount a successful vocational program—in equipment, an industry-savvy faculty, and maintaining employer connections—may be more effectively implemented when it is trained on a larger catchment than a high school.

The community college option speaks to two different needs that sometimes overlap: students who cannot afford the tuition and fees at

four-year colleges and those whose performance in high school was problematic, putting more prestigious institutions out of reach.[1] Federal
financial aid is not enough to support the cost of attendance at residential schools and hence good students looking to avoid debt, including
many who are the first in their families to venture beyond high school, turn
to community colleges. Many hope to complete their community college
two-year programs as a prelude to transferring into four-year institutions.
The total cost of a college degree is considerably less when half of it unfolds
in community colleges.

In the United States today, there are more than twelve hundred
community colleges. In 2013, they enrolled over 12.4 million students (7.4
million in for-credit programs and 5 million in noncredit programs), or
46 percent of all undergraduate students in the country.[2] As open-access
institutions with low tuition fees and flexible scheduling options, community colleges enroll higher proportions of students who are older,
female, from underrepresented groups, and from low-income families
than the traditional, residential four-year colleges and universities.[3] In
2013, African American students made up 15 percent of the student body;
Hispanic students, 18 percent; Asian/Pacific Islander students, 6 percent;
and Native Americans, 1 percent, all of which eclipse the enrollment
figures for these groups in four-year institutions.[4]

Community college students also tend to have graduated from high
school with grade point averages below 2.5, which would disqualify many
from four-year institutions. In part because they also are significantly older
(on average) than the traditional college students,[5] those at community colleges often find themselves juggling the roles of parent and student.[6] At this
life stage, few are able to attend full-time. Instead, at least twice as many
(62 percent) are part-time students. By facilitating flexible schedules, community colleges have made it possible to obtain college degrees for students
who might otherwise have left education behind at the end of high school.

There is evidence that the credentials that graduates earn from these
institutions pay off in the labor market. Researchers followed a cohort
of students enrolled in thirty-four community and technical colleges in
Washington State in 2001–2 for a number of years after they completed
their degrees. Their certificates and associate degrees increased the
chances of finding full-time work and enabled higher wages ($3,000 to

$4,000 more), especially compared to students who took a few courses but didn't complete a degree.[7]

Yet the community college has its critics. As far back as the 1960s, skeptics argued that community colleges appeared to foster equal opportunity through their open-door policies but in reality perpetuated the inequality that emerges in the K–12 system. As late professor of education Burton Clark argued, students found themselves in remedial classes that led nowhere and, over time, lost much of their ambition for higher education. When asked to identify the reasons why they enrolled in a community college, over one-third of students reported that they had higher ambitions, especially moving to four-year colleges.[8] Unfortunately, poverty, parenthood, and a host of other problems often intervene to thwart their intentions. Community colleges let student expectations decline slowly rather than confront them in a sharp shock as they emerge from poor high schools. He coined the phrase "cooling out" to describe this masking process.[9]

Of first-time college students who enrolled in a community college in the fall of 2008, 39.1 percent earned a credential from a two- or four-year institution within six years,[10] 16.2 percent of students who started at community colleges in 2008 completed a degree at a four-year institution within six years, and 60.4 percent of these bachelor's degree earners (or 9.8 percent of the total cohort) did not obtain a two-year degree before transferring.[11] These high noncompletion rates are worrisome because amassing a few credits does not pay off very much in the labor market.[12]

The multitude of forces responsible for these low completion rates—from the impact of poverty to the competition between school and family responsibilities to the confusing curricular organization of many community colleges—have been the subject of attention from major foundations, federal and state government, and the higher education systems themselves. The problem has proven remarkably difficult to budge. Yet we know that leaving young people with nothing more than a high school diploma will put them at a lifelong disadvantage. Hence we must continue to work on policies ranging from financial aid to child care for student parents to streamlining programs and boosting academic advising so that students do not lose their way.

These drawbacks aside, no other country (except, to a degree, Canada) has created comprehensive community colleges that offer not only vocational training but also an academic transfer program, continuing education, developmental education, and customized training. By including different programs within the same institution, community colleges allow students to move among basic skills, vocational, and transfer programs, although, in reality, there are often institutional obstacles to smooth transitions. Still, this sounds like the ideal setup, something verging on what our competitors in Europe have developed at the high-school level.

Two problems stand in the way of declaring the workforce training problem solved. First, precisely because community colleges are comprehensive, vocational education is often sidelined as less important, becoming a second-class concern. And when, in periods of financial downturns, millions of people stampede the system, community colleges simply cannot manage the demand. They turn people away in droves, and the vocational tracks that are costly to support are often shuttered to absorb budget cuts even though their outcomes, in terms of job placement, may be far more favorable than the less costly academic tracks.

The second-class citizen problem is particularly acute when academic faculty are in charge. Those faculty members often are committed to the idea that the main purpose of community colleges is to prepare students to graduate from four-year colleges with BAs in political science or Spanish literature. And academic faculty are often the majority in community colleges. Their perspective is even more persuasive when the alternative is a budget-busting investment in technical laboratories full of costly equipment. What's more, those labs need to be updated continuously if they are going to do the students in them any good; hence ongoing expenses are steeper in vocational parts of a community college, even when the payoff to the students is commensurately higher. New English instructors don't need such support. Moreover, their objectives may be more in line with the high prestige side of community college education that values the ability to stream students toward four-year colleges. If the transfer rate to "real universities" is high on the list of institutional priorities, equipping mechanics shops or kitchens for chefs may fall to the bottom.

De-emphasizing vocational education in the community college has a long history. As sociologist Jerome Karabel explains in his account of its origins, the institution was an adaptation designed to excuse elite colleges and universities from the obligation to accept the "wrong" kind of student. At the turn of the twentieth century, elite American universities sought to rid themselves of the first two years of university training in an effort to imitate the German university, with its focus on research and scholarship. William Rainey Harper, president of the University of Chicago, was the first to divide the university into a junior and senior college. He convinced a nearby high school to offer college courses, and in 1901, Joliet Junior College opened as the nation's first community college.

In the succeeding decades, a number of universities sponsored junior colleges as extensions of high schools or as new institutions designed to reduce overcrowding in the universities and divert unprepared students from the rigors of university education. Harvard president Abbott Lawrence Lowell clearly saw the advantages of this strategy. "One of the merits of these new institutions," he wrote in 1928, "will be the keeping out of college, rather than leading into it, young people who have no taste for higher education."[13]

From 1900 to 1925, the majority of community colleges provided an academic curriculum that transferred to the university. The vocational emphasis was entirely absent. When leaders of the American Association of Community Colleges sought to bring their institutions out from their subordinate role as handmaidens of elite institutions,[14] they became convinced that junior colleges could take on a new role. They would provide training for occupations lodged between the recognized professions, which were dominated by the universities, and trades that did not require training past high school. This would provide junior colleges with a new status and an expanded role.

It didn't work. Students and parents continued to enroll in community colleges as a more affordable stepping-stone toward a university degree, and expressed little interest in that secondary purpose. Even in the post–World War II period, 75 percent of junior college students were enrolled in transfer programs and one-third actually made good on them.

But federal government officials saw the advantages of the training mission. In 1947, the Truman Commission produced a report on higher education that affirmed the role of the community college in preparing young adults for middle-level jobs, which further increased enrollment. With the baby-boom generation entering college in the 1960s, enrollment continued to grow, with new campuses opening at a rate of more than one a week.[15] Their student populations more than tripled between 1960 and 1970, from 451,000 to 1,630,000. The 1963 Vocational Education Act and its amendments broadened the scope of federal funds for vocational education from secondary schools to postsecondary schools, which significantly increased their budgets.

By the 1970s, students started to follow government's lead. Between 1970 and 1977, the proportion of students enrolled in vocational programs in junior colleges increased from less than one-third to over one-half. A full 1.6 million of them were enrolled in 1970; by 1980, that number increased more than threefold, to about 4.5 million.

A goodly part of this boom could be chalked up to the demands of employers.[16] Eighty-five percent of community colleges had developed occupational programs at their request. Coincident with these changes, junior colleges were renamed community colleges—a term first proposed by the Truman Commission—to reflect their focus on terminal degrees and their connection to localities.[17]

Fueling this popularity was the stunning growth in part-time enrollment of nontraditional students, including older, less academically prepared, minority, and female students. Between 1970 and 1995, part-time enrollment in community colleges increased 222 percent.[18] Higher education was no longer solely the province of eighteen-to-twenty-two-year-olds, and with these new demographics came the demand for a broader definition of purpose for community colleges. Jobs were opening up that did not require four-year degrees.

At the same time, the white-collar labor market was convulsing and could no longer absorb the supply of college graduates. Deep recessions in the early 1980s drove unemployment up to double digits, hammering the college-educated (and blue-collar labor), leaving millions looking for a place to start over again. The community college became a critical node not only in the training of young workers looking for their first foothold but a means of enabling mature Americans to reboot. Its very affordability made it the ideal place for those who needed a second chance. Today, what started out as an appendage of elite four-year universities has become one of our most important sources of human capital. And vocational programs enroll between 40 percent and 60 percent of community college students.[19] They are looking to enter middle-level semiprofessional jobs in fields that include trades, industry, and agriculture, where the majority of American vocational students were headed forty years ago, as well as domains such as advertising, entry-level electronic engineering, and nursing.[20]

The Budget Bottleneck

Whatever their weaknesses, it is clear that for millions of Americans the more productive road should lead to a community or technical college. Yet in recent years, it has become more difficult for these institutions to educate the very people they were built to serve. The Great Recession sent state education budgets into a tailspin. In California, home to the largest community college system in the country, the budget has been trimmed by nearly $1.5 billion in recent years, which provoked an enrollment crisis (enrollment declined by half a million students between 2008 and 2012, even as the college-age population grew). The Public Policy Institute of California concluded that enrollment fell to a twenty-year low in the wake of unprecedented cuts in state funding. Colleges "have reduced staff, cut courses, and increased class sizes—all of which have led to declines in student access."[21] Thus this lifeline for low- and moderate-income students, veterans, and older workers who need to retrain when their employers turf them out has now been cut.

San Mateo Community College in northern California had a booming program in welding in the 1990s. Its graduates were snapped up by the manufacturing firms, local airports, transit systems, and construction industries in the Bay Area. But because it is so costly to equip a welding studio, the program closed down in 2005 despite the robust demand for trained welders. Welding classes require a trained craftsman to teach, tools and heavy equipment, protective gear, and liability insurance in case of injury. When the budget cuts began coming thick and fast, the college had to make tough decisions and find ways to conserve its funds. A nearly surefire avenue to a skilled blue-collar job disappeared with the stroke of a pen.

Nursing is another field in which demand is high. Indeed, hospitals all over the United States are screaming for more trained nurses and resorting to hiring trained staff from the Philippines, even though there are thousands of American students who would jump at the chance to be trained for such a rewarding career. Faced with an avalanche of demand and insufficient resources, nursing programs are jacking up their admissions standards. One of the key portals through which job candidates can qualify for a nursing career is turning thousands of people back because colleges cannot afford the labor- and equipment-intensive training (and clinical training opportunities, which are often in short supply). What was once a reasonable career option for many modestly skilled students is being placed out of reach.[22]

Given these pressures, students from low-income or working-class households are often shut out of the only reasonably priced public, non-profit alternative. The lucky ones who have been able to get in often find they have to fight for space in overenrolled classes, delayed for semester after semester as they wait to complete their requirements. The problem is serious in districts that are normally well funded, but it is even more acute in rural areas where there may be few alternative options for a student in need of a community college program.

As the *Chronicle of Higher Education* noted recently, costs that would be routine in many institutions can be impossible for rural community colleges to manage. Interviewing officials from an Arkansas institution, the *Chronicle* notes that replacing a computer lab is an "insurmountable" cost because there are few opportunities for partnerships with private business, there are costs that are beyond the college's ability to meet, and the local tax base is too meager to afford much relief.[23] It is little wonder that the end result, particularly in regions that are opposed to tax increases to support community colleges, is either enrollment bottlenecks or tuition hikes.

In recent years, community colleges have also suffered from rising competition from the for-profit sector, which aggressively courts the same audience. With their marketing focus, the for-profits work overtime to persuade would-be students that they can give them both the credentials and the financial support they need and guarantee success in the labor market, promises that often lead to disappointment on all counts.

Yet in spite of these significant obstacles, community colleges, overall, have grown and become increasingly important to our national training effort, a point underscored by President Obama, who has supported the sector with treasure and publicity. In the summer of 2013, Obama proposed an $8 billion "Community College to Career Fund" to train two million workers for high-demand industries.[24] He followed with an unprecedented $12 billion to fund community colleges to help stimulate the economy through worker training and partnerships with businesses. Even more recently, he has proposed making the first two years of community college free for students who attend at least half-time, maintain a 2.5 GPA, and make steady progress toward completing their program. The cost of this proposal is estimated at about $60 billion over ten years and would also require state governments to pick of 25 percent of the bill.[25]

Can the community colleges continue to serve their mission? The Great Recession revealed vulnerabilities these institutions share with the rest of higher education. Economic downturns create "countercyclical" pressures: when unemployment rises, individuals looking for a new start need to retrain. They turn to the least expensive institutions that can satisfy their needs effectively, and community colleges often fit the bill. At the same time, high levels of joblessness drain state coffers both because there are fewer employed people to contribute to payroll taxes and because spending declines and sales tax on goods, gasoline, and other fiscal mainstays follows suit. Just when educational institutions are most critical to the human capital equation, they find themselves hammered by budget cuts.

Do Community Colleges Work?

Determining whether an educational institution is doing its job is a complex matter. Is the main criterion whether it is making a positive difference for its students, given their characteristics? Or do we want to ignore those inputs and just ask whether its graduates are successful? Much of the debate in the press is based on the latter question: Are students graduating on time, and are they getting jobs?

Community college graduates do not do as well in the labor market as students who attend four-year institutions. Perhaps we should not expect otherwise since they are, on average, less affluent and not as academically qualified to begin with. What we would hope to see is that the same kind of student fares equally well. And here the news is less encouraging. When compared with similar students who enter four-year institutions, community college graduates are at a disadvantage in terms of their long-term employment prospects. They end up with positions that are less prestigious and not as well paid.[26]

However, a more appropriate benchmark might be to compare community college students with high-school grads who do not go any farther in school. And by this measure, the picture looks far more favorable. For every year a student completes in a community college, she sees a 5 percent to 10 percent increase in annual earnings, which is comparable to the returns on a year of education at a four-year institution.[27] Finishing a degree is important. The "sheepskin effect" of earning an associate's degree boosts annual earnings by 15 percent to 27 percent.

Not only is the degree itself important to earnings, but so is the opportunity students at community colleges have to develop connections that may help them land a job. Despite all the criticism that has been piled on four-year colleges that make heavy use of adjunct teaching staff—people without regular or recurring contracts—in the world of community colleges teachers who are not career faculty can be a boon. This is so largely because they are more likely to keep one foot in the industry they are training students for. Having well-connected up-to-date references is a godsend for students who have no other ties to rely on. Not all community college faculty take this on as a sacred responsibility. Some think that the colleges' career services or internship coordinators, specifically charged with forging these connections, are sufficient. But those who take this mission on, even when it is not required, can make a world of difference given their networks.[28]

The labor market for students without bachelor's degrees tends to be local and hiring is done through informal connections.[29] Given the importance of finding employment that is related to the field a student has studied, community colleges should play a critical role in connecting students to employers. Although they generally have stronger ties than high schools do, community colleges face similar problems helping students make the transition to the work world. Unlike their German counterparts, who are so closely connected that they are always on top of the latest technical demands and needs of the employers with whom they partner, American community colleges are often slower to respond to changing labor market conditions, and programs tend to be self-perpetuating.[30] Links between community college faculty and employers are often ad hoc and based on individual relationships, and the quality of these relationships varies across departments and schools.

High-quality private "occupational colleges," such as Wentworth Institute of Technology in Massachusetts, do better on this score, as sociologist Jim Rosenbaum has documented. Their livelihood depends on burnishing connections with employers through active advisory boards, job placement services, and relationship building. Although community colleges have some of the same characteristics, they are less tailored and tend to advise their charges on general job search strategies such as résumé writing or interview skills. Rosenbaum argues that community colleges act more like four-year institutions in assuming that the associate's degree provides a credential that employers will recognize, whereas occupational colleges actively create programs collaboratively with particular employers. In part, this is the result of the narrow, career-oriented missions of occupational colleges, in which a school's reputation depends on its successful placement of students into jobs. In contrast, community colleges have broader missions to meet a variety of student needs and prioritize other goals, such as program accreditation, over employer connections.

These problems aside, community colleges do pay special attention to a crucial aspect of vocational education, and that is apprenticeship. This occupies a greater pride of place in the community college system than anywhere else in American education. Twenty-four percent of construction apprentices attend community or technical colleges for some aspects of their training.[31] Forty-two percent of apprentices in other fields do so. Nearly all the sponsors of automotive manufacturing and hospitality apprenticeships make use of this option, as do 61 percent of apprenticeships in the health care area. Apprenticeship sponsors may be especially invested in community/technical programs if they pay directly for the courses, and over 70 percent of sponsors do pay for their apprentices to enroll in related instruction at community-technical colleges.[32]

Short-term training programs that are strictly job-oriented and often custom-designed for employers have continued to grow in community colleges. Some customized training programs are self-supporting through student or employer charges, while others rely on special state funds. "Contract training" of this kind is generally not credit bearing and the students are often not seeking degrees, though certificates are becoming more popular as a portable statement of mastery. Community colleges are starting to develop a reputation for more nimble responses to state and local labor market needs, though they often segregate these offerings from their traditional academic and occupational units. Nearly all states have funds for workforce training, and thirty-five states designate community colleges as the fiscal agent for these funds or as the preferred training provider.[33]

The community college occupies a pivotal role in the workforce preparation system of the United States. Is it sufficient? To answer this question, we have to ask who we would lose if we vested all of our training eggs in this basket.

One group that would not be served are high-school dropouts. Without a high-school diploma, they are not able to enroll in community colleges and hence are stuck unless they can complete a GED (general equivalency diploma) somewhere along the line. This is a not insignificant segment of the country's low-income people. While some dropouts do complete GED degrees and find their way back into higher education, we lose millions—especially millions of men from low-income minority families—along the way when we delay access to vocational education beyond high school. We build up a lot of scars, a lot of disappointment, in the Rust Belt cities when we come at the task of workforce preparation this way.

We have seen high schools all over the Northeast, Midwest, and Southeast trying to move into the vocational space in order to provide the kind of positive alternative that set Wesley Buress from the Bronx on his educational path from the age of fourteen onward. We would probably do better as a country if we provided robust support for our high schools to capture the imagination and motivation of students who want to work yet find higher education uninteresting. But given the political barriers to a wholesale move in that direction, it makes sense to support community colleges as regional institutions that can take advantage of economies of scale (especially in industries where training requires expensive equipment), as well as switch points for mature workers who need to make career changes in the wake of economic downturns.

A truly robust vocational system would find both institutions—high schools and community colleges—to be essential.

6

What Vocational Education Could Be:
The German Model

With his peach-fuzz blond beard just blooming across his chin, Johan[1] is a typical German teen. He attends a vocational high school in Osnabrück, a medium-size city in Germany with a long industrial history. Johan's father and grandfather worked their entire lives in the Georgsmarienhütte (GMH) steel mill on the outskirts of Osnabrück, and one of his cousins has been employed there for several years as well.

When Johan was fourteen, he joined millions of other young people across the country in a two-week "practicum," an exploration of the work world. Every year, eighth-grade students drop what they are doing in class to shadow adults in private firms near where they live to get a feeling for what companies do, the role unions play, and how careers unfold. Those two weeks see German students in auto factories, hospitals, agrobusiness farms, hospitals, beauty parlors, and pharmaceutical companies. Johan decided to spend his two weeks in the steel mill where his family works, and he persuaded several of his classmates to join him. It took very little to convince Johan that GMH was the firm he wanted to work for. Two years later, he was chosen as an apprentice there, along with nearly thirty other sixteen-year-olds. Since then, for three or four days a week, he has made his way to the steel mill and put in a long day's work.

Now eighteen, Johan dresses in protective gear—goggles, gloves, and bright orange overalls—when he ventures out onto the shop floor. Back in the day when Johan's grandfather was on the shop floor, this was a dirty, dangerous job. Steelworkers could make mistakes that cost them an arm or even their lives. Accidents happened all the time. Today, those accidents are rare because virtually no one works on the shop floor anymore. Robotics has seen to that. Human hands are nowhere near the tubes of steel that are ejected out of furnaces and travel at high speed around the factory, shaped by pressure rods that squeeze the steel until it conforms to the right shape and is then set aside to cool. At most, when there is a disruption in the production process, workers emerge in protective gear, descend from an enclosed platform high above the factory floor, and scoot along in a small truck to the spot where the glitch has occurred to make an adjustment to one of the electronic instruments.

The emergence of robotics and mechatronics ensured that the labor force of the GMH firm would shrink drastically. Machines are able to run twenty-four hours a day and they can produce far more than any human being, and with no injuries. But someone has to program those machines and stop them instantly when something goes wrong.

Breakdowns are infrequent, but when they happen, the workers are alerted to the problems by flashing red indicators on the computer screens that surround them, just behind the glass windows that separate them from the factory floor. Monitors record every conceivable measure of the temperature, surface quality, and strength of the steel beams. The sensors that line the tracks guiding the steel bars on their journey from the furnace through the molds are wired to send a constant stream of information to the control towers that sit high above the workers and the manufacturing floor. Suited up in their orange jumpsuits, Johan's supervisors spend the entire day watching numbers cross their screens. Graphs appear and fade away, alerts register and then dissolve as the repairs are made. This is not his grandfather's steel mill.

Yet the camaraderie of the blue-collar world remains. And that is one very important reason why Johan picked GMH for his apprenticeship out of the five offers he received when he was sixteen. He wanted to be part of the culture that his family had embraced. GMH management is especially interested in young people—men and women—whose family members are longtime employees. They know that loyalty counts, that people in the region are attached to the industrial history and heritage of the great German steel companies. And they also know, as these large family firms often do, that if you have entire families on the payroll, the divisions that might erupt between management and workers are tempered by durable loyalties. This helps to account for the fact that there are only about thirty-five or forty family names on the GMH payroll. The company relies on local kinship networks to bring in the apprentices and the adult workers and has done so since the company's founding in the mid-nineteenth century.

Johan wasn't thinking about such distant history when he chose this pathway in his young life. "I didn't want to go to college," he told Katherine. "School was never very interesting to me. I wanted to get to work, earn real money, and do it with my friends, cousins, and uncles all around me." The other boys in his class made the same decision and they headed into manufacturing companies in the region together. He considered working for the Volkswagen company, which used to produce the Carmen Ghia car in the Osnabrück plant. In the end, though, he followed his family's tradition and settled into his apprenticeship at GMH.

At eighteen, Johan was earning the euro equivalent of $1,200 a month, well above the poverty line for a family of three in the United States. For every twelve months he works in the apprenticeship program, he receives a thirteenth-month bonus, a routine benefit for trainees across industries. For a young man with no kids, living at home with his family, this is a very comfortable wage for a first job. "I bought my first car and started saving money for a house," he explained. He is no doubt a long way from that house, but one has to marvel that this teenager knows he has a solid job waiting for him when he finishes his training.

In addition, he enjoys a suite of benefits, a soccer group drawn from the apprentices, and a working community to belong to. Johan can expect to earn three times what he makes now when he finishes his apprenticeship. He is basically assured steady work as long as the mill survives.

One hundred and twenty young people—mostly men on the factory floor and young women in sales and backroom offices—train at GMH at any given time. About a third of them are officially apprentices and the rest are preparing for jobs at firms that are too small to make an apprenticeship program cost effective. Those companies contract with GMH to provide training for them. This has become a profitable sideline for GMH. The company expects to hire permanent labor only from among their own apprentices, and 80 percent to 90 percent of its workforce was trained in this fashion. Only the managers and a few technicians have been recruited "from the outside."

Of course, no one in the world of manufacturing can be certain that any track record will continue indefinitely. Twenty years ago, the firm employed nearly seven thousand workers on three shifts. They produced high-quality steel for auto plants around the world. Today, the same factory employs only twelve hundred workers, although they can produce three times the amount of steel—in excess of one million tons—they typically manufactured decades ago. To compete with firms worldwide, the firm was pushed toward robotics, automation, and computer-intensive work processes.

That evolution has changed dramatically the kind of person who makes for a suitable apprentice. It is not enough to be a blue-collar guy who gets along with his mates and knows how to handle hot steel. Today's steelworker is a computer jock—not a programmer, but someone comfortable with numerical machine control and quality metrics. Johan, who has known for some time that he wanted to be a steelworker, realized that this meant he had to take his mathematics classes seriously and that the physics of materials matters. Certain kinds of white-collar skills are as important to his future as they are to the students in his high school who aspire to be medical assistants or accountants.

He has had classroom experience with precision lathes and predesigned computer programs, electronics and graphing calculators. But if Johan's experience was only school-based, he would not have been very helpful to GMH. To shape him into an apprentice who could add value, he was paired with Thomas Eckhardt, his Meister (or master), who is a full-time employee of GMH.

A tall, burly man, Mr. Eckhardt put in twenty-five years as a worker on the shop floor at GMH, coming to the company originally with no more training or education than Johan has now. He has seen the steel industry through many ups and downs and remembers well when GMH had thousands of workers and the factory floor was hot and choked with soot. A lot of dangerous work was done by hand and more than one of his friends suffered grievous injuries. Today's technologies are easier on the body, but because they demand more skill, many of Thomas's coworkers have been let go in favor of mechanization.

The unions, which represent 98 percent of the workforce, have had to manage a difficult transition to a slimmer labor force, to a new kind of worker, and to a different model of remuneration. Apprentices of the twenty-first century hover between a white-collar culture based on individual mobility and a blue-collar ethos that favors group solidarity. Unlike the wage workers of the past, today's GMH employees are entitled to 10 percent of the profits no matter what their rank. Their individual bonuses are scaled only by the hours they work and range from 1,500 to 4,000 euros a year, depending on the company's profits. This pioneering profit-sharing arrangement was developed in the early 1990s, and the firm was one of the first to undertake it, with the support of the government. Today this is a common arrangement in German manufacturing companies.

As he rounded the corner to his twentieth anniversary with GMH, Eckhardt started thinking about a career change. He liked the idea of teaching and decided it would be fulfilling to help young people learn the skills needed to make a good living. With the support of GMH, Eckhardt was admitted to a course in engineering based solely on his long years of work experience. (GMH's private foundation covered his tuition of 200 euros a month.) Every three weeks, he made the trip to a university of applied sciences in Osnabrück for classroom instruction and examinations. He completed the program over a four-year period, studying at night and submitting his work by mail.

Every three years, Meister Eckhardt takes in a new cohort of apprentices, most of whom are young men who work on the shop floor, and trains them to operate the computer systems that monitor steel production. He schools them in the technical aspects of mixing steel, heating it to astronomically high temperatures, and pouring and molding the results. These workers need to understand the underlying mechanical process that yields cold steel bars, from the beginning to the end, up to and including their shipment around the world. He spends some of his time at the local vocational high school conferring with his counterparts who provide in-class instruction to students like Johan. This constant contact ensures that the students have the foundational knowledge necessary for them to absorb the advanced applications Eckhardt will teach them in the workplace. The company is a constant presence in the high school, as are all the other firms that draw apprentices from among the students.

Fredericka works at GMH in worldwide sales and distribution. Like Johan, she arrived at the firm as an apprentice. Unlike the average apprentice, she attended an academic high school—or *Gymnasium*—and completed the *Abitur*, a diploma that is more demanding and hence elevated in prestige. Nonetheless, she decided to pursue employment in manufacturing because the GMH apprenticeship has a good reputation and the wage offered when she finished her apprenticeship two years ago was high enough to take care of a family. The company helps her with the cost of child care and her parents lend a hand, but she is very practical about what she needs to do to be financially secure.

Unlike Johan, who came to GMH steeped in the culture of blue-collar work, Fredericka knew nothing about this world when she started her apprenticeship. She was the only person in her school to go into manufacturing. It took time for her to become accustomed to electrical work and welding; she was more adept at the computer programming side of heavy manufacturing. She knows that the Abitur would permit her to jump back into higher education, while Johan's high school degree would not qualify him for admission to a university, but she does not expect to go that way. She anticipates remaining in the most white-collar part of the steel business: the back office.

Although she does not work in production, Fredericka shares Johan's pride in those giant bars of steel that roll off the shop floor and onto ships bound halfway around the world. She thinks of herself as part of a great machine that does remarkable things with technology, that outproduces other steel mills because it is adaptable, that it is fueling the industrial growth of countries far away, like China. Most workers at GMH share her sense that the meaning in what they do goes well beyond the limits of their own specific jobs. That commitment is an important part of the so-called German secret of highly trained and loyal workers.

From the moment they walk into the training section of the precision manufacturing companies where they hope to work, apprentices are asked to become highly skilled in most aspects of what the production process requires. Mechatronics technicians, who will end up watching for production mishaps, also learn how to run high-speed lathes and mount engines. Volkswagen technicians learn how to troubleshoot electrical faults, even if they are destined to monitor the painting process for the exterior of cars. The rotations apprentices go through during their training years ensure that they keep that bigger picture in mind. They are trained in skills that they may rarely, if ever, use but that allow them to develop a more capacious understanding of what the company does. This is one of the benefits of the German system of apprenticeship, but it is also a liability. Workers are, in a sense, overprepared, so much so that one of the great dangers German firms encounter is boredom with the actual jobs employees hold at the end of their training.

Keeping a workforce like this happy in jobs that are fundamentally repetitive is a challenge and management freely admits this is a problem. They try to deal with it through job rotation, challenges, support for further education that enables upward mobility (as it did for Eckhardt), and involvement in workers' councils in the large firms that have significant influence over company policies. But boredom is a risk firms such as GMH are willing to take because what they most desire is the high skill level of workers they produce through apprenticeship and continuous training.

One of the most important assets employees gain through this kind of training is the ability to train a critical eye on the production process. Every year GMH runs a problem-solving contest and awards big prizes— cars, cash—to the winners. In 2012, the company posed a challenge to the workers involving the disposal of scrap metal. A train loaded with wagons carrying the metal moves through the complex and has to be unloaded with the use of magnets. If the magnetic force is too strong, it picks up the wagons as well as the scrap metal. If it is too weak, it won't harvest the metal. GMH also was having trouble with trains that were crashing, costing them a fortune. Workers formed teams to debate alternatives to both problems and submitted their ideas by e-mail. The winning solution saved GMH nearly a million euros a year.

From an American perspective, where cost cutting and efficiency are more important than cultivating workers with a 360-degree view of the firm, the German system seems luxurious, almost wasteful. Does it really take three years to train a steel worker? Is it necessary to limit the responsibility of Meisters to five or six students at a time, a ratio unheard of in any educational enterprise in the United States? Why invest so much in training beyond what is necessary, however that might be defined? The answer is that this is what excellence costs to produce.

A highly skilled workforce, able to contribute to process improvements, is one of the reasons why German firms have become the dominant manufacturing power worldwide. Their high labor costs force them to remain lean in number, while putting a premium on productivity.

These factors fuel an ever-increasing emphasis on skill and on the ability to be competitive in high-margin international markets. German manufacturers have excelled at positioning themselves well for those markets. They have been instrumental in building manufacturing and transportation infrastructure in high-growth developing countries such as China. With international sources of demand, German firms can command relatively high wages for their employees as long as they are more efficient than anyone else. They do not even try to compete at the low-wage end of the international labor market. That is left to poorer countries.

The Dual System

The long history of the German dual system of vocational education and apprenticeship training can be traced back to the Middle Ages and the first regulations that German guilds developed for qualifying tradesmen. Formalized training regulated by the state is of more recent vintage. It commenced in 1830 with the creation of vocational schools. Today's dual system—which produces workers with nationally certified skills in construction, electronics, nursing, cosmetology, and 345 other occupations—is a balancing act involving three parties: private firms, the school system, and the unions. The national and regional chambers of commerce are in the middle, coordinating the interests of these three sectors.

The German tradition relies on a variant of economic statism, not through direct control over the economy but by casting government as an agent of cooperation, a convening power that brings unions and private industry together to bargain for optimal conditions. This does not mean that labor and management see eye to eye about everything. Indeed, there is plenty of push and pull going on as unions argue for better wages, benefits, and worker security, while management tries to limit costs and worker power. But instead of going to the brink, these two actors are moderated by government, especially through regulatory mechanisms like the national standards imposed on apprentice training courses. Cooperation of this kind is almost unheard of in the United States, where labor unions are often at odds with management. At most, government's role is an arbiter of disputes between these parties. Education, especially at the high school level, is kept at arm's length from private industry and has virtually nothing to do with unions.

In Germany, government, unions, and educational institutions function as public regulators and overseers of the training. They have statutory responsibility for developing the part of the curriculum that unfolds in the workplace. They put participating companies through rigorous paces as part of an accreditation process; they assess and certify student qualifications in partnership with the state. Together they set national standards for the roughly 350 occupations that are certified through rigorous annual examinations that vocational students study for, sweat over, and exhale only when they are over, on an annual basis. While there are differences in the way Volkswagen and BMW train the mechatronics specialists who produce their cars, they are all required to pass the same demanding examinations that assure both employers that certificate holders have mastered certain skills.

High rates of unionization are essential to the operation of the vocational education and apprenticeship system in Germany. Companies gain from the investment they make in training low-skilled employees who they don't want to lose; employers gain from the regulation of wages, which means very productive workers are paid less than they would be in a more flexible employment system.[2] As we have seen, unions are also important, as they can shape how firms train and then subsequently employ workers. Also with highly centralized collective bargaining, unions and business groups are better positioned to lobby the state to enact policies that promote vocational training.[3]

Beginning at age sixteen, German students in the vocational and educational training (VET) sector attend school one or two days a week and spend the rest of the week in the workplace. A Vocational Training Act outlines detailed rules for establishing occupational titles, training content, and duration, as well as examination or assessment standards and certification requirements. The students who successfully pass the rigorous national exams gain the legal right to call themselves "qualified professionals" (a legally defined and protected term in Germany) in their field of concentration. The diploma they receive signifies not only a social status but a particular wage grade. Because of this standardization, the skills trainees obtain through the VET system are highly portable. And because employers can rely on a worker's credentials, they can operate firms with less supervision. Managerial hierarchies are "flatter" than they would be in companies where it is necessary to exercise more oversight. This lowers the cost of manufacturing and services by eliminating the cost of middle management, the expense of inspection, and the waste that results when workers are less well trained.

In 2013, Hermann Nehls was responsible for national policy in the field of vocational education and apprenticeship for the High Council of German Trade Unions.[4] We visited with him in the council's offices, high atop a large office building with a commanding view of Berlin below. From this location, Nehls develops policy for the trade unions in Germany but also works to promote apprenticeship and high-quality training throughout the European Union.

Hermann explains that the dual system has become increasingly important as a demographic decline has created instability in the labor force. Even as recently as 2011, firms could find skilled labor fairly easily. No longer, Hermann remarks, especially where midskill engineers and technicians are involved. German firms are picking up and moving to Spain and Italy in search of more of these less expensive workers. The response of German workers has been to support EU-wide organizations like the European Alliance for Apprenticeships, a cooperative group of member states looking to spread both best practices and the kind of constraints that make it harder for German firms to bust wages or reduce the quality or duration of training.

While vocational training in the United States is a poor stepchild of conventional high-school institutions and captures the attention of only a modest number of students, in Germany it is the majority experience. Fifty-five percent of upper secondary students take part. This translates into 1.6 million student trainees at any given time. About 23 percent of all companies—484,000 firms—are involved in providing training; as with GMH, many of the larger firms take on the process for smaller firms in the same region.

As is true in most countries where students encounter a fork in the road that is consequential for their futures, Germany sorts its students into different types of middle schools. In Germany's case, the divide occurs after the fourth grade. The students who are academically strongest go to Gymnasium, and their path leads to an Abitur diploma and the ability to enroll in a university. This is the elite path and, while it is formally open to all, it is most likely to be traveled by young people from highly educated and affluent families. Practically speaking, students who are advantaged in their early years are the ones most likely to make the grade. Notably, 17 percent of Abitur students elect to enroll in the dual system after they graduate from high school so that they can obtain a vocational qualification before deciding whether to go on to college.[5]

A middle group of elementary school students are placed in the *Realschule*, where at age sixteen they receive a certificate that allows them to pursue further academic education or vocational training. If their grades are good enough, they may be permitted to enroll in a Gymnasium. The students whose academic performance is weakest attend a *Hauptschule*, where, after ninth grade, at fourteen, they receive a certificate that entitles them to pursue vocational training.

In 2010, the federal government, the *Länder* (states), and the municipalities, together with the Federal Employment Services, spent a total of 7.2 billion euros on vocational education and training in Germany. The Länder paid an additional 3.3 billion euros for vocational training in vocational full-time schools. German businesses footed more than three-quarters of the cost of apprenticeships in Germany while the federal government and Länder paid about one-tenth of those costs and the Federal Employment Services about one-seventh. The Länder outspent both the federal government and Federal Employment Services on vocational training, but the federal government and Federal Employment Services contributed much more than the Länder to supporting further vocational education and training.[6]

Germany invests heavily in training its master teachers, equipping its secondary schools with expensive equipment that enables students to learn the latest technologies, and then devotes even more through the commitment of private firms who hire the Meisters, pay the apprentices, and then hire them once they graduate.

It should not surprise us that this investment has a dramatic impact on the job prospects of Germany's young people, which has the lowest youth unemployment rate among the world's industrialized nations. Their national devotion to training is largely responsible for this good fortune, but the Germans are not alone in their emphasis on vocational education. Half or more of secondary school graduates in Europe enroll in a vocational-oriented program (in which they earn 25 percent or more of their total credits). Even in Korea and Japan, with their strong academic traditions, a quarter of secondary graduates concentrate in vocational education that meets OECD (Organization for Economic Cooperation and Development) standards. By contrast, since the early 1980s the percentage of US secondary students meeting OECD standards for vocational education enrollment declined from about 18 percent to 6 percent.[7]

German Apprentice in ZF

ZF is a worldwide producer of auto parts; its most important product is the chassis for automobiles; the company supplies Mercedes and BMW, among other auto manufacturers. ZF has 121 production facilities in twenty-six countries. Ten of them are in the United States, including plants in Michigan, Alabama, and South Carolina. Its facility in Lemförde, a municipality in the German state of Lower Saxony, ships 17.3 million euros' worth of chassis, produced by seventy-five thousand employees. In the Osnabrück region alone, there are forty-five hundred workers, making ZF Lemförde the biggest employer in the area, larger by far than Volkswagen.

Martin Waitz is the senior manager and head of apprenticeship training at the facility in Diepholz, one of the constituent facilities of the Lemförde branch of ZF. He began his career with ZF thirty-five years ago as an apprentice and has risen up in the ranks. He now heads the group that supplies apprentices for all of the ZF plants in the region. There are more than 200 apprentices at any given time; 110 of them are ZF trainees, while approximately another 90 are being trained by ZF for placements in smaller firms who pay the company for their training services—a lucrative side business. Martin's role is to ensure that all of the apprentices are trained to the point where they are sure bets for permanent positions.

Because ZF is a multinational and a leader in mechatronics and other applications of computer-based technology, its labor needs are on the high-skill side. They are particularly interested in hiring people who can advance the applications of new methods and go beyond focusing simply on increasing the efficiency of the tried and true. Accordingly, ZF encourages a blend of traditional apprenticeship and partnerships with universities. Forty of Martin's trainees participate in a dual program that links them to a university-based engineering qualification that takes 3.7 years to complete. Tuition is fully paid by ZF and they give students a stipend to boot. Standards are set high and qualifying for this opportunity is demanding, but the rewards are significant, including guaranteed jobs in engineering and management. Apprentices also have the option of enrolling in training modules for six to eight weeks in ZF plants outside of Germany; for anyone expecting to enter a management track, it behooves them to take advantage of this opportunity.

Martin supervises an experienced and highly credentialed training staff of six. All of the ZF trainers are licensed by the national Chamber of Trades, having sat for a rigorous examination after they have had three to four years of teaching experience. As a group, the trainers start the apprentices out in the training center, where they master a common curriculum of machine tools, electrical circuits, and welding, among other things. When they are proficient in these skills, they are sent out into ZF's plants, of which there are half a dozen in the Osnabrück area, to train with Meisters.

Though ZF is careful in the selection process, every year some ten to fifteen students drop out of the plants and come back into a less demanding industrial training system within the company that is state-funded. The failure cases are not random; they are often from depressed areas of

Osnabrück and families that are not part of the ZF kinship system. The company intentionally works with young people who would be called "at risk" in the United States and adds to the mix of resources for them, including social workers and additional basic math training. These trainees are more heavily subsidized by the government, but they are otherwise totally integrated into the apprenticeship system and about 80 percent of them are eventually employed by ZF.

While ZF perceives that it has a social responsibility to train students who are not necessarily destined for high-skilled jobs, the investment is not only charitable. Like other German firms, the company has an interest in trying to make this work because it is getting harder for them to access the traditional source of apprentices.

One of the reasons is that German youth have absorbed the prejudices and aspirations common in the United States and began to see manufacturing as uninteresting, dirty, or dangerous, with few possibilities for advancement. Blue-collar jobs remain fairly secure and certainly well represented by industrial unions in Germany, but the cultural spillover of the prestige hierarchy is dissuading increasing numbers of youth from seeking apprenticeships in manufacturing. Apprenticeship is still the majority experience, but it may not remain that way forever. Even now, as the hiring manager of GMH explained, "It is not so easy to persuade young people to come into manufacturing today."

> Times are changing. Parents want their kids to work in offices, not in steel mills. We have to build a positive identification for them with our firm. They want to balance work and life today. It is no longer sexy to produce steel. But our jobs pay well and they are stable.

For this reason, Germans are trying to create a loop that will give its young people another shot at higher education after they have traveled the vocational pathway. This "second chance" has become all the more important. Another reason for the shortage of trainees is that the present generation of teenagers and twentysomethings is very small by historical standards. Due to labor shortages of native-born German youth, a young man like Johan might receive five attractive offers to choose from. Thus the assisted apprentice who completes the program, despite the problems posed by his or her background, is well worth the investment.

Unemployment among Germany's immigrant and second-generation youth mirrors the American experience with low-income minorities. In both cases, entry-level job seekers who have fewer family resources to draw on[8] have a more difficult time finding work since they lack robust connections to the labor market.[9] They are thus particularly reliant on what formal institutions like schools can do for them. Institutions that can give them a leg up, especially in finding a first job, are critical for the less advantaged.

Immigrant youth in Germany, many of whom were born in Turkey or who came from that country as young children, are more likely to find themselves on the outside of the apprentice system unless they are fortunate enough to find their way into a very large company. Indeed, research has found that immigrant children in Germany have lower educational achievement in general than their German counterparts and, in the case of some immigrant groups, are overrepresented compared to German youth in Hauptschulen. For example, in 2008 only 14.8 percent of German-born children attended Hauptschulen as compared to 45 percent of their Turkish immigrant counterparts. And while these schools are supposed to prepare students for a trade, in some regions of the country, according to a 2008 article in the *Economist*, they are little more than dumping grounds.[10]

Even within the VET sector, young people with what the Germans call a "migratory background" are at a disadvantage. Immigrant youth have less of a chance to get into the system than German natives. This inequality of access is particularly pronounced in the area of apprenticeships. Workers' councils have the right to be involved in screening applications for apprentices and may be inclined to favor the native-born, although in larger companies they may play a critical role in insisting on a minimum rate of migrant youth in the program.[11] This problem was identified as far back as the early 1990s and researchers point in part to antecedent difficulties immigrants face in learning the German language and the attendant problems with school performance, as well as anti-immigrant prejudice to explain it.[12]

A 2010 OECD report noted that one of the reasons Turkish youth in particular have difficulty getting access to good training places has to do with the fact that these immigrants are also concentrated in a few segments of the German labor market, which can hamper their children's ability to break into other areas.[13]

Big firms like Volkswagen make more of a deliberate effort to diversify the ranks of their apprentices. Smaller firms, especially family-owned businesses, are less likely to do so and are not subject to public scrutiny for evidence of commitment to progressive values. Unfortunately, companies owned and operated by immigrants are less likely to participate in the dual-education system compared to the national average of German firms.[14]

In spite of the increasing difficulty in recruiting apprentices, localism and the traditional penchant for recruitment within family lines persist. We asked employers in Osnabrück who complained about having a hard time finding qualified apprentices whether they ever advertised in eastern Germany, where unemployment is much higher and opportunities are fewer. They looked at us with puzzled expressions as the idea clearly had not occurred to them. Of course, the tradition of taking apprentices at the age of sixteen or seventeen, when the vast majority of young people are still living with their families, makes geographic movement somewhat more difficult.

Given the scramble to find local labor, ZF knows it cannot be complacent but must instead reach out to young people earlier in their school years, in the eighth grade, when they are first beginning to debate what kind of apprenticeship they should pursue. ZF is generous to the local schools, providing each of them with a significant grant every year to support a robotics program. The company has an entire department that is responsible for educational relations. It organizes opportunities for students to do class projects and arranges for current apprentices to return to their middle schools to run workshops that showcase what they have gained from their training experience at ZF. Those role models encourage succeeding crops of eighth graders to choose ZF for their two-week shadowing assignments.

It was just that kind of opportunity that led Franz to ZF three years ago, when he was seventeen. He didn't have any family members in the company to pave his way, but Franz had long been fascinated by electronics and was attracted to the idea of pursuing a training opportunity in mechatronics. His vocational school prepared him well with courses in practical physics and math, classes that appealed to Franz because he had always had a technical mind, interested in concrete problems.

At ZF, Franz and Josef, a friend he met at the company, began their training with fairly advanced electronics, building on top of the more basic skills they had already learned. Our visit occurred in their third and final year as ZF apprentices, by which time both young men had graduated to working on the latest in computer-controlled metal lathes. Each of these machines costs over 200,000 euros and was produced by Siemens specifically for the purpose of training advanced students of mechatronics.

Trainees learn to program the high-speed lathes, inputting the instructions appropriate to the kind of metal part they aim to produce. Franz and Josef know how to troubleshoot and need that capacity because as sophisticated as this equipment is, it is not foolproof. The sound of blades cutting into steel at high speed has its own rhythm and they rely on sight and sound to figure out when something has gone wrong. They can watch the machine operate through a hard plastic shield and must learn to let the machine come to a full stop before they reach in to retrieve a part or adjust an angle.

Martin Waitz is particularly proud of the capacities for independent thinking he has developed in Franz and Josef. As Meister, his job involves devising complex exercises to test their problem-solving skills. These are not simple tasks, either. From their second year forward, apprentices are expected to produce real value added for ZF. The problems they take on are related to actual glitches in the production of automobile power trains that ZF encounters in the manufacturing process. Solutions the apprentices devise are incorporated—after thorough testing—into standard company production methods. In this ZF follows a common practice in all German apprenticeships: The trainees pay for themselves because they are part of the work flow, not an auxiliary to it.

Franz and Josef earn about 600 euros a month (approximately $1,000) as apprentices. When they finish, there will be jobs waiting for them at one of the ZF plants in the region at four times this salary. The company has invested a great deal in all of its apprentices and hence hires 100 percent of those who finish the course.

The School Side of the Equation

Franz and Josef were well positioned for the ZF training experience because the skills they learned at their vocational high school, the Beruts-kolleg Techlenburger Land, prepared them well. Lutz Kornau is the director of vocational education at the school, which is incorporated into a system of vocational schools within the state of North Rhine–Westphalia. There are sixteen such states in Germany, and they provide a portion of the funding for the vocational schools, where the standards are guided by national occupational guidelines and the tests that certify them. There are four such vocational schools in the Osnabrück region, where the population is about 160,000. Nearly three thousand students are enrolled in the Berutskolleg, though there are never so many actually on-site since most are out working in the companies for three to four days a week by the time they enter their third year of high school.

The atmosphere in the *Kolleg* is serious and respectful. Although kids are dressed in T-shirts and jeans, they do not stroll around casually or hang out in the hallways. The students are attentive and behave in a professional manner. Teachers know the students well and follow their progress not only during the school day but in the firms where they are working, since the Meisters and the teachers must collaborate to ensure the students are prepared for the national examinations for their trades. Equipment that the students work on in class is as up-to-date as the machines they use on the shop floor where they are apprenticed. Innovations spread quickly back to the schools so that the training is synchronized and the students remain at the cutting edge. Employers come to the Kolleg with specific objectives in mind and hence create contracts with the school for particular kinds of training. Students move through the school in cohorts that stream out into the firms in groups, which reinforces a sense of belonging and connection in both settings.

Typically, apprentices who are attending vocational school one day a week (and working the other four) will take four-hour classes that are divided into two-hour hands-on workshops and two hours of classroom instruction where they learn the mathematics, electronics, or physics needed to understand the underlying principles that govern their practical work. They also take courses in English, German, history, and religion, a curriculum devised locally but with state-level standards in mind.

An electronics class is learning the physics of electrical currents in order to understand how energy is created, the relationship between revolutions and currents. Sixteen boys and one girl are bent over their notebooks. Having studied the principles in this class, they file down the hallway to an industrial mechanics workshop where there are electrical grids and fuses mounted on pegboards. The instructor forces a mistake into the system and then watches as the students diagnose the fault, putting into practice what they have learned in theory. Students work in small groups and problem-solve out loud, while the instructor moves from group to group, monitoring their progress, calling students over to observe when a cluster gets a demanding problem right.

In a more advanced workshop, students work on lathes for aluminum. As they program and simulate the milling process, they put to work the three hours of vocational mathematics they take every week, calculating the optimal speed for the equipment. They work in classes of about fifteen, under the supervision of teachers who have had long experience in companies where this technology is the stuff of everyday life. They trade on that background to guide students through course projects that have been codesigned by companies and teachers.

One class worked on the design of a conveyer belt that had to handle the automatic sorting of parts. Programming a robotic arm was integral to the project. It took thirty-eight hours in the company and even more time in school to complete the project. Apprentices moved back and forth between the shop floor and special courses in programming.

Students who are successful will be able to demonstrate both practical and theoretical understanding, display their prototypes, and document the design process. When they finish this apprenticeship, they will be qualified as medium-rank technical managers, below the skill level of university-qualified engineers. Their skills are analogous to those of workers at the kind of middle-skill jobs that are predicted to grow in the United States.

Not every class in the Kolleg is directed toward manufacturing. The kitchen serves healthy and elaborate lunches to the entire school population every day. Cooking and serving hundreds of meals, students also go to the local markets, purchase meat and produce from local suppliers, and transport it back to the campus, where they prepare it according to industrial scale recipes. Consumer scientists at the University of Osnabrück work with them to craft a food-processing curriculum. "Kitchen math" is required, since students have to calculate unit prices, weights, and caloric values. They put this training to use in the school's kitchen, which cost nearly one million euros to design and outfit with industrial ovens, stoves, and fume hoods.

We had the opportunity to sample their wares in a five-course meal the students prepared for us, their teachers, and a group of seven students who joined us for a bit of biographical conversation. Georg, the first young man to speak, is at the end of his apprenticeship. At twenty-one years old, he has now mastered what he needs to work full-time for a packaging company where he is an industrial mechanic. "I loved to play with Legos as a kid," he explains in fluent English. "My father is a truck driver and my mother works as a house cleaner, but I wanted to go into industry." The next young man is twenty-two and completed his national service obligations before coming back to the Kolleg to learn joinery. He had always wanted to be a teacher but went into the family's blue-collar trade instead. His long-range ambition is to fuse the two and become a vocational school teacher.

Benedict, who is now twenty, comes from a family that has long worked in one of the local automobile manufacturing companies. His father is an electrician and his mother is a clerk in a social work agency. At sixteen he started an apprenticeship in maintenance but has graduated to a training course that is preparing him to be an extrusion technician in a plant that makes pipes out of synthetic materials. William is the son of a facilities manager who took him around to construction sites to familiarize him with the work. But at fourteen, William decided he was more interested in mechatronics and hence is pursuing the training his needs to master numerical control machines.

As these examples suggest, one rarely encounters children of middle-class white-collar workers in industrial apprenticeships. These young people are mainly the sons (and some daughters) of the skilled working class and they hope to equal their parents in income and social status or perhaps slightly exceed them in skill. Upward mobility is less their goal than stability, security, and a good wage. And that is precisely what they get. They understand the value of the training they are receiving and that matters most to them.

The Family Firm

Hermann Mohle (HM) is a building trades company that has been in one family for more than a hundred years. This is not unusual in Germany, where the law—especially tax law—encourages the preservation of family enterprises by making it financially worthwhile to hold them through the generations. The company installs electrical and solar heating, plumbing systems, and waste water treatment. A small company of only thirty workers, it exemplifies some of the difficulties firms of this size have in attracting apprentices. Mr. Mohle, the president (and grandson of the original founder), is in his early sixties and is grooming his own son to take over as the fourth generation to operate the company. "I am proud of our work," he explains, "but it isn't sexy. Apprentices prefer to go to bigger companies and everyone seems to want to do white-collar work these days." The "small trades," he notes, "have a hard time attracting young people." Yet it is the small family firms that often offer the greatest stability since they don't compete against the international conglomerates and tend not to go through the waves of downsizing that typically affect industries like steel or automobiles.

In the last year, Mohle has had to raise the wages of new apprentices by about 20 percent in order to land his fourth or fifth choice. This year, his sole apprentice was not a native speaker of German but an immigrant from Hungary who arrived in Germany with his family when he was about ten years old. Before finding Zsazlov, Mohle had made offers to six or seven other people who turned him down. Not that long ago, he had one hundred applicants for every apprenticeship. Last year he had sixty for three places and most received multiple offers. The company scrutinizes applicants for their performance in school, especially in math and physics, because the work they do involves calculation, especially for volume. In the end, though, it is the soft skills that count the most: motivation, follow-through, punctuality. The company's customers expect responsible and personable service.

Apprentices begin their tenure with the company on a kind of probationary contract for four months, after which time the law requires the company to offer a full three-and-a-half-year training course. Virtually everyone who gets that far is guaranteed a job for which the starting wage is about $20 an hour. Apprentices take home about $900 a month, which, while not as generous as the wage of the steel mill trainees, is nonetheless a fair amount of money for a teenager living at home.

HM has now combined what were once two different kinds of apprenticeships, one in heating and the other in electronics. They have eliminated training in welding because the pipes they use now are all made of plastic. Zsazlov expects to complete his training and get a steady job in the family firm. He is particularly happy about this because every worker at Mohle owns his or her own home. The apprentices and workers build those houses together using the technology and materials they employ for customers and their networks in the construction industry to cobble together the rest.

No doubt this is one reason why Mohle's apprentices think of themselves as part of a family. This year the company will celebrate the forty-fifth anniversary of several workers and many are at the thirty-five-year mark. "People stay forever in our company," the president says with pride.

Amazone is also a fourth-generation family firm that got its start making machines that cleaned grain. They take satisfaction in having won awards frequently ever since 1891, when they received a prize for the best agricultural machines at an exposition in Bremen.

Pride is very much in evidence in the grand foyer that welcomes visitors to Amazone. Every machine the company makes is displayed there: giant tractors with wide plows that till and seed fifteen rows of upturned soil at a time, mounted irrigation equipment that sprays water across a thirty-foot plot, fertilizer spreaders, and harvesting machines of varying sizes line up in an impressive row. Americans accustomed to John Deere equipment in neon green and yellow do a double take because Amazone's machines are in exactly the same colors.

When Amazone got its start, every part in its agricultural machines was handmade. Today, of course, they are stamped out by machines that can produce over one hundred parts an hour. Unlike other companies that outsource this work, Amazone makes its own tools and manufactures 70 percent of the parts they use, which now total about 3.5 million a year. Injection molding technology makes this fairly straightforward and, because it involves plastics, Amazone can recycle their mistakes to avoid waste. And they are quite successful at containing waste, as 98 percent of what they make is used in production. Farmers in Germany, France, and Russia constitute the largest market for Amazone equipment and the annual revenues from those sales run at around 460 million euros. Amazone is growing at the rate of 20 percent to 30 percent a year because one of the principal crops it supports—wheat—is commanding ever higher prices both because of its role in the food system and because of its value as a source of bio fuels. The company has seven factories, four of which are in Germany and the others are in Russia, France, and the United Kingdom. They export 80 percent of what they produce to seventy different countries. The factory near Osnabrück employs sixty apprentices at a time, twenty per cohort. The German plants hire both engineering and apprentice labor; in the other countries, workers merely assemble the parts. Amazone doesn't trust anyone else to follow their quality standards.

An entire section of the factory floor is carved out for the apprentices, with row upon row of gleaming equipment. The machines the students use are exact duplicates of the ones that regular workers run on the main shop floor. Each of the giant lathes is worth more than 250,000 euros, an enormous investment for the company, but one they feel is worth it to ensure that the labor force is training on the most modern equipment. Apprentices take three and a half years to complete their course of study. While a few go on to take the Abitur to become engineers, all of the apprentices who finish the training are guaranteed jobs at about 35,000 euros a year (approximately $40,000).

Jorg and Stefan, first-year apprentices at Amazone, are about six feet tall, blond, and dressed in overalls. Both were from farm families and were used to getting up at the crack of dawn, a good thing since apprentices have to get up early in the morning for shifts that begin at six a.m. and end at two p.m. They explained that they had done their eighth-grade practicums in this Amazone plant and hoped they might work in the company someday. Both had completed the Abitur and then applied for eight to ten apprenticeships in the region. Luckily, they were exactly what Amazone was looking for: farm boys who know how to work the land and see agrobusiness as their way of life.

Like the labor force they will join at the end of their training, Amazone apprentices are part of the organized labor system. They are represented by the metal workers union; they have negotiated a good wage and a thirteenth-month bonus. They can look forward to a long, prosperous, and stable future at Amazone as one of the eight hundred workers in the plant. Turnover in the labor force is very low because laborers and Meisters alike spend their entire working lives there. This kind of investment— which would be extraordinary by American standards—pays off over the long run because it is this high-quality training that ensures Amazone's future labor force will be at the top of the skill pyramid. They are competing at a high level, and that requires workers who can be relied on to produce the highest-quality machinery, contribute to process improvements, and stick with the firm to realize the value of the investment. This is what it takes to remain a top contender in industry and that is where Amazone intends to stay.

The Auto Behemoth

The largest auto plant in Germany—and indeed in the world—is the Volkswagen production facility in Wolfsburg, just west of Berlin. One of one hundred production plants worldwide—in the United States, South Africa, Argentina, Brazil, and Mexico, to name only a few—the Wolfsburg plant boasts nearly sixty-five miles of streets. VW employs 250,000 workers in Germany and another 400,000 throughout the rest of Europe, a labor force that has grown by leaps and bounds with the development of the European Union.

Architecturally, the Wolfsburg plant is a jarring sight. While driving its streets, one cannot help but notice the carvings on the buildings' walls, which are hallmarks of German National Socialism. Built in 1938 as part of the Nazi war effort with the confiscated resources of the German labor unions, Wolfsburg has a history that its current leadership keeps in mind. They feel strongly that the company's origins should never be forgotten.

The interior hallways of the main administration building are lined with photos of VW executives making their yearly pilgrimage to what is left of the concentration camps of the Second World War.

Volkswagen is run with a policy of "codetermination," in which the unions and internal company or works councils—institutionalized bodies recognized by company management to advocate for worker rights and provide advice to management—play a robust role uniting management and labor in virtually all policy decisions, an approach fueled by the desire to overcome the company's beginnings. The company board is by statute made up of half labor and half management. In Lower Saxony, the state where Wolfsburg is located, there is a somewhat unique addition of public ownership in which two representatives of the state participate in the supervisory board. A two-thirds vote of this board is required to authorize the building of a new plant anywhere in the world.

This power-sharing arrangement prevents VW from escaping the strictures of codetermination by setting up shop in other countries and it ensures the representation of workers not only from VW but from the hundreds of suppliers whose employees are also affected by any decision the company makes to start or stop production, close or open a plant, cut or extend a shift.[15] Codetermination strikes a balance between economic efficiency and employment security, production strength and the ecological responsibilities that the works councils regard as integral to decisions over plant locations.

Works councils in every plant oversee the decision making on all aspects of plant operations. All employees below the level of senior management are represented in the councils, and they are paralleled by the trade unions, who appoint shop stewards whose main responsibilities involve provisions of the collective bargaining contracts. A Europe-wide works council deals with agreements that go beyond workplace policy. In 2002, the European Works Council developed a social rights charter and a platform that guarantees freedom of assembly. These are rights taken for granted in Europe, but in China, where VW was interested in setting up a number of new production facilities, this was hardly the case. In 2006, the firm's international works council developed a policy of sustainability designed to govern supplier relations. In 2012, it developed a temporary worker charter. In this, VW is a little more like a nation-state and a little less like the industrial firms we are familiar with in the United States.

Codetermination has seen the company through the worst of times. The early 1990s were among them, when international competition and economic downturn threatened to topple VW, but because management and employees weathered the storm together, without waves of strikes, they feel the model is battle-tested. The company kept open plants in order to protect jobs that even the works council agreed should have been closed. Plants around the world redistributed work rather than watch their coworkers lose their jobs. Workers voluntarily (and temporarily) gave up wages to support those threatened with unemployment. Today, it is the intention of the apprentices, workers, managers, and public owners to see VW rise from its current position as the number three automaker in the world to number one by 2018. (Volkswagen may have a more difficult time recovering from a 2015 scandal in which it became clear that the company deliberately incorporated software into its diesel cars that led to false emission readings and hence increased pollution. The news plunged VW into a crisis, leading to the resignation of high-level management, plunging stock values, and sharp declines in sales.)

The experience of the '90s showed that codetermination is not the same thing as harmony. There were powerful managers who argued strenuously at the time for the more conventional approach of cost cutting through plant closings. They lasted only a year and then left VW. Even today, there is a tug and pull of divergent interests. In 2013, management attempted to cut the cost of the apprenticeship program by reducing it to two years. The works council resisted this approach and it disappeared from the agenda.

Because Wolfsburg is such an enormous facility, its apprenticeship program is one of the largest and best organized in Germany. Young people from all over the country vie for an opportunity to become part of it both because it has an excellent reputation for training and because the company is regarded as a "flagship" firm emblematic of German precision manufacturing. Wolfsburg alone takes in some 650 apprentices a year; countrywide there are 16,714 working for Volkswagen. They are training for thirty-one occupations and pursue nineteen separate degree programs, in fields from automobile sales to accounting to mechanical process engineering, and construction mechanics. Seventy-five percent of the apprentices are men. As a large and very visible company, VW makes notable efforts to include young people from migrant backgrounds; nearly one-third of their apprentices are either foreign-born or have immigrant parents, far more than at smaller German companies that provide, by far, the largest number of apprenticeships.[16]

It is hard to land a job at VW without passing through this training program, and it produces a strong internal culture and a degree of flexibility in the workforce given their common training. One hundred percent of the graduates of apprentice programs are hired by the company and 90 percent of them are awarded permanent contracts, based on their marks in school, assessments conducted every three months, and the fit of their personalities with the company's expectations. Ten percent are given two-year positions.

Their wages are high. Indeed, they would be regarded as good pay for regular workers in many parts of the industrial world. In 2013 entry-level, first-year apprentices earned 924 euros (about $1,200) a month, typically at age seventeen. In the fourth and final year, that wage rises to 1,119 euros (about $1,400). Apprentices are also given bonuses of about 4,000 euros, while full-time workers see 7,000 euros in their paychecks at the end of the year. Apprentices who complete the training and are hired on for permanent positions could expect a starting wage of 3,000 euros in 2013, or $50,000 a year plus full benefits. The workweek is only thirty-four hours long and most employees head into retirement with full benefits at the age of fifty-six, fifty-nine, or sixty. Mandatory retirement is set at sixty-seven.

"People want security," explained Stephan Wolf, VW vice president and deputy chair of the Wolfsburg Works Council. "They want a program that rewards talent, an opportunity to travel to other VW plants, sponsorship for degree programs for advanced training at the master's level, and the ability to reenter our workforce at the same level if they take time off to start a family." That kind of stability and opportunity is the reason why the VW apprenticeship is coveted.

Julie, a first-year apprentice, started out at VW because her cousin Karl encouraged her to follow him. Where once the firm was entirely male, today there are many young women who see a future for themselves in auto manufacture. Julie was working with a Meister who was teaching her some of the intricacies of spot welding. Karl is now a second-year apprentice who says he was almost born to this work. Even in the midst of this enormous facility and one of the largest companies in Germany, it feels like home to him. Both of his parents work at the Wolfsburg plant: his father is a mechanic and his mother is on a clerical support staff for the works council. Karl spent his early years in a child care center run by the company and knows many other young people who are apprentices here, following in the footsteps of their own parents.

Another group of apprentices was learning how to move car parts through enormous "baths" that apply a finish to the painted side panels, roofs, and wheel covers of VWs. Parts are hoisted by magnetic arms that move along a track, dipping them into each bath for a period of twenty seconds, ending in a high-temperature "oven," the size of a house, to dry. Notable for anyone not accustomed to modern factories is the small number of people working on the shop floor. The process is highly automated and very little human labor is visible from the viewing platform.

A group of fourth-year (and final-year) apprentices proudly displayed a car they had designed from stem to stern, a white sports car, low to the ground, with a slick red and black stripe down the side, and the largest set of stereo speakers ever inserted in the back of an automobile. This project was the crowning glory of this class of apprentices and it sits proudly on display for all of the others to admire.

The skills these young people have developed in the course of their training were cultivated through a blended learning model of Web-based instruction and face-to-face instruction. Their Meisters are looking to cultivate in them a desire for lifelong learning, especially in high tech. Andreas, who has been a Meister for VW for a decade, accepts a cohort every three and a half years and stays with them for their entire period of apprenticeship. "They really aren't blue-collar workers," he explains. "It makes more sense to think of them as computer diagnostic technicians." That shift may help to explain why we find more girls on the shop floor today. There is a tremendous amount of book learning, math, and measurement. Apprentices must be able to write reports and document orders; they have to work in teams. These qualities are hardly exclusive to the boys, Andreas notes.

Conclusion

There are many reasons why Germany has been one of the world's most successful industrial powers. The undervaluation of the euro, especially relative to the old deutsche mark, artificially depresses the cost of its exports and makes them highly competitive in world markets. They have also insisted on wage moderation in the industrial sector in order to exceed the mandated targets set by the European Union. The country's specialization in both luxury goods—Mercedes, BMW—and the precision manufacturing that has built Chinese industries and high-speed rail systems around the world is also critical to their national success.

None of this would have worked, however, if the Germans had not been able to deploy the world's most skilled labor force. High quality, efficiency, disciplined delivery—these are the attributes of a national manufacturing system made possible by the investments the country has made in the training of its workers. What it takes to create and then maintain a workforce of this caliber is a deep investment in a first-class vocational education program, coupled with a serious, time-consuming commitment to training on the shop floor, in thousands of companies, all across the country. German apprentices are schooled with state-of-the-art equipment and expected to master complex and intellectually demanding curricula. They must prove they are capable by passing rigorous examinations that are developed nationally and signify mastery of the occupations they have trained for.[17]

The stigma that attaches to vocational education in the United States is a problem that is beginning to bedevil Germany, but it faces a stiff headwind because of the country's long-standing respect for this kind of training and the occupations for which it prepares people. In the United States, this is (somewhat ironically) being addressed by insisting on the simultaneous focus on college preparation rather than a concerted effort to alter perceptions about the value of middle-skill work. This approach authorizes the continuing emphasis on standardized testing, which vocational teachers and administrators see as a mixed bag: A strong performance on standardized tests can demonstrate to the world that vocational education is neither "lesser," nor is it meant for students who can't cut it academically. At the same time, the mania for testing not only fails to capture much of what vocational students learn and know—and, in so doing, devalues that learning—but also takes time away from the training itself.

Apprentices in Germany are compensated handsomely for their time, promised long-term employment in exchange for those years of vocational training, and given expert teachers who are also well paid and well respected for the skills they transmit. To be a Meister is to be honored. And that extends not only to the mighty manufacturing fields but to the masters who teach young people to become nurses, hospital technicians, and for countless other service occupations. The German system epitomizes an old, and thoroughly American, adage: You get what you pay for.

7

The Math Puzzle

From Andrew Hacker in the *New York Times*, July 29, 2012:

A typical American school day finds some six million high school students and two million college freshmen struggling with algebra. In both high school and college, all too many students are expected to fail. Why do we subject American students to this ordeal? I've found myself moving toward the strong view that we shouldn't.

My question extends beyond algebra and applies more broadly to the usual mathematics sequence, from geometry through calculus. State regents and legislators—and much of the public—take it as self-evident that every young person should be made to master polynomial functions and parametric equations.

There are many defenses of algebra and the virtue of learning it. Most of them sound reasonable on first hearing; many of them I once accepted. But the more I examine them, the clearer it seems that they are largely or wholly wrong—unsupported by research or evidence, or

based on wishful logic. (I'm not talking about quantitative skills, critical for informed citizenship and personal finance, but a very different
ballgame.)

This debate matters. Making mathematics mandatory prevents
us from discovering and developing young talent. In the interest of
maintaining rigor, we're actually depleting our pool of brainpower.[1]

Andrew Hacker's broadside against the gatekeeping functions of the
mathematics curriculum is a response to the anxieties that underlie the
"college for all" movement. The rationale for the current curriculum is
that all students need to understand pure math—rather than the application of mathematical ideas for real-world problem solving—because it is
a fundamental form of knowledge. Without this mastery, students will be
unable to function in modern society. Hence the traditional mathematics
sequence should be required for high-school graduation and augmented
by additional requirements in the early years of college.

The federal government's Common Core initiative is based on this
premise. Its advocates believe that a rigorous high-school education, especially in math, will ensure that American students will be able to head
for higher education if they want to, but will also equip them if they want
to enter the job market immediately.[2] But, as Hacker notes, the evidence for
this position is as limited as the conviction about it is strong. The "Survey
of Workplace Skills, Technology, and Management Practices (STAMP),"
funded by, among others, the National Science Foundation, makes clear
that only a very small number of occupations make use of any mathematics beyond what most of us learn in the first few years of high school:

Nearly all workers use some math and 68 percent use fractions, but less
than one in four uses anything more advanced than fractions. Only
19 percent use the skills developed in Algebra I and only 9 percent use
the skills for Algebra II. Even among upper white-collar workers, professionals and managers, the use of middle to upper level high school
math is strikingly low. Only 14 percent of these managerial, professional
or technical workers report using Algebra II and only 22 percent report
using statistics. The share using these math tools among workers in all

other job categories is generally in the single digits. Upper blue collar workers use Algebra I (36 percent) and geometry and/or trigonometry (29 percent) at rates higher than all other groups of workers, including upper white collar workers. The Common Core mathematics standards encourage states to mandate upper level math for high school students on topics that are used by a very small percentage of the workforce.[3]

More important, the same study shows, is the ability to read. If we are going to put students through their paces and hold them to a high standard to graduate from high school, this is where we should put most of our energy: Nearly all workers have to read on the job and about half (53 percent) read work-related books or instruction manuals or reference materials. Writing requirements are exceedingly low. Except for workers in upper white-collar jobs, less than half write anything at least one page long. Less than 15 percent of these workers write anything five pages or more; for upper white-collar workers, the proportion is only 4 percent, a surprisingly low figure.

For workers in middle-skill jobs in the manufacturing sector, among the most important abilities are those that are neither mathematical nor reading-related per se but might be described as a "visual information" skills. They need to be able to absorb and produce information from "maps, diagrams, floor plans, graphs, or blueprints." Upper blue-collar workers are the most likely to read and create such visuals (82 percent and 62 percent, respectively), rates far higher than among upper white-collar workers. Even among lower blue-collar workers, "55 percent commonly read these visuals and 22 percent create them."

Nonetheless, we are willing to let all kinds of roadblocks stop students who fail to pass math requirements dead in their tracks. This is one of the primary reasons that millions of American students drop out of high school altogether. "To our nation's shame," Hacker laments, "one in four ninth graders fail to finish high school. In South Carolina, 34 percent fell away in 2008–9, according to national data released last year; for Nevada, it was 45 percent. Most of the educators I've talked with cite algebra as the major academic reason."

The City University of New York, where Hacker has taught for decades, is wrestling with the consequences of poor preparation in math among its 250,000 undergraduates. Fifty-seven percent cannot pass the university's mandated algebra course. The discouraging conclusion of a faculty report indicated that "failing math at all levels affects retention more than any other academic factor." A national sample of transcripts found mathematics had twice as many Fs and Ds compared to other subjects.[4]

A depressingly large proportion of students who cannot pass those classes give up on college altogether. Thousands more who struggle through remedial math finally pass but, given their low performance, may be permanently blocked from careers where the actual use of math beyond arithmetic is rare. Hacker points to "a definitive analysis by the Georgetown Center on Education and the Workforce forecasts that in the decade ahead a mere five percent of entry-level workers will need to be proficient in algebra and above." In short, in the name of giving everyone a crack at high-prestige jobs that only a small number of people will ever seek, we are strangling the educational objectives and career prospects of thousands for whom this skill will never be relevant.

This is particularly troubling because the kinds of occupations for which many students are preparing do not require abstract mathematics beyond what most of them master in the early years of high school. A strong grasp of arithmetic, complemented in some of the more sophisticated fields of precision manufacturing and nursing with geometry, trigonometry, and elementary algebra, will more than satisfy the demands of these jobs.

Math on the Job

Education researchers have looked at the kinds of math people use on the job and how they use it. For example, John P. Smith III, professor of educational psychology at Michigan State University, studied seventy-five hundred autoworkers in sixteen plants, including facilities that supply Japanese factories. According to the American Association of Mathematicians, he "found three kinds of mathematical domains embedded in workers' activities: measurement, numerical and quantitative reasoning, and spatial and geometric reasoning."

Ten sites involving high-volume assembly work required only minimal mathematics; most workers repeatedly did the same small set of actions, such as bolting on components using air-pressure wrenches, with manual dexterity, eye-hand coordination, and visual acuity being very important. The mathematical demands on the majority of these workers were limited to counting, measurement, arithmetic with whole numbers or decimals, and interpreting numerical information; only a small number of quality control workers did jobs with more mathematical content. At three sites having a "team" structure which included the two Japanese "transplants," there were higher mathematical demands— more diverse numerical calculations including ratios and rates, translation among fractions, decimals, and percentages, and evaluation and interpretation of simple algebraic expressions.

At the remaining sites where machining and quality control lab work was done, the mathematics included substantial spatial and geometric reasoning mediated by "smart" tools such as a Conturograph, composed of an input device, a personal computer, and a software package that measured two linear dimensions and two angles of anti-lock brake valves. The workers had to match the "lines of best fit" to the profile which affected the reliability of the final measurements and judge whether the critical dimensions fell outside the design tolerances.

Smith determined that these jobs require essentially an eighth-grade education, albeit one that illustrates the use of quantitative concepts in problem solving rather than abstract or pure mathematics. He argues that the standard curriculum should focus more heavily than it does in most middle schools and high schools "on visualizing, orienting, plotting, locating, and reasoning in two- and three-dimensional coordinate systems and an introduction to trigonometry as soon as students can conceptualize ratios."[5]

Medical fields are growing in demand.[6] Accordingly, the math needed by nurses, dieticians, and other support staff is relevant to what kind of curriculum we need in high schools and community colleges. Researchers in the United Kingdom followed twelve pediatric nurses around a children's hospital in order to observe how they used math in the everyday problem of measuring quantities of drugs:

A simple within-measure scalar strategy was observed as two nurses prepared a morphine prescription. They needed to administer 1.5 mg of morphine packaged in 20-mg ampules diluted in 10 ml of fluid. The mental calculations of one nurse at the time were verbalized as, "Ten in five; five in two point five; one in point five. . . . Zero point seven five." When interviewed later, she explained that she had made the following parallel computations: Given 20 mg in 10 ml; that's 10 mg in 5 ml; so that's 5 mg in 2.5 ml; 1 in 0.5; and 0.5 in 0.25; and then 1.5 in 0.75. The usual explanation for employing such seemingly awkward calculations is that they tend to preserve the proportion in the (situated) quantities, rather than having to work abstractly to calculate *(1.5/20) x 10. . . .*

Another nurse needed to give 120 mg of the antibiotic, amakacine, prepared in 100 mg per 2 ml vials. When interviewed, she explained, "With amakacine, whatever the dose is, if you just double the dose, it's what the mil is." In effect, this amounts to a transformation of dose mass (120 mg) to dose volume (2.4 ml) by doubling and moving the decimal point. Since the relationship of mass to volume is fixed for a given concentration of drug, one can calculate *(120 x 2)/100* instead of *(120/100) x 2*, obtaining an ml answer by beginning with the number of mg.

What these examples suggest is that the nurses had developed rules of thumb that worked for them as calculation strategies. Their similarity to or divergence from the rules they learned in school were of little importance.[7]

The same UK research team studied the ways in which employees in London banks thought about the work they do to calculate interest rates and other routine transactions. Unused to thinking about these problems as applied forms of mathematics, they too had to develop informal rules. Richard Noss and Celia Hoyles, both professors of math education, were on-site to develop a program called Time Is Money, "which included a small number of modifiable programs modeling future value and present value."

These were not clerical personnel or janitors, but rather ranged from administrators to one fellow in charge of computer equipment support, whose budget ran to some million or two pounds a year. They used spreadsheets or the bank's theoretical models, often involving functions from R^n to R, designed by the bank's "rocket scientists," the term used for the mathematics PhDs responsible for them.

The bank employees spoke their own specialized language; they saw dozens of distinct financial instruments whereas [the researchers] saw them all as more or less the same. For example, Treasury bills were considered distinct from certificates of deposit because of the way interest was calculated. Indeed, when asked the question, *Suppose you want $100 in one year. You have the chance of buying a simple instrument (say a CD) paying 8% or an instrument (like a Treasury bill) which offers a discount over the year again of 8%. Which would you choose and why?*, many employees gave situated, rather than abstract mathematical, answers. For instance, one person rejected the artificial world of simple interest and answered in terms of the bank's practice of compounding interest, *I would choose the Treasury bill. The discount will take account of the compound interest and will make the Treasury bill cheaper to buy than the simple interest instrument.*

Bank employees have to master different kinds of interest rates, but they do not calculate them from scratch. Instead, they tweak computer programs, "switching variables and parameters to model various financial situations." These manipulations may make mathematical ideas more meaningful, but it is just as likely that they remain somewhat formulaic since the software was designed to make the math invisible.[8]

How We Teach Math

In conventional American high-school programs, students are led through a one-size-fits-all pathway designed to prepare those who are bound for four-year universities. They start with the basics of arithmetic in elementary school, graduate to prealgebra in middle school, and then move into algebra, geometry, and trigonometry in high school. The most advanced and elite high-school students take calculus in their senior year, though many will need to repeat it in college. This cumulative curriculum is organized such that every step along the way is critically prerequisite to the next. Stumbling in one subject poses huge problems for mastering the next. Failure to master algebra effectively forecloses the rest of the sequence, which is tantamount to closing the door on college altogether unless a student is willing and able to spend as much as a year full-time in remedial math.

Vocational education—in both Germany and the United States—employs a very different approach to the study of mathematics. Math is embedded in classes that have a practical bent and make use of its principles in the service of problem solving. While there are abstract ideas in play, they are in the background. The relevance of mathematical ideas is there, but the emphasis is application. Technical education students we spoke to in both countries say that they do not find math (or elementary physics) to be an obstacle and are not intimidated by their studies in these fields. Understanding what they are good for is their primary goal.

According to Rudolf Straesser, an expert in math education, all German students—no matter what form of secondary education they are pursuing—are expected to understand how mathematics figures in professions and fields of study as well as how it matters in the vocational subjects they pursue. They should "acquire general competencies, for instance the ability to argue, to solve problems, or to translate between the real world and mathematics." German students should "be comfortable when facing new problem situations" and, in a wider cultural framework, to see math as a "source of philosophical and epistemological reflection." Their teachers should help them by "generating a balanced . . . picture of mathematics as a science and part of human history and culture."

Math that is taught in vocational classes is supposed to enhance the transfer of mathematical skills to the real world. In practice, this means that vocational students are expected to be fluent in the use of arithmetic calculations, especially percents and fractions. They are exposed to "elementary calculations with numbers and technical magnitudes."

German vocational students need to know how to derive information from tables and diagrams and represent it in the same form. Technical occupations make use of basic geometry and algebra, especially where metalwork, electrical circuits, and construction are concerned. Simple equations, formulas, and functions are taught by embedding their use in classroom exercises in which students search for electrical faults. Two- and three-dimensional geometry is taught to apprentices in technical drawing classes, as well as specialized courses that make use of computer aided design (CAD) and numerical control machines (NCM). Business students are expected to understand ideas like interest rates and their use in calculating "discounts, bank drafts, bills, credit and loans."[9] For many other domains, especially administration, nursing, and social work, the use of statistics is of greater importance.[10]

Vocational students in Germany encounter these topics first in their general education courses prior to the age of sixteen. But they are covered again when they become apprentices both because they need a refresher since the original exposure and because, the second time around, the emphasis is less on the theoretical and more on the use of algorithms in the form of recipes for solving mechanical or technical problems. Teachers "adjust their teaching style to the motives and competencies they expect from their students."

One critique often advanced against this kind of training is that it will enable apprentices and workers to solve routine problems, cases where a formula can be invoked and things work without a hitch. But can they solve problems when something goes wrong? Where the formulaic answer fails? This kind of critic is arguing that without a command of the underlying mathematics, problem solving that is out of the ordinary will be impossible. That is debatable. While workers are relying on geometry or Ohm's law, they are not particularly aware that this is what they are doing: "By integrating mathematical concepts, relations and procedures into various types of procedures (be it rules to follow, charts to fill in, computer technology to handle or other machines to use) mathematics tends to gradually disappear from the attention of the worker."[11]

Indeed, this is precisely the point of many in-house forms of information technology that are based on mathematical models but need not plague the user with their intricacies. What they need to know is when to lean on a particular solution, not how it was devised it in the first place:

> Banking software . . . has been developed by high-fly specialists and completely hides the inherent functional, mathematical relations between the numbers processed. Even in the number driven world of banking, numbers and commercial arithmetic disappear from the consciousness of the average employee. Mathematics hides in computer

algorithms which are applied without paying attention to the underlying mathematical model of the banking process.[12]

American CTE (career and technical education) courses have taken a page from the practical or embedded math book and have produced a pedagogy that is less demanding than its German counterpart but bears a family resemblance to it both in the classroom and on the shop floor. Automotive High School offers both traditional academic classes and CTE classes that combine hands-on work with theory. CTE teachers tend to use—and modify—existing materials developed specifically for their classes, along with developing their own materials. In the pre-engineering class at Automotive, students might start a class session by doing some calculations regarding the costs of "green" materials for home construction and then go on to begin an exercise that requires them to design the most energy-efficient home possible given certain constraints.

The state of Oregon devoted three years to figuring out how to develop mathematical skills in their CTE students. They brought together nine teams, partnering CTE and math teachers from schools and districts throughout the state who worked together to formulate a new curriculum in the "Industrial and Engineering Systems career area." Aimed at students interested in manufacturing, construction, and engineering, the curriculum embeds as much math as possible into the kinds of practice problems real workers in these fields encounter. For example, they wanted students to figure out how "manufacturers determine the precision of measurement needed for the production of interchangeable parts," or how to use what they learned about energy transfer and conservation to determine what kind of insulation is most efficient and cost-effective in a building.[13]

Instructors designed problem sets that required students to figure out how three-dimensional items are produced from two-dimensional patterns, how to use math to design a set of stairs within a specified area, or how to calculate the electrical power needs of an office tower. Students were asked to show how geometry is used in the building of bridges, specifically how triangles, angles, and linear relationships are used in construction and architecture. Marketing classes were designed to explore the use of statistics for discerning consumer preferences. The Oregon instructors drew from algebra, geometry, and statistics to build problem sets that required students to link conceptual ideas to practical problems.

Nonetheless, the point was less to develop the skills young people would need on the job and more to ensure that in exploring CTE domains they would exercise as much of their pure math muscles as they could. The outcomes they hoped for were therefore quite different from what Germans seek in their vocational classes, which are far more intensive in duration and put students through the paces of actual construction tasks or electrical repairs. For the Germans, one must demonstrate facility with these skills in practical problem solving.

In Oregon, success was measured by how well students performed on college-level math placement exams, reflecting the continued concern, even anxiety, over whether CTE students are college ready. This does not mean that CTE students in Oregon cannot read a wiring diagram or construct an electrical grid. It means that our benchmarking process remains wedded to traditional conceptions of mathematical knowledge.

Teachers working hard to equip their students with both knowledge and enthusiasm for construction or nursing are encouraged not to focus exclusively on the intrinsic value and worth of the buildings their charges might construct or the patients whose well-being they might enhance. These trades or semi-professions are fine, but students should be equipped to aim higher, to become architects or doctors, both of which require a college education.

Expressing these high expectations simultaneously communicates something else: the less prestigious route is deficient. This ambivalence is underlined by federal standards embedded in the fourth iteration of the Perkins Act. Perkins IV called on the states to "integrate rigorous and challenging academic and career and technical instruction." As with No Child Left Behind, Perkins IV demands accountability. States must show that students are reaching proficiency in both academic content and technical content. The quality of math standards within career paths is an important one, as it can indicate whether CTE students are receiving a rigorous academic and technical curriculum.[14]

To ensure that a state or a district is on the right side of Perkins IV, it is necessary to cross walk the math standards between CTE and the academic curriculum. Are they comparably demanding? Do they require a mastery of the material taught in algebra or geometry in order to be proficient in a CTE course in construction? In the years since the legislation was passed by Congress, states have been scrambling to satisfy this demand.

It has not been a simple process, not least because teachers responsible for the CTE curriculum are rarely specialists in math. Instructors who handle classes in construction, electronics, or medical assistance are recruited for their experience in those fields. They are dedicated to making sure that their students learn these trades well enough to follow blueprints or detect and repair faults. CTE faculty try to stay abreast of new technologies that affect their fields and to burnish the ties they have to industry, both to remain current and to advantage their students by exercising their contacts for internships or entry-level jobs. None of these responsibilities includes expertise in mathematics.

In many states, the requirements of Perkins IV encouraged partnerships between math teachers and CTE instructors. In New Jersey, a multiyear program intended to increase the rigor of mathematical content in CTE courses relied on teams of this kind since CTE teachers did not have the training to do so on their own. The impact of these interventions has been modest: not zero—just not overwhelming. Students in CTE classes that have been reimagined to enrich the math content do seem to garner slightly higher scores on traditional math exams designed to assess mastery of the Common Core. But the alignment is still weak, the teachers under stress to deliver content that is not their expertise, and the gains slight.

While it sounds reasonable to keep college options open for students in these programs while training them in practical problem solving, in truth this is a complex balancing act, and it often fails. The more pressure we place on faculty and students to pass academic examinations like the New York State Regents exams, the more we place them in jeopardy of labeling them as failures. As Mitch Almonte, an engineering teacher at New York's High School for Construction Trades, Engineering and Architecture (CTEA), puts the matter, "I think a lot of CTE schools fall through the cracks because the state requirements for graduation don't exactly line up."

They probably do, but they are not articulated in such a way where it's all clear. At our last department meeting, we held it together with the math department. That was our goal, really just trying to put together the math in CTE classes with what they are trying to teach for the Regents. To teach it so that the students can make the connection.

Teachers who were themselves prepared along different pedagogical tracks are struggling to bridge a divide that is there for a reason. The skills a technical instructor needs to guide students in electronics is not the same as that of a math teacher. They are trying to impart different kinds of expertise that are intentionally divergent. The effort to fuse them, spurred on by the desire to avoid pigeonholing a student into a life without college, is exhausting and almost inherently delegitimizes CTE education. It telegraphs to all—students, teachers, and parents alike—that mastery of practical skills is not enough. If it won't see students past the Regents hurdle, it is substandard.

On a gray December morning, the academic math class in trigonometry at CTEA is working through a problem comparable to what they will be expected to solve on the Regents exam later in the academic year. The students are all very engaged, calling out potential answers to one step after another. They are looking for a solution to an abstract problem that has no explicit connection to anything practical except the test. The teacher, a stocky, energetic Latino man with a commanding voice, paces around the front of the room and invites students up to the Smartboard. He cautions those who seem to be headed in the wrong direction and urges on the students who seem to be getting it. "I don't just want your answer, but how you got there," he says more than once. "I want to see how you're thinking."

Down the hallway, students in the electrical shop are learning about how to bend conduit, the tubing that is used to protect and route electrical wires and often must travel around corners and permanent structures and up from the floor at a 90-degree angle into electrical boxes. When conduit is bent in the direction of another plane, length is lost and that affects how one calculates the total amount of conduit needed for a job.

Bending conduit properly so that nothing is wasted involves the use of trigonometric principles, but electricians who do this day in and day out may or may not understand the underlying mathematics. Students are given formulas and tables that electricians rely on to guide them in making these calculations. Some come to a point where the theory and the practice meld together and click, even if they could not lay out the mathematical principles.

Angel Texidor, a slight, friendly teacher, explains that whether the kids in his class fully understand the trig behind bending the conduit or not, going through the exercise helps them grasp it conceptually and practically. Indeed, doing the bending, as opposed to just learning about it, teaches them not only how it feels to do it but also the importance of doing it right, and the ramifications of cutting corners or making mistakes. "It's a real-life problem. It has consequences. You bend the conduit beforehand so you don't waste it. You have to measure it out before bending it."

This exercise will help to make Texidor's students better electricians. But will it ensure that they can pass the Regents examination and pick up their high school diplomas? That's the rub. CTEA instructors have been hard at work—spurred by Perkins IV and the Regents tradition in New York public schools—to integrate CTE and academic math, but they often remain far apart. Common concepts may not be covered at the same time, forcing the CTE teachers to introduce mathematical or scientific concepts that the students have yet to learn in their academic classes. "Measurement in math is often an abstraction," Texidor commented.

> Most kids don't know what a meter is. They don't know what a Newton is. I give them a practical situation. If you pick up an apple, that's a Newton force. Take the theory and make it practical. They all hear about gears. I give them a real-life situation. Take a bicycle. Then move on to cars. I want them to have a theoretical insight. They have to draw from their previous knowledge. And then they put it together in a way that makes it more functional.

In the engineering CTE class, students are working in groups following step-by-step directions for making a small winch, which in this case consists of a chain winding around a small, rotating gear turned by a small motor. The aim is for the students to learn about efficiency in mechanical systems. The particular project is part of Project Lead the Way, the national, nonprofit provider of K–12 STEM curricula and teacher professional development. Keith Williams has modified their instructions a bit, as he often does. He is looking for lessons that do not start from abstract math or scientific concepts but from a problem or a need, in this case the need to design a weight system that converts electrical energy into mechanical energy.

But what do Williams's students think they are accomplishing? One young man explained they were using "basic knowledge" as well as formulas from physics related to weight and mass to complete the exercise. Another noted that in the engineering class he feels that they are "using math in real life" and that in the CTE class he gains a "deeper understanding" of certain concepts he has learned in math or science. For Williams, who started out his teaching career in industrial arts in schools in the Caribbean and the Bahamas, "Engineering is the application of physics and math. We either reinforce what they are doing in those classes, or do it here." But it is not easy to apply ideas in his class if students have not already learned them. "They need to know about vectors, and some trig. They should know it before they come in but they don't always."

On another floor, students in the architecture class are in the middle of a project that involves designing a house renovation according to client specifications. Groups of students are huddled in front of computer workstations where they are doing three-dimensional modeling using Autodesk Revit, modeling software for architects; structural engineers; mechanical, electrical, and plumbing engineers; and designers and contractors. They are trying to figure out how to calculate square footage: The client wants certain rooms to retain their size while others could be reconfigured by moving walls. Danny Adegbie, their instructor, has just finished walking the students through an explanation of the difference between rentable and gross building square footage and asks the students how these different measurements relate to New York City building codes (which permit building only within a certain space).

The CTE classes in this school vary in how much math they require and how they make use of it. It is entirely possible that students who are at the high end in academic math master CTE in ways that provide them with greater depth and facility for creative work, while students who struggle are less likely to be innovators but can handle the more formulaic aspects of the trades they seek to enter. All of the CTEA engineering students go on to college. About half of the architecture students go on to college (though not necessarily to study architecture). This is not the case for the kids in the construction trades, who typically get jobs after graduation and may go back to school for some postsecondary education or training later on in life.[15]

Yet it is not clear that mastery of mathematics is important for CTE students outside of the hurdle placed before them by the state of New York. That is not to say that analytic ability is unimportant. It is to say that application and analysis are not the same animal. Math is an abstract language of symbols. But its importance in most careers, including many very skilled, demanding, and high-paid jobs, is minimal. What is more important in many rewarding occupations is the capacity to exercise deductive reasoning.

This is what CTE teachers mean when they say the students are engaging in problem solving. Can students eliminate potential explanations for a problem and home in on the right one? That requires a "testing logic," in which they come to recognize that if the "answer was X," they should see "Y," and if they don't, they can set X aside as a likely possibility. They have to assess what they can see or measure and in this fashion "diagnose" surface characteristics or symptoms as clues to an underlying condition or problem. This kind of analytic thinking is on display when plumbers try to figure out where leaks are coming from or when electricians try to trace a fault. It is this deductive logic that is critical to the kind of conceptual work they need to be able to do if they become middle-skill workers.

And it is also the need to solve problems that might get students who are otherwise put off by math interested in it, because it's a means to accomplishing some sought-after end. Kim Guzowski, the executive director of the Technical Artisans Collective (TAC), a nonprofit organization whose mission is to "bring production professionals and youth together in project-based learning experiences grounded in the skills and knowledge of theatrical and event production," describes this process well:

> What most bothers me about my own education is that every teacher, especially in high school, knew that theatre was my passion. Yet, instead of

teaching me to build with my geometry, I was banned from the theatre for flunking geometry. Without building something, geometry made no sense to me. As a teacher who has taught several subjects, it is my opinion that if a student does not understand the relevance of a subject, then the educational system has failed, not the student. Why should a student learn something if that student does not understand how what they are learning is useful? We understand the usefulness of what we learn by using our learning in ways that have meaning to us. Our educational system often does not emphasize the real application of concepts through making things that matter to us as students. TAC is an attempt to help bridge this gap. By bringing designers and technicians together with educators to create project-based lessons, TAC aims to create learning experiences that inspire students and deepen their understanding of what they are already learning in their classes by linking theory to practice.

Indeed, Mike Rose, author of the best-selling book *The Mind at Work: Valuing the Intelligence of the American Worker*, points to the ways in which we overlook the cognitive skills and intellectual abilities of ordinary workers. In a commentary he provided on the tenth anniversary of the book's publication, Rose reflected on why he needed to write it in the first place, on what it is that we are so unable to see when it comes to recognizing the demands of deductive reasoning. We quote at length from his interview because it expresses so well precisely the problem we face in developing full respect for the work middle-skilled employees do:

> What struck me as I did the research for *The Mind at Work* was the number of instances of reasoning, of problem-solving and of learning that fell outside of what gets assessed in an intelligence test or the traditional school curriculum. There is the waitress at rush hour prioritizing on the fly a number of demands from customers, the kitchen and the manager. And the plumber diagnosing a problem by feeling with his hands the pipes he can't see behind an old wall. And the hair stylist figuring out the cut a customer wants through talk and gesture. These kinds of smarts surround us, yet might not be considered when we talk about intelligence. . . .
>
> But I think the huge challenge that faces us is how to undo the

vocational-academic divide itself. The divide institutionalized what in some cases is a pretty arbitrary separation of kinds of knowledge and skill. To develop into a good cabinetmaker, for example, you need to know about mathematics, have a historical and aesthetic sensibility about tools and cabinetry and understand things about economics and markets. The ideal occupational program would realize and build on these "academic" subjects within the context of the occupation itself. Dewey called for such an approach a century ago, and some contemporary programs are attempting it now, but such work is difficult, for so many institutional barriers and cultural biases constrain our educational imagination.

Analytic work of this kind is crucial not only to the completion of ordinary tasks but to innovation on the shop floor. German apprentices in ZF Lemförde, who are training in mechatronics and expect to join a workforce that produces drive trains for sophisticated cars, are not experts in algebra or calculus. But the last phase of their training involves complex problems that require them to use skills—including the application of computer numerical control machines—to solve vexing problems that have cropped up that year on the shop floor. What ZF is looking for in an apprentice, particularly one they plan to take on as a full-time worker, is that deductive logic and the ability to deploy it to a problem that is unfamiliar, where there is no ready-made solution.

Pure mathematics may not help with that challenge. ZF's highly trained apprentices are valuable instead because they can draw on the experience they have racked up over the previous three years, fixing things that have gone wrong under the guidance of a Meister who has had to fashion solutions before them. Sometimes those solutions involve mathematical principles and the apprentices express no sense of intimidation about that requirement. They are matter of fact about integrating math into their daily work lives.

8

Bringing the Dual System
to the United States

Nigeria Williams is a slender, elegant African American teenager whose family has lived in and around the small town of Aiken, South Carolina, for several generations. Her godmother, Lula Brown, with whom she lives, retired after eighteen years working in a factory owned by GlaxoSmith-Kline running machines that manufactured feminine products. Her godfather put in thirteen years working for Carlisle Tire and Rubber. But manufacturers like the ones where Nigeria's family worked and the textile industries that employed thousands of others in the Aiken region began shutting down and leaving the United States decades ago. Today, as Lula explains, teenagers who are not college-bound graduate from Aiken's high schools and "get stuck working at McDonald's." Until recently, there wasn't much else to look forward to in Aiken.

Happily, fast-food jobs are not in Nigeria's future. In the fall of 2013, her junior year in high school, she heard an announcement on the intercom. "Anyone interested in earning money this summer should come to the office and apply for an apprenticeship." "I thought they were going to

offer us yard work," Nigeria laughed. "I thought we'd be picking up trash."
She applied anyhow.

Instead of doing manual labor, Nigeria was introduced to an innovative program run by the diesel engine manufacturer MTU, a subsidiary
of Rolls-Royce Power Systems. MTU hails from Friedrichshafen, Germany, and had arrived in Aiken in 2010. The company had acquired
Detroit Diesel and decided to move the plant out of the Midwest. South
Carolina, the region where Nigeria was raised, was perfect for MTU. It
boasts a mild climate, a competitive wage structure, and plenty of old factories that have been abandoned but could be reclaimed. In short order,
the company purchased an old factory that had once belonged to SKF, a
manufacturer of ball and roller bearings that had closed up shop five years
earlier and decamped to Mexico. SKF was only too happy to sell the obsolete facility and one hundred acres around it to MTU for $40 million.

MTU moved the engineers, production supervisors, and vice presidents from Detroit to Aiken, but they planned to find their hourly workforce
right there in the local community, where they could pick and choose
from the workers who had been let go by the firms that had moved to
offshore locations. As Arjonetta Gaillard, the HR director who runs
MTU's training programs, explained, the company took in over six hundred applications for the available line jobs in March 2010. They interviewed 250 people and picked 60. The company could select from among
experienced mechanics who had once worked in the auto body shops, car
dealerships, and Jiffy Lube stations. With those 60 they started producing engines and the first ones rolled off the production line in October
that year. But once they were done with that initial wave of hiring, the
company came to the conclusion that it had tapped out all of the labor
that was skilled enough to meet their requirements. "Our director, Jörg
Klisch, came from the parent company in Friedrichshafen," Gaillard
explained.

> When asked where we were going to find the skilled labor we needed
> to expand, Jörg said, "I've got just the ticket." He had experience with
> apprenticeship programs in Germany. He thought we could certainly
> do the same thing here in the United States. That's why we started our

apprenticeship program here with high school students; we modeled it directly after the dual program in Germany.

Because the company lacked a training center of its own, Jörg and his colleagues began canvassing the community colleges and high schools in the area. The Aiken County Career and Technology Center was a promising candidate. The center serves the entire Aiken County School District, consisting of seven high schools. "We found their program was open to jointly developing a curriculum that students can use," Gaillard remembered. "We realized we had great partners to pull this off." MTU sent some of their new Aiken employees to Germany to learn how to become expert instructors. They returned to help organize the vocational program at Aiken County Career and Technology Center and the companion training program on the shop floor at the MTU plant.

When Nigeria responded to the announcement over the intercom at school, little did she know that she was about to join one of the few apprenticeship programs in the United States that offers opportunities of this kind to teenagers in high school. Most of her friends thought she was a little nuts. Those dirty factory jobs aren't for girls, they told her. "I just figured I'd fix my nails if they broke." Nigeria smiled. She flashed her dark red nails in the air for illustration. "There's money involved and I could use it."

Twelve students from five of the high schools that feed into the Tech Center vied to get spots in the program. MTU put them through an online math course and then tested them to find the best applicants. Nigeria had taken prealgebra, algebra, algebra II, and geometry and found the tests relatively straightforward assessments of the aspects of math she knew well already. Only six students survived the testing phase to go on to company interviews. Nigeria was one of them.

Production apprentices at MTU need math skills because they have to be able to work within the European metric system and read blueprints coming to Aiken from the parent facility in Germany. It was the firm's intention to create an apprenticeship program that would enable young people not only to build diesel engines but to pass the same rigorous tests their German counterparts take to gain national certificates in industrial mechanics.

The first cohort to pass through the program, the group just ahead of Nigeria, consisted of five young men, all seventeen years old when they started. Three days a week they attended regular district high schools in the morning and the vocational education program at the Tech Center in the afternoon. The Tech Center introduced them to the basics of machining, but the equipment was old and the exposure fairly perfunctory, with teachers "running around trying to introduce kids to a lot of different kinds of equipment." Two days a week they apprenticed in the factory. In the first year of the program, that shop floor training consisted mainly of rapid rotations from one part of the factory to another, providing the students with a general overview. When the German trainers descended on MTU to assess whether this first cohort was ready to take the stringent examination in industrial mechanics, the answer was a resounding "No." It was a rude awakening for Gaillard.

The faculty recognized that students weren't learning enough in school and in the training process. While at the factory, they were moving around, spending relatively little time in each spot. In response, the faculty changed the curriculum so students could spend more time in each of their rotations and develop more skill. Gaillard explained:

> We had to bring in more equipment to the school program and rearrange the structure of the classroom so that the teacher could really work with the student. We realigned all the equipment, workbenches and tools. . . . The quality of the equipment needed to be upgraded. They weren't teaching metrics at first. We brought in tools, calipers and gauges because that's what we use in the workforce and then had to train the teacher in what we needed to get out of the program in the Tech Center.

MTU soon realized that it would never be able to train its American apprentices to the same standard as their German counterparts. The requirements of South Carolina's education board meant that the company could only have the apprentices for two days a week for two years, plus full-time in the summer. In Germany, an apprentice in this field would be working four days a week full-time and one day a week in school for three years. While they too have summer vacations, they are short by

American standards. It was simply not possible to jam enough training into the truncated schedule in Aiken to qualify students like Nigeria. As a result, "our program is one step below the German program," Gaillard explains. "We are doing the skilled trades as opposed to the full industrial mechanics program we were trying to do. We started off with industrial mechanics and had to scale back."

By the time Nigeria's cohort began the apprenticeship program, MTU had worked out most of the kinks. Her trainer, Jonathan Galantin, is a parts assembler working in the machine department. His son is a student in her high school, and Galantin is friendly with Nigeria's godfather. Galantin had trained new workers at a previous job and he put that experience to use showing Nigeria the ropes.

He taught me how to work the computer numerical control machines. I had never seen a machine like it before. He showed me from the beginning how to check the parts with the CNC machine. He walked me through it.

We ran the tests for an hour and then turned the part around, deburred it to grind the sharp edges off. He showed me how to do all the measurements according to the blueprints on the wall. You find out if the part is right or not by using height gauges, for example.

Most of the time, the machine will catch a mistake. It will flash at you if the part is wrong; you have to check the screen, you see x's, y's, and z's and it is set to a particular decimal point of tolerance. You have to check the blueprint on the wall to see if the part matches what's on it. They have models that we know are right to check against.

Nigeria has been an apprentice for two years. "I still have a lot to learn, but I've been like everywhere but not as in-depth. Now I am in each department for three months." She was so successful as a student of machining and as a worker with a strong ethic of responsibility and seriousness of purpose that the company nominated her for a national award. She was placed into competition alongside all the other trainees nominated by the thirty-eight hundred German subsidiaries in the United States. To her amazement, Nigeria was selected as the Trainee of the Year by the German American Chamber of Commerce, which represents those companies.

For the moment, MTU is the only company in South Carolina that mimics the German approach of taking on apprentices in high school. Yet because it has been successful, albeit on a modest scale, the state is trying to get other companies to follow MTU's lead. They are encouraging Bridgestone, the tire manufacturer, and Kimberly-Clark, which makes personal care products from paper, both of which are in the state already, to set up similar programs so that more kids can be hired. The biggest obstacle, apart from funding the training, is that health and safety regulations make it difficult to place sixteen-year-olds in a factory. But South Carolina is starting to get traction by agreeing to regulations that protect students, developing exemptions, and extending the liability coverage carried by the school districts themselves.

In 2012, the German embassy in Washington announced the launch of a major effort to bring the German vocational education system to the United States. Two years later, in December 2014, representatives from over four hundred German subsidiaries gathered at the annual meeting of the German American Chamber of Commerce in the Thomson Reuters Building in New York. The attendees listened to a rosy report on the state of their firms in the United States. Based on a survey of more than a thousand German companies the news was good. Confidence levels among German business leaders were at a five-year high, with 98 percent expecting growth in 2015. New product lines were ready to launch. European growth is at a standstill but the American market for German goods is healthy and the companies anticipate higher sales volume. Accordingly, 64 percent of the firms have increased their strategic focus on the United States, "driven by close customer proximity and fueled by strong demand."[1]

While German firms see major advantages in locating manufacturing facilities within the United States, they are hampered by the inability to find workers who meet their high skill standards. Sixty-five percent of the firms surveyed for the annual German American Business Outlook report say that they are suffering skill shortages of the kind they would not face on their home turf. And that is up from 49 percent from the previous year. The shortage of skilled workers is beginning to bite and threatens to slow the expansion of these firms. When asked their highest policy priorities, the German respondents answered: "investment in K–12 education, more affordable university education, and dual training grants"—that is, the sort of pioneering apprenticeship system that Williams participated in.

Wisconsin is one of the states that has stepped up to meet this demand through a homegrown system known as Youth Apprenticeship. The Wisconsin program involves cooperative education, which is a one- or two-year, school-supervised, paid work experience for high school juniors and seniors. Students are trained based on statewide "youth curriculum guidelines" that are endorsed by business and industry. They are simultaneously enrolled in academic classes to meet high-school graduation requirements and, in a Youth Apprenticeship–related instruction class, are employed by a participating employer under the supervision of a skilled mentor. Program certification provides a mechanism for the credentialing of competencies identified by business and industry that are necessary for the workplace. Youth Apprenticeship–related classroom instruction is taught by qualified instructors at high schools, in technical colleges, online, or through an employer; specific skills-related classroom instruction is taught only by a career and technical education teacher certified in that specific skill area.

The program has two levels: Level one, in which a junior or senior can participate, involves a minimum of 450 hours of work-based learning and two semesters of related classroom instruction, while level two requires enrollment in both the junior and senior years and involves a minimum of 900 hours of work-based learning and four semesters of related classroom instruction. These programs are overseen and administered by a local consortium of partners representing school districts, technical colleges, employers, and organized labor. Parents of youth apprentices or other community representatives may also be included in the partnerships.[2]

Wisconsin spent $1.8 million on apprenticeship grants to serve twenty-two hundred students from 227 school districts in 2013. The following year, the grant program grew to $2.2 million to support twenty-nine hundred youth apprenticeships. All kinds of employers participate, from city public works departments to credit unions to machine companies.[3] By and large, these programs have won the admiration of employers.[4]

"We think Youth Apprenticeship is valuable," noted Andy Preissner of A to Z Machine Company of Appleton, Wisconsin, "because it provides direct experience and exposure for students who are interested in the [computer numerical control] machine trade."

> This is a great opportunity for students to spend a year or more of school learning and experiencing the trade, and figure out if it is right for them, while we get some time to see if we would like to hire them on once they graduate. We are utilizing this program to not only develop our own CNC machinists, but to also increase exposure for the field. Instead of accepting status quo and succumbing to the constant news that less and less individuals are pursuing skilled trades, we are proactively working to develop the professionals of tomorrow. Manufacturing is not what it once was and we need highly skilled and passionate individuals to join our team and help our business grow. This is an excellent opportunity to change the perception of manufacturing one student at a time.

Ron Polum of Pointe Precision in Plover, Wisconsin, agrees:

> Currently 19 percent of our machine operators are either previous apprenticeship students or currently enrolled in the program [which began in 2008]. Some of our most valued long-term employees are developed through this program. By being involved with the students when they are beginning their careers, we can tailor the training to meet our company's needs and beliefs.

Of course, this tailoring is precisely what many progressive critics of career and technical education fear. From their perspective, students should be free to sculpt themselves and schools should not become the handmaidens of industry. It is a difficult balancing act. Firms want loyal and cooperative employees and they know that the earlier they start to cultivate those sentiments, the stronger they become. German firms are of the same mind. At the same time, the labor movement is much stronger in Germany than it is in the United States, hence starting young hardly guarantees a workforce that rolls over in the face of management.

Above all, the Wisconsin program enables young people to find their way in manufacturing because they have the skills employers are looking for. Dave Bemowski of POWER Engineers, Inc., in Plover, put the matter well in 2012:

POWER's Plover office has been hiring YA students for more than ten years. The time it takes to find qualified students is reduced through the YA-Engineering program, dramatically reducing the cost to POWER in finding new hires. POWER has benefitted from the YA program by finding low-cost employees who are able to perform drafting and other duties, freeing up office staff to perform more difficult engineering and designer tasks. Liability has not been a factor in hiring students because all work is performed by students with POWER supervision and the completed work is approved by a designer or engineer. The first YA student POWER hired is currently a full-time employee. Past YA students, now attending college, contact POWER when they are on breaks looking for work. This gives POWER the opportunity to hire trained workers if the workload at that time requires more help.

While Wisconsin may be the state most like Germany, the Southeast of the United States has been the site of some of the more innovative experiments in apprenticeship in this nation. The region has been a beneficiary of the movement toward reindustrialization, in part because of its lower labor costs and weak—almost nonexistent—union presence. This is not good news for the union movement, nor does it contribute to any improvement in the wages of manufacturing workers. This form of reindustrialization will not measurably address the problem of growing wage inequality in the United States either, since the wages paid in the Southeast are generally lower than in the Midwest, especially in states where union density is higher.

What it does do is add to the employment base of the United States as a whole, especially when these jobs have "come home" from offshore locations to which so many heavy manufacturing industries fled. When these firms decide where to relocate, they fully recognize the advantages to them of landing in the Southeast. Accordingly, we should not look at their decisions through rose-colored glasses. But we should recognize that when they make choices, the options for creating a skilled labor force factor into the decision. States like North and South Carolina have recognized that this is a competitive advantage and hence have established and funded youth apprentice systems. Georgia's program is structured along the same lines as Wisconsin's, except that it involves a minimum of 2,000 hours of work-based learning and 144 hours classroom hours of related instruction.[5] Georgia spends about $3 million a year on youth apprenticeship programs, while Wisconsin spends about $2 million.[6] This is not a small amount of money, but it is modest compared to the rest of what these states spend on education and training.

North Carolina also has a program called Apprenticeship 2000, which began in 1995 and offers technical career opportunities to high-school juniors and seniors and jobs after graduation. Students must have a minimum GPA of 2.8 and have completed courses in algebra and geometry. The partner companies, which include Ameritech Die and Mold, Blum, Inc., and Chiron, host the on-site apprenticeships, which provide training for four years while students earn an associate's degree in mechatronics from Central Piedmont Community College and a journeyman's certificate from the North Carolina Department of Commerce. Siemens, the German engineering conglomerate, has a plant in Charlotte, North Carolina. The company offers a youth apprenticeship program in which rising high school seniors can enroll in a four-year machinist training course.

Not to be outdone by southern rivals, Michigan has launched as similar program: the Michigan Advanced Technician Training program, or MAT2. Established in 2013 and inspired by the German system, it is a three-year program for high school seniors and recent graduates in which students alternate between classrooms and labs and work sites, obtaining hands-on marketable skills in high-tech fields such as mechatronics or IT. Students get on-the-job training, with their salaries and college tuition (four community colleges participate) paid by the employer, as well as an associate degree and a job upon successful completion of the program. In its inaugural year, ninety-seven apprentices and twenty-nine companies participated.[7] While most of the employers were local operations of German companies, such as Volkswagen and Eberspächer, state leaders are hoping to expand participation.

In 2014 the Minnesota legislature created an apprenticeship program, the PIPELINE project, which is based also in part on the European model. Specifically, the project is designed to give people a path to obtain a degree and prepare for a career through classroom and on-the-job training in advanced manufacturing, agriculture, health care services, and information technology.

The Swiss firm Bühler, which makes manufacturing equipment for the food industry, has been offering apprenticeships in the state through the Bühler Apprenticeship Academy in Plymouth, Minnesota, since 2012. The program was created in response to the company's need for qualified customer service engineers—people who can install and repair equipment and provide on-site training for its customer operations' personnel—and currently enrolls fifteen students.

The program, which takes three years to complete, is divided into segments of eight to twelve weeks, with alternating courses given at Dunwoody College of Technology in Minneapolis and Bühler's Apprenticeship Workshop in Plymouth. The courses, each of which serve only five apprentices, are tailored to Bühler's needs. The first year of the program focuses on mechanical training, the second year on electrical and electronics training, and the third year on training in the field.

Bühler pays for the apprenticeship program and also pays the apprentices a stipend while they are training. Each apprentice earns certificates from both the technical college and Bühler, as well as a journeyworker card from the state's Department of Labor. ("Journeyworker" refers to someone who has attained a level of skill, abilities, and competencies recognized within an industry as having mastered the skills and competencies required for the trade or occupation.) Bühler is in the process of getting the program accredited so that apprentices would be able to earn college credit and an associate's degree.

Mike Bryan is the guru of a high school robotics program at the Bosch plant in Laurens, South Carolina. Bryan started a robotics team (distinct from the company's apprenticeship program) for his county's school district, located in a very poor region with a high proportion of students eligible for federally supported free lunch. His budget comes from federal sources since the local high schools cannot afford the cost. It has been exceptionally successful in recruiting low-income students, and through its offices they have been able to participate in FIRST Robotics, a well-known international competition.

The students and their high-school teachers come to the Bosch plant at 4:30 p.m., Monday through Thursday, and Saturday from nine to five throughout the school year. In order to be a part of the program, they need good grades and a good attendance record. The high-school students work in a section of the plant next to the older apprentices. Often the students say until 10:00 p.m. "I have to kick the kids out," Bryan notes with pride.

Bryan talks to the kids "like they are apprentices" and says he gets goose bumps seeing how well they do. They have a lot of "moments where the kids learn about workplace maturity, performance, behavior, and attendance." He has two or three students who are autistic and he is amazed at how well they do because, although they are socially awkward, they tend to have a laser-like focus and absorb information quickly, even if they don't speak much. Bryan finds that "kids who are overlooked or labeled thrive here. If you want to get kids to get interested in a career, get them involved with robots."

The robotics team has won numerous contests within and outside the state. When they go to these competitions, they have "the coolest pit," which Bryan has dubbed the Robotz Garage, modeled after his father's garage. His dad had a hobby of restoring old motorcycles and jeeps, the kind of tinkering that many older blue-collar men remember from their childhood. The pit's frame is covered in paper made to look like wood siding. Its walls are covered with photos, stickers, posters, and mementos of past competitions. The tools are hidden behind a secret door through the back of the pit.

In all, Bryan has mentored about four hundred kids. It took him a long time to convince Bosch that the robot team is a good feeder for skilled labor and engineering, but he now has a lot of success to show.

Companies like Bosch have found that they need to adapt their programs to the realities of the American educational system. German firms wish they could persuade more American school systems to let them in because they believe the training is more effective in molding superior employees if it takes apprentices in during their formative teenage years.

But they have found it difficult to break through the US penchant for a pure academic model and hence have made do with more limited, part-time hours or older, full-time trainees. They have also had to do their share of "reeducation," trying to improve American attitudes toward and respect for blue-collar work.

Adult Apprenticeship Programs

The modest size of many of these youth apprenticeship programs alerts us to the complexities of forging bonds between firms and high schools. We face headwinds in developing these bonds in part because Americans are not as comfortable as Germans with the notion that childhood should give way to adult responsibilities or that people should be sorted at sixteen into technical work. Having learned this lesson about American culture, many German manufacturing firms have instead turned to older students.

In 2012, Mercedes-Benz set up an apprenticeship program in its Tuscaloosa, Alabama, plant. The program was born from a partnership between Mercedes and AIDT, an independent agency under the supervision and oversight of the secretary of commerce that encourages economic development through job-specific training at no cost to new and expanding businesses throughout the state. Mercedes was looking to solve its principal problem in building a factory in the United States: the lack of skilled labor able to keep up with advances in technology and the pace of US sales. (Indeed, when Mercedes came to Alabama in the early 1990s, Alabama had no auto industry.) In 2012, forty Alabama high-school graduates began a seven-semester program at the plant.

VW also has a three-year training program at its plant in Chattanooga, Tennessee. The 160,000-square-foot training academy opened in 2010—two years after VW selected Chattanooga over Alabama and Michigan for its plant—to train workers to use and maintain tools and give them access to "learning laboratories and simulated production lines."[8] The students also learn how to measure, troubleshoot, and solve problems, as well as gain exposure to myriad valuable manufacturing concepts.[9] Most of VW's trainees at the Chattanooga plant are between twenty-five and thirty years old, compared with a typical starting age in Germany of sixteen to seventeen. As of February 2015, twenty-five people had completed the program and all but two work at the Chattanooga plant.[10]

According to Ralph Linde, head of Volkswagen Coaching, the carmaker's training subsidiary, "outside Germany we tend to find either no training model or a 100 percent [school-based training system]."[11] The facility planned to train two thousand people in the months after its opening. Siemens in North Carolina also foots the bills for a community college mechatronics degree for employees who get paid to train on the job as well as an apprenticeship program for high-school graduates. This college program was developed after Siemens opened its plant in 2011. At the time, the company was hoping to train fifteen hundred workers but found that only 10 percent of the applicants were able to pass a math and science aptitude test.[12] Students can't work at the plant until they are eighteen, but there is no age restriction on learning.

Estevan Torres was one of the first to join this program. He expected to emerge with an AA degree in mechatronics, "no student debt, and a job" at Siemens "paying at least $34,000 a year."[13] The starting hourly wage for Torres and six others was $9 but would go higher with incremental raises. Siemens invested $165,000 per apprentice and expected to hire about nine hundred employees between 2011 and 2013. For the firm, this was the beginning of a German-style program with the same aims: a workforce capable of performing to their high standards. "Siemens considers the apprenticeship program a community investment in work-force training," management maintained. "Apprentices will learn math, computer and technical skills at CPCC [Central Piedmont Community College], augmented with time in the factory."[14]

Bosch Rexroth is a German manufacturer of hydraulics for heavy equipment. The company began offering two-year apprenticeships for adults in its American plants (located in South Carolina and Pennsylvania) in 1989. In South Carolina, trainees spent twenty hours a week at a local technical college and twenty hours per week at Bosch, with a full forty-hour-a-week salary. But after investing in these workers for two years and paying for their degrees, the company had trouble retaining them because their skills made them desirable and mobile. Their loyalties lay mainly in their own careers, and they took jobs with the highest bidder. Accordingly, Bosch ended that program in 2006 and also disbanded the youth apprenticeship program for rising high-school seniors that had been started in 1997. These apprentices took high-school courses and some courses at Tri-County Technical College in Pendleton, South Carolina. But retention "was bad" with high school students and the program stalled out.

Bosch has replaced these more ambitious programs with a much shorter, four-month in-house training program for their employees. Participants have already graduated from technical college when they sign up for the course. To be accepted as an apprentice, graduates must have a B average coming out of the tech college. The math taught at Bosch includes calculus and trigonometry. These entry-level positions pay $60,000 a year with a 3 percent increase annually.

Bosch also hires Clemson University (South Carolina) engineering grads into this apprenticeship program, although some of the company's managers are skeptical about these college kids. Clemson students are smart, they say, but have very few skills and virtually no knowledge about how systems actually work. Textbook principles do not help them figure out how to solve problems, how to apply their knowledge to real-world situations, and how to avoid safety hazards. Craftsmanship, the trainers argue, cannot really be taught in any college. It is inculcated on the shop floor.

The company also worries about how to attract more black apprentices. One trainer we spoke to argued that African Americans have moved away from "tinkering" culture as the population has urbanized. Big cities don't have space for kids to fiddle with car engines or even to fix bicycles. But even in rural black communities, the obsession with cars that was so common fifty years ago seems to have eroded. We heard the same lament about a generational divide from Aviation High School teachers, who did not express the concern in terms of race but observed the difference in young people who have grown up with fathers who could introduce them to the pleasures of taking machines apart and putting them back together. That blue-collar culture, often passed from father to son, yielded thousands of young men who liked to work with their hands. They were also good at using their minds for the deductive reasoning that fixing mechanical problem requires.

Ken is a second-year apprentice in the Bosch Rexroth Apprenticeship Program in Fountain Inn, South Carolina. That his profile appears on the Bosch website illustrates how much store the company puts in its apprentices. An African American, Ken is training to become a machinist in keeping with the guidelines issued by the US Department of Labor certified apprentices. This two-year course is an intense skills training program with a focus on computer numerical control machining. Based on the traditional German apprentice training model, the program begins with basic hand and machining skills and quickly moves to complex close-tolerance multifaceted large assembles.

At the end of his second year, Ken is focusing on quality control, machine maintenance, tool preset, product assembly and testing, as well as the manufacturing turning and milling centers. He is doing extremely well in his advanced training and the managers in some departments at Bosch have requested that he be placed in their areas when he finishes up. Often the first to complete his projects, Ken is also at the top of the academic courses taught at Greenville Technical College and has made the dean's list multiple times.

Ken invests in his studies, devoting extra time to ensure that he stays at the top of his class. Because he is quick to complete his work at a high level of quality, he is a resource for production groups that need someone to design, build, or repair parts for manufacturing equipment. With his help, these teams are able to meet their goals of high quality, reduced cost, and timely delivery of products to their customers. During his stint as an apprentice, Ken has been asked to teach other apprentices when the regular instructor is on vacation or away on business. His honesty and integrity are so widely respected that he has been given his own key to the apprentice shop so he can access tools and equipment at any time. He is safety-minded as well. Ken makes it a priority to see that the shop maintains a "5S environment," a form of training that was coined by the Japanese to refer to *seiri* (tidiness), *seiton* (orderliness), *seiso* (cleanliness), *seiketsu* (standardization), and *shitsuke* (discipline).[15]

The Need for National Integration

Germany has fueled the creation of new youth and adult apprenticeships in the United States, either indirectly by example or by opening up plants and importing the training ideology and methods. But the United States does in fact have its own modest federal government–based registered apprenticeship system,[16] a brainchild of the New Deal, unrelated to high-school—or community college–related—programs. The US Office of Apprenticeship, a division of the Department of Labor, oversees the program. Uniform standards of training and quality control are enforced by this office, lending at least the air of a federal government presence.

Initially, registered apprenticeship programs involved mainly the manufacturing, construction, and utilities industries. After World War II, they began to expand into training of health and safety workers, including firefighters, police, and emergency medical technicians. In 2008, the program guidelines were revised to allow for greater flexibility to respond to economic conditions, and apprenticeships now exist in construction, manufacturing, telecommunications, IT, service and retail industries, health care, the military, public utilities, and the public sector.

Upon completion of a registered apprenticeship program, participants receive an industry-issued, nationally recognized credential that certifies occupational proficiency. In many cases, these programs provide apprentices with the opportunity to simultaneously obtain secondary and post-secondary degrees.[17] According to the US Department of Labor, the number of active apprentices nationally fell from 469,238 in 2002 to 287,750 in 2013. (These numbers do not include the US Military Apprenticeship Program, which has actually grown from 20,200 apprentices in 2008 to 51,001 in 2013.)[18] According to a 2014 Brookings report, apprenticeships account for only 0.2 percent of the US labor force.

A combination of interrelated ideological and practical obstacles has kept this number low. Perhaps because of the historic role of organized labor in developing apprenticeships, many employers are wary of these programs because they fear they will inevitably lead to unionization. Ironically, South Carolina, a right-to-work state and a leader in high-school and community college programs, as we have seen—today boasts one of the most successful apprenticeship programs in the country, in part, once again, because companies are attracted to the state for its industry-friendly labor laws.

Federal investment in apprenticeships is also modest. We commit about $100 to $4,000 per apprentice versus $11,400 per student in two-year public colleges.[19] Overall, the government spends less than $30 million a year to "supervise, market, regulate, and publicize" the apprenticeship system. To say this is shortsighted is an understatement. The value of apprenticeship for both workers and employers is significantly greater than this. As one researcher put the matter:[20]

> The returns to apprenticeship training far exceed the returns to other types of training, including two-year, community college programs. For apprentices, the present value of their post-program increases in earnings, net of any earnings forgone during the training period itself, amounted to over $50,000 for the first 2.5 years after exiting their program. In contrast, estimates using the same approach for workers entering community college occupational programs indicated gains of only about $8,000 or less in the short term. The estimated long-term gains to community college occupation programs are certainly substantially higher ($104,000 to $130,000 for workers through age 65), but still far less than present value of long-term gains to apprenticeship training of about $266,000. Moreover, the public costs of community college were about $5,000 more than the public costs of apprenticeship. Of course, as in the case of any postsecondary education and training, the net gains are likely to vary, depending on the occupation and geographic area.

Employers seem to see the wisdom in apprenticeship.[21] Department of Labor surveys of the sponsors of registered apprenticeships show that 86 percent "strongly" recommend it and 11 percent indicate they would recommend it with reservations, due primarily to "problems with accessing related instruction." Even so, some apprenticeship sponsors expressed concern over the costs of training and a perceived inability to recoup those costs because other firms will drive up the wages of these newly skilled workers. Poaching was, somewhat surprisingly, not seen as a significant problem.

Even states where apprenticeship had a rocky beginning have found this form of training to be worthwhile. In 2002, South Carolina lagged behind other southern states, with about 800 adult registered apprentices in 57 sponsoring companies/organizations compared to 5,000 to 12,000 in Tennessee, North Carolina, Georgia, and Florida.[22] In 2007, the state created Apprenticeship Carolina, which has played a key role in increasing participation. The program started with 90 companies and 777 apprentices. As of late 2014, more than 10,000 apprentices have been trained for 678 companies.[23] With a state budget of $1 million a year, this is a modest price tag for a proven pathway into the labor market. It is complemented by a tax credit for firms of $1,000 per registered apprentice, an amount available to firms for up to four years per trainee.

South Carolina's well-established technical college system (there are sixteen technical colleges in the state) contributes to the stream of qualified workers. While these institutions can serve as bridges to four-year universities, their primary aim is to provide for career and technical education by granting associate degrees and engaging in corporate and community education. Between the education sector and the apprentice programs, South Carolina has gone a long way to helping companies train and expand their workforce.

Alex Rickett is a registered apprentice in mechatronics for Cooper Standard, a global automotive parts supplier. He graduated from high school and spent one year in community college before dropping out to work at a textile factory when his girlfriend got pregnant. At some point Alex heard about a job at Cooper Standard through the engineering manager at the plant. Because he has always been interested in mechanical engineering and works on cars as a hobby (he says he is a "visual, hands-on person"), he jumped at the opportunity.

Rickett, who is trim with dark brown hair and eyes, began his apprenticeship in August 2013 and puts in full-time hours while also attending technical college full-time, where he is studying toward his AA degree. He works from 7:00 a.m. to 3:00 p.m. during the week, and attends school from 4:00 p.m. to 9:00 p.m., Monday through Thursday. His schedule is made a little easier because his apartment is right across the road from the plant (Cooper Standard also has an in-house medical clinic and offers workers free preventive care, such as flu vaccinations and breast cancer screening). Alex pays nothing for his schooling—CS foots that bill. He would like to keep working for them and ultimately get an MA in mechanical engineering. If he gets his way, he will stay at CS "as long as [he] can."

At the plant, Alex can be found in almost any area of the large, clean shop floor, troubleshooting and doing repairs on the press injection molding machines that shape plastic for the car parts that CS makes. He has learned from working with experienced technicians, taking machines apart to see how they operate and fixing them. His mentor, a senior technician, "treats me like an adult." Alex feels that the job has given him more motivation than he's ever had before.

John Hayes is an apprentice at Cornell Dubilier, who was enlisted, along with several of his peers, while in high school. He began by sweeping floors, working in the machine shop, and "wiring up" programmable logic controllers. After he graduated from high school, he stayed on at the company and enrolled in technical college.

Hayes is "sitting pretty" and his family is thrilled with his accomplishments and success. "My mom, she flaunts it to people," he says with a grin.

> She tells people, I can't believe my son did this. I don't know where he got it from. My grandpa builds cabinets so I guess that's where I got my building side. I guess in my brain I guess I'm mechanically inclined. I find it fun to take stuff apart and put it back together. See a couple of lights come on.

"I didn't think I would fall into third in the nation," Hayes continues, referring to his 2013 bronze medal win at a national mechatronics competition sponsored by SkillsUSA. "But it's a really great field. A lot of people are in need of maintenance techs. Production jobs, you've got to have people to keep the lines running."

> They treat me very, very, very well. I enjoy it. I have a good relationship with my bosses Patrick and Will both. I am very comfortable working here. There is money to be made. I don't have any intentions of leaving. I don't want to have to drive all the way to Spartanburg to work at BMW or something when I can just work here and still do really good.

For a young man for whom high-school academics were less than captivating, it is clear that the work world inspires an appreciation for rigorous problem solving.

"We work with hydraulics, pneumatics," John says. "It's a little bit of everything."

> If there's a task to do I don't really limit myself. As long as we have the prints we can usually fix whatever is wrong with it. It's a very broad field. It's machining, electrical, pneumatics, hydraulics, robotics. That's why I enjoy it because you're not doing the same thing all the time. You constantly have something different to do and you don't get bored.

He tries to put in forty hours a week at Cornell Dubilier and then drives over to Greenville Technical College to put in yet more hours into technical education.

John's training and classroom education have opened up a variety of possibilities for the future, which is why he is not sure what he will end up doing. "I may not be stuck doing the actual mechatronics side," he muses. "I may go into the electrical side. That's what's so good about mechatronics. You learn a little bit of everything. You can then further your education in one specific field. I still have opportunities."

The Role of Technical Colleges

South Carolina's technical colleges play a central role in the apprenticeship programs flourishing in firms of German and American origin. A network of public technical schools offering industry-specific training and education, these sixteen schools are an important part of the state's economic development plan. Technical colleges offer a variety of programs and credentials, including AA degrees, certificate programs, and tailored "contract programs" that they design and implement for companies upon request. At Piedmont Technical College's Center for Advanced Manufacturing in Laurens, South Carolina, fifteen young men (no women) are working in small groups, building model conveyor belts using a combination of sensors (inductive and optical) and a software program. Most of them are in a two-year AA program, working toward a degree in mechatronics, which one of them describes as "the study of factory automation."

Some of the students in the class came to Piedmont Technical College (PTC) right out of high school, while others took a less direct route: They held low-wage fast-food jobs or low-skill factory jobs. PTC's promotional materials emphasize that its graduates will be "career ready" the day they graduate and will earn 30 percent more than high-school graduates (they also note that some graduates start out earning more than $50,000 a year). They may do even better if they find their way to four-year institutions and obtain more advanced degrees, something that is facilitated (rather than impeded) by completing an AA degree.

The college provides limited financial aid for students, but many of the area companies pay for this degree for their apprentices. This is a cost-effective way for the firms to see to it that their workers are highly skilled. An apprenticeship program with accompanying classes that leads to a two-year certificate in mechatronics technology costs about $6,500. The state kicks in $3,600 from the proceeds of the state lottery. The companies can claim tax credits of $2,000. With all of these subsidies, the actual cost per employee for the two-year degree is only $962. The next certificate, Mechatronics II, adds $152, and training for operators of computer-operated numerical controls is a mere $75. Of course, these low numbers are possible only because the taxpayers and lottery players in South Carolina have authorized this public investment in industry.

James enrolled at PTC because his high school didn't start offering a course in mechatronics until after he graduated. Tall and skinny, dressed in a red flannel plaid shirt, James sports a wispy beard and a strong southern accent. He noticed when the area around his hometown started attracting new industries and he has set his cap on working for the ZF plant. He is drawn by the same opportunities as the German apprentices we met in the ZF training facility near Osnabrück.

But unlike his German counterparts, James has no skills to offer ZF. He loves mechatronics and hopes that by pursuing an AA degree he will be able to secure a job on the floor at ZF, because "there's money and it's fun," and he wouldn't have to be mopping up blood, like one of his cousins does at a nearby Louis Rich meat-processing plant. James understands, however, that ZF is going to want to train people like him to their specifications. "They want young people instead of older people who come in and say, I want to do it my way." They need people who want training but don't have "that much experience so that the company can mold them."

James is trying to talk his younger brother, Dave, into nailing this training in high school. If he follows through, Dave could graduate from high school with a certificate in mechatronics and will need only one year at Piedmont.

PTC's Center for Advanced Manufacturing is located in a building the college acquired after ZF contacted Rusty Denning, the associate vice president for continuing education and economic development. ZF was on the lookout for a training facility that could accommodate twelve hundred people. Although Denning didn't have the space at the time, he told ZF that housing its program wouldn't be a problem and then hustled to make it work, successfully appealing to the college's foundation, which ponied up the money to purchase and renovate the facility. Denning sees this as being all about "giving companies what they want."

In April 2013, Zeiss donated a million dollars' worth of software and support to expand the curriculum at the Center for Advanced Manufacturing. The software, for use with Zeiss's coordinate measuring machines, enabled the college to start a precision metrology (science of measurement) training program, the first and only of its kind in the state. Area companies using CMM technology include BMW, Bosch, and ZF.

This investment is fueling job opportunities in a region that sorely needs them. And it is taking a page from the German system of dual education in extending training to students as young as sixteen. High-school juniors are enrolling in district-wide career centers in order to spend part of their day taking classes at the technical college. These dual-enrollment students, who are typically not in the honors-level STEM programs that aim to send students into four-year colleges, can graduate with a mechatronics technology certificate and credits equivalent to about half of an AA degree. This will make them attractive hires for companies like ZF, who will pay them $18 an hour for twenty hours per week, and also foot their technical college tuition bills.

These collaborations represent two legs in what is, in Germany, a three-legged stool comprised of business, education, and labor. Historic antagonism between the labor movement and southern politics has sidelined the unions, though that story may not have come to a conclusion yet. Some German unions are strong enough to insist that companies like Volkswagen adopt governing structures in the United States that look like the ones they are used to at home.

This requirement was put to the test in 2014, when the VW plant in Chattanooga, Tennessee, narrowly failed to adopt the United Auto Workers as its representatives for collective bargaining. The plant, which opened in 2008, first became the subject of controversy in 2013 after the UAW attempted to unionize the labor force, drawing opposition from right-wing politicians and others who feared such a move would deter other businesses from setting up shop in the state. In that right-to-work state, many workers were just as resistant to the entreaties of the UAW.[24]

Ultimately the union vote (narrowly) failed, but in November 2014 VW—apparently under pressure from its labor union in Germany—announced a new policy that would allow employees to be represented by several labor groups, among them the UAW.[25] The new rules require that at least 15 percent of the workforce must join up for their union to have some level of representation. The recognition by the UAW of minority unions is considered by some on the left as a potentially important development in organized labor.

As this example illustrates, there are features of the German system of labor organization—including apprenticeship—that do not transfer seamlessly to the US context. However, we are taking strides in that direction, led by the example of subsidiaries that are bringing the apprenticeship model and some forms of certification to our shores. They have been met with a warm welcome not only because the training pays off for German firms but because American companies face the same problem of skills mismatch and have moved on their own to improve training. It is an investment long overdue and, unfortunately, uneven in its application, subject to regional economic and political realities.

For most of American history, the federal government has played a weak role in the development of education at all levels. It is quintessentially a state and local enterprise. However, Washington is concerned with workforce preparation and as such has entered the debate periodically about the nation's competitiveness and the role of labor in our international position. Wartime production has also tended to mobilize at the national level, and in those periods federal government has been critical to a unified response to manpower demands. But the commitment waxes and wanes. It is easily caught up in the tension between equal opportunity on the one hand—which tends to lean away from workforce training because it eschews "college for all"—and both workforce preparation and poverty alleviation on the other.

The time has come for rededication on a more consistent basis to the goal of a national system of high-quality vocational education, with national standards for occupation-related skills, certification to go with them, and a renewed attempt to link America's teenagers to the world of work. This is the direction the whole country needs to pursue if we are to support the aspirations of millions of young Americans who need a leg up in the labor market.

9

Where Do We Go from Here?

The ebb and flow of American interest in and support for work-related education has yielded different visions for vocational education, none of them entirely satisfying. Vocational education has been offered in separate schools and tracks, comprehensive schools, and integrated academic and vocational programs, and has involved an assortment of school-based and work-based learning activities. The enterprise has evolved from manual training to narrow skill-based training for specific occupations to general career education for all.

None of these strategies has been successful in producing the kinds of labor market outcomes we need. That record of confusion—not failure but not the kind of success that inspires confidence—has led many policy makers to argue that we should just walk away. In 2006–2008, President George W. Bush attempted to do just that by taking steps to eliminate or reduce spending on vocational education on the grounds that it was a ticket to nowhere.

But have we really tried hard enough? To this day, we have failed to create an institutional body trusted by the various stakeholders—schools, employers, and workers—to coordinate and help sustain a national system of vocational education, and this has surely hampered our past efforts. Another obstacle has been the lack of a unified certification system. Further, scholars have pointed out that, for the most part, American employers worry more than their German counterparts about investing in training that some other firm might benefit from if it steals their trained labor. They tend not to envision themselves in the training business and are typically ill-equipped to perform it anyway, at least not without making important changes in their own corporate culture.[1]

Our ambivalence toward blue-collar work, our postwar obsession with white-collar occupations, the national religion of upward mobility, and—it must be said—a degree of selfishness on the part of the middle and upper middle class when it comes to investing in the future of other people's children all play an important role.

Ambivalence toward vocational training is reflected in the way we spend our education dollars. In fiscal 2014, the Department of Education received $67.3 billion in federal funds. Most of that money ($48.6 billion) went to general funding for elementary and secondary education, to local education agencies dedicated to poverty relief, to disability accommodation, and to the Pell Grant program for college students. Career, technical, and adult education claimed a mere $1.75 billion, which is simply not enough to run a credible program. In September 2015, the US Department of Labor awarded $175 million to winners of the American Apprenticeship grant competition who have pledged to train and hire more than 34,000 new apprentices in industries like IT and advanced manufacturing.[2] It is the single largest investment of its kind, but given the scale of the American labor market this is a modest contribution.

Vocational funding in the United States comes primarily through the Perkins Act. Perkins IV, its fourth renewal, was signed into law in 2006. In so doing, Congress recognized that technological changes along with shifts in global markets are the sources of evolving demands in the labor market. It also wanted to improve the faculty who teach technology subjects. Thus, the federal bill speaks explicitly to the importance of career and technical education, but, as in the past, implementation is largely left to the states.[3] Perkins IV allows some flexibility in how states and local entities spend their funds, but, for the first time, the legislation makes it clear that the purpose of the act is to prepare American youth for "high-skill, high-wage, or high-demand occupations in current or emerging professions."

While this is a helpful emphasis, it does little to cure one of the enduring flaws in our educational structure: Its decentralized nature makes it very difficult to develop anything approaching a uniform system of training. Hence credentials earned in Florida may bear little resemblance to ones with similar names in Wisconsin. To the extent that labor markets are local, this may not be such a problem. But they aren't. Skilled workers need to be able to move where jobs are opening up and if they cannot easily signal their qualifications, this will restrict their geographic mobility and their employability in general.

Of course, the American labor market also has its decentralized elements. Most employers search for a labor force close to home and judge the qualifications based on local needs and standards. Yet when regions suffer losses, as the Midwest and the Eastern Seaboard have for decades in manufacturing, localism is a liability for those who need to find new jobs. In certain high-demand occupations, such as welding, plumbing, masonry, electrical work, and HVAC, this might be less of a problem as employers desperate for workers may overcome their skepticism about the value of out-of-state training. But it is an impediment for those trying to enter crowded labor markets where credentials may matter more.

Creating a more uniform signaling system is a challenge in the United States not only because we spend too little on this kind of education but because education funding is barely a federal responsibility. Congress allocates only 9 percent of what we actually spend on education. Under these circumstances, the action lies largely with the states and, predictably, some are more enthusiastic than others about technical and career education.[4]

At the federal level, the Obama administration began implementing a job-driven action plan, allocating $2.4 billion in discretionary funding to a range of employment-training programs. By August 2014, the administration had awarded $950 million in job-driven grants, with another $1.4 billion to come in 2015. The government has already funded partnerships serving the long-term unemployed, supporting community colleges and employers who train workers who have lost their jobs as a result of foreign trade. Additionally, Youth CareerConnect grants link high schools, employers, and the public workforce system. The remaining $1.4 billion will underwrite a $30 million initiative to improve "within-state alignment of workforce policy and programs; new pilot testing strategies for [food stamp recipients], disconnected youth . . . and expanding apprenticeship programs."[5]

These are all important steps in the right direction. But they are not going to train a twenty-first-century workforce unless we realize that developing quality at that level means starting in high school and enabling teachers who come out of industry to educate their students without looking over their shoulders every day in fear of declining test scores.

We are unlikely to be able to afford to place state-of-the-art equipment in most vocational classrooms, since no school district in America has the resources to purchase cutting-edge technologies, much less update what they have as the industries they are preparing their students for surge ahead. For access to such equipment, American students need to be able to do what Nigeria Williams is doing every week: train on the shop floor, with the right equipment, in the hands of an American Meister who is experienced on the job and qualified to teach. They need to be able to do that for three years full-time, in combination with their classes, so that they can pass the equivalent of the German industrial engineering exam and not have to fall back to a lesser qualification because they have only two years and two days a week to accomplish their goals.

This will only occur if we soften the rigid division of labor between school and work, which has meant that, at least until recently, industry has not seen itself as having the primary responsibility for preparing people for work. As such, companies haven't wanted to invest in vocational education and training that lasts for more than a few weeks or months. In other countries, that role is heavily subsidized, with taxpayers picking up about 70 percent of the overall costs in Germany. The political economy of government/private firm/union relations means that no one seems to worry about the "free rider problem," in which a company invests heavily in training someone who may end up working elsewhere. The national investment in producing the most capable labor force in the world is enormous and politically sacrosanct.

Corporate commitment to training in the United States is much weaker. American firms generally oppose the kind of government oversight of training programs that is mandated in Germany, where unions also play a powerful role in terms of management, education, and policy development. German apprentices are also eligible for the same benefits and protections that full-time employees enjoy, which would surely be difficult to replicate here.

Until we turn this around, the dedicated students at Aviation High School will be working on instruments that were new during World War II, while their counterparts in Europe are training on state-of-the-art equipment. We will have instructors who are struggling against the odds, fighting against a prestige system that places greater confidence in abstract calculus than in the ability to accurately bend a conduit.

If we are going to get serious about preparing a competitive labor force and paving the way for young people who want reach the middle class through technical employment, we must develop more intentional, permanent, sustainable relations between industry and education. Right now, to the extent that these relations develop, it is almost accidental and often temporary. It depends too much on the motivations of individual teachers and administrators who are trying against the odds to smooth the road for a few students whom they can connect to employers they know. It does not help matters that apprenticeships—just like education policy and spending as a whole—are ultimately developed, implemented, and overseen at the state and local levels. And while state governments have done the most to foster linkages between educational institutions and industry, the system of vocational education and training really is—in many states—not a system at all. It is a hodgepodge long characterized by unresolved conflicts over roles and turf and subject to political winds.

This is in contrast to other countries, where the stakeholders all have defined roles to play in the systems and work together in a coherent way. In Japan, maintaining robust ties to employers is part of a vocational teacher's job and instructors are benchmarked by how well they place students. In Germany, the seamless web that embeds teaching inside the workplace ensures that those connections are as strong as steel.

We cannot afford to make this a hobby or an accident; it has to be hardwired into a training system. MTU in South Carolina is on the right track, blending vocational education and shop-floor training, but state regulations preclude them from implementing a three-year-long, full-time, and fully integrated program, a model of the kind that would be routine in their parent company.

Imagine how much money we would save on incarceration, poverty-related expenditures, and lost opportunities due to urban blight if we could boast a 7 percent unemployment rate among youth instead of the nearly 50 percent rate our inner-city minority youths suffer right now. Our investment policies are out of kilter with our needs. To improve the situation, we have to set aside the traditional wariness and fully private orientation of our leading firms and our uneasy relationship with government more generally. Government is a tool for reform, for channeling investment into national needs. We knew that when we had wars to fight: We handed over a massive amount of power to government to mobilize, train, and produce everything from tanks to uniforms. We have another war on our hands now, but it is quiet, insidious, and has been slow-moving, to the point where we are unwilling to recognize its devastating consequences for productivity, mobility, and national prosperity.

Skeptics might ask why we should imitate the German model, when so many of their firms seem to be headed in the direction of the United States. European economic growth is not exactly the shining example we should follow either. The reasons these firms are headed our way are many, ranging from the more prolonged duration of the Great Recession in Europe to the much higher levels of unemployment and sharp "austerity policies" in the European Union, both of which impact consumer demand. Bringing production of cars, which are expensive to ship, back to the region where the demand is high makes sense, especially in light of the (unfortunate) decline in manufacturing wages in the United States. These conditions are helping to propel manufacturing firms to set up shop in the United States, but we must recognize that this is not likely to continue if we cannot raise our productivity and that, in turn, comes down to the quality of our workforce.

The advice from German subsidiaries in the United States is that we must begin to provide more affordable university education and invest in dual training. That is at the very top of the agenda (alongside predictable calls for the elimination of tariffs and better regulatory cooperation). They are bullish about the prospects for economic growth because, as tough as things are coming out of a long recession, American consumers represent a massive market for everything these firms produce, from diesel engines to chemicals. But the thirty-eight hundred German companies that have facilities in the United States are looking for every way possible to import their own training system because they know that ours is not up to the task. When asked for his advice to young Americans interested in a career in industry, James Sharp, the president of Carl Zeiss Microscopy, suggested that they leave the country for a year or two to go someplace where people take training seriously. Zeiss has five hundred employees in the United States and twenty thousand worldwide. We will not see more of those jobs coming here unless US workers can produce what Zeiss workers in Germany do every day.

At the policy level, the government has addressed anxieties over academic standards and premature tracking by making it a requirement of Perkins IV that CTE programs focus on the academic achievement of their students, strengthen the connections between secondary and postsecondary education, and improve state and local accountability. In theory this seems wise and certainly mollifies those who worry about tracking as a limitation on the freedom and potential of students, especially those from less educated or low-income households. But in less than competent hands, this can mean watering down both CTE and academics; attempts to integrate the two can be superficial and the emphasis on standardized testing creates a further obstacle to creating meaningful connections. Further, even dedicated CTE schools express a need to retain their independence from industry, which, while a source of employment for their students, can also be a source of suspicion among both educators and parents (are they exploiting students?), the latter of whom have also bought in to the pervasive college-for-all perspective.

While the fear of tracking is not unfounded, it need not come true. Unlike in Germany, in the United States there are many on-ramps that allow young people and adults to return to education and credentialing programs. Americans aren't stuck in the way people may be in countries with more de facto tracking and educational stratification and thus fewer such opportunities. Indeed, the US adult education system is more flexible than the German system in general and may allow for more innovation and agility. The advantages of our second-chance society are so significant that the Germans are now developing more on-ramps back into higher education for their own dual-system graduates.

That said, there is no doubt that the college-for-all mentality has affected America's perceptions of CTE, including perceptions about what it signals about a child's intelligence or ability and what vocational training may mean for his or her social status and future prospects. This needs to change. Whether it will or not is an open question.

The fact is, in parts of the United States where young people—high-school students—have had the opportunity to engage in serious, well-designed, and well-implemented training and work, through either youth apprenticeship or high school co-op programs, the benefits can be striking. This is true not just in terms of employment prospects but, as writer, teacher, and education scholar Mike Rose so powerfully demonstrates, of cognitive development, the ability to diagnose, analyze, and solve complex problems, and to operate with social intelligence.

But even in places where CTE is embraced, we still need to make sure we are giving both technical and academic teachers in CTE schools the support and the respect they need to do their jobs. We cannot prepare a workforce if the people who do the teaching are at arm's length from the firms that will employ their students. We should pay teachers to get updated industry experience in the summers, incentivize them to place their students, and provide ongoing support for their connections to the industries they are training people for. Taking a page from the German national skills exams, we should define high standards and enable industry-experienced people to teach to them. These standards need to mean something definitive at the national level, so that employers know what the entry-level workers they are searching for actually know. And we are also going to have to change how we evaluate students and schools. As the de Blasio report on vocational education in New York (discussed in chapter 1) made clear, we need to improve an inadequate system for monitoring programs and student outcomes, which ties our hands by making it difficult to evaluate them and assess their impact.

As long as schools are evaluated based on standardized test scores, we are going to need a way for students to substitute an academic-based exam like the Regents with something that demonstrates proficiency in a CTE area (perhaps the passage of industry certification exams or some other kind of test developed by people knowledgeable about industry requirements). This, of course, is exactly what students in Germany are doing: taking rigorous, union-certified examinations that measure their proficiency in technical applications. New York will be doing this in a small way now that new Regents rules have been passed allowing students to get Regents credit for CTE courses. But we would be wise to invest in national standards that will certify the skills that our high-school students have learned so that employers across the country have a way of understanding what job seekers can do.

With better evaluation methods may come a more congenial understanding, of not only what these students really know but the value of this kind of education more generally. We may well find that students who go through serious vocational training have a better grasp of math and science than those kids who are great students and test takers but cannot apply what they know. The CTE student uses what she learns day in and day out in ways that the academic students do not. Indeed, more and more universities are stressing what they call "active learning," to engage college students in problem solving and move them away from passive lecture-style education. Vocational students have been busy pursuing active learning right under our noses.

We have lauded the German system throughout this book, but it bears notice that it is not perfect. Germany has its own forms of inequality, even with a more robust respect for vocational education. Their apprenticeship system is not as capacious, especially toward immigrants, as one might hope. Turks of Muslim origins, in particular, seem not to find their way into the dual-education system in nearly the numbers their demographics would warrant. Just as African Americans have a hard time cracking the barrier of union employment and the higher wages that go with it, the children of immigrants in Germany are often unable to make their way into the more highly skilled occupations. The preference of many firms, including GMH, for hiring multiple generations within the same families encourages exclusivity. Some of this is based on ethnic or religious prejudice. But the same localism discourages young people from the former East Germany from migrating west, where the economy is stronger. They are native-born Germans yet their absorption into apprenticeship opportunities in regions like Osnabrück is limited, which is surprising given the complaints employers in the western region of the country voice about the difficulty of landing good apprentices nowadays. It may be that the German desire to get to students when they are young, at age sixteen or seventeen, is the biggest barrier to geographic mobility. Few kids of that age are ready to leave home.

In the United States, status dynamics of race and class have left a deep crevice and have been responsible in large measure for our hesitation to invest in vocational education, despite the questionable track record that college for all has had among working-class students, especially the minority poor. One might imagine that in Germany, where nearly 60 percent of high school students elect the dual-education system, that respect for blue-collar vocations is stronger.

Germans do have greater respect for the blue-collar worker than Americans do. Yet our European counterparts are not immune to the siren of white-collar prestige, notwithstanding the fact that manufacturing is now far cleaner and more computer-laden than ever before. In a period when the birth dearth has meant German firms are scrambling more than they once did to find apprentices, the problem of status is growing. Indeed, we are starting to see an increasing number of parents and kids who reject the apprenticeship pathway in favor of university education and the lure of a white-collar job. This shift has been slower to gain ground in Germany compared to the United States in part because the wage differential between blue-collar workers in Germany and their white-collar counterparts is not as large as it is in the United States, especially after decades of deindustrialization, declining union density, and falling wages in America. Nonetheless, even in Germany, we see younger people wondering about whether they want to devote their lives to blue-collar work. Industry looks on this development with dismay. Time will tell whether these changing attitudes will open up opportunities previously unfulfilled for German youth or lead them into the dead ends that many of their American counterparts have experienced.

If we do follow this new path in the United States, we must be mindful of the need to incorporate those who are often left behind, especially young black men. Their unemployment rates are catastrophic. The Great Recession took a bad situation and made it far worse. These are the people who are in greatest need of the intensive skills investment that a new dual-education system could produce. For those who are still in high school, something like the apprentice model should be encouraged. For those who did not make it that far, the route that leads from a GED to a community college–based training system like those sprouting in South Carolina should be a high priority.

It is essential, not only for their long-term economic security and the well-being of their families but for the cities and rural regions they live in. Spending time in cities like Baltimore, Syracuse, Detroit, Newark, and dozens of other major metropolitan areas that are struggling to find a next economy to pursue is all one needs to become convinced that business as usual is no longer good enough. Employers will not locate firms in cities whose young people have such profound skill deficits. We cannot abandon those regions as there are too many people trapped in them who need to benefit from a next act in the economic evolution of their hometowns. Right away.

Scott Paul, president of the Alliance for American Manufacturing, believes that certain policy changes could prevent another Detroit. In a 2013 article[6] he outlines steps that can be taken to "grow exports, rebuild the middle class and put us on a path to a better fiscal position." Among his highest priorities is to:

> Rebuild our system of vocational education. Creating a seamless system of training from high school, to community college, and on to the factory floor for a new generation of manufacturing workers will boost American manufacturing's competitiveness and provide a viable career path for millions of Americans.

A *Time* magazine interview[7] with Rick Snyder, the governor of Michigan, about the rescue of the city of Detroit, is particularly germane to the role of vocational education in the rebuilding of a bankrupt city on the brink of complete industrial collapse. When asked about his next priorities, Snyder identified as among the most important, "filling skilled trade jobs and re-establishing a career/technical education track in our state second-to-none."

We're number one in adding manufacturing jobs and it's coming back strong. But we also need to redefine the skilled trades, because historically people tended to think of them as the welder, plumber, electrician, and those are great professions, but if you're in manufacturing today, you're a skilled tradesperson most likely. If you're in agriculture today, you're driving a $250,000 tractor, a $500,000 combine, you're a skilled tradesperson. So, this is a very pervasive issue. A lot of times we overly encourage people, and tell all of our young people to go get a university degree when in many cases, they would be just as well off if they'd have looked at a career tech-ed track and being successful there. So we need to have two parallel tracks that are both well-respected and honorable.

The possibilities for a state that heads in the direction of high-quality CTE are extraordinary as students at Fraser High School, twenty miles northeast of Detroit, have discovered. In the spring of 2014, fifty-four welding students at Fraser had a chance to qualify for certification from the American Welding Society that would mark them as qualified professionals. I. F. Metalworks in nearby Roseville linked up with the high school's welding instructor, Brent Brasure, putting him to work with the company's certified welding inspector/educator, Jeff Maxwell. Together they created a program tailored to the high-school welding students at no cost to them:

> This qualification verifies that students are capable of performing specific materials joining processes in accordance with international industry standards. Successful qualification requires completing a joint according to parameters defined on a print and passing evaluation by way of visual inspection, macro etch testing, and destructive bend testing. Just over half of the students who attempted qualification received this valuable credential.

This program should speed the careers of those successful students, placing them immediately in line for welding jobs that are, right now, going begging. The combination of training, certification, and employer engagement is exactly the right strategy.

Collaborations of this kind bear fruit for those well past high school. In northeastern Ohio and western Pennsylvania, the Oh-Penn Manufacturing Collaborative is bringing together educational institutions, labor unions, private-sector firms, chambers of commerce, community organizations, municipalities, and economic and workforce development groups to market and provide local training for the region's machine-building jobs.[8] A similar effort is under way in Chicago, through Skills for Chicagoland's Future (SCF), a nonprofit that is coordinating an effort to connect unemployed job seekers with employers and workforce development organizations and educational institutions that provide training. According to SCF, since its inception in 2009, 1,300 unemployed job seekers have been hired through partnerships with over forty employers. Further, more than 170 unemployed job seekers have been enrolled in train-to-hire programs leading to immediate employment upon successful completion of the programs. SCF's employer partners have signed commitments to hire more than 1,000 unemployed job seekers in 2015.[9]

If we want to see programs like this become the state of play rather than an occasional accident, if we want to avoid the need repeatedly to revisit the issues that have animated this book, we have to make these reforms permanent and insulate them from the winds of political change. We may never have a system like Germany's because we have fundamentally different attitudes toward the role of government as it relates to both education and industry—not to mention how the latter two relate to each other—as well as the rights of workers and the obligations of employers. Americans are also ambivalent about appearing to steer teenagers into tracks, even though those inequalities have already emerged as a consequence of the segregation they experience according to family wealth, race, and educational background.

The presidential primary season for the 2016 elections suggests there may be a public appetite for a reboot of vocational education and apprenticeship. In June of 2015, Hillary Rodham Clinton, the Democratic front-runner, proposed a plan that would offer companies a $1,500 tax credit for every apprentice they hire. Senator Marco Rubio of Florida, one of the Republican hopefuls, promised he would expand apprenticeships and vocational training if he lands the presidency. His rival Scott Walker, Republican governor of Wisconsin, may be permanently on the outs with

Appendix

What's Growing?

The fields where we can expect the greatest occupational growth going forward provide us with a road map toward sensible investments in vocational education and apprenticeship. Below we provide a quick survey of the occupations and industries that are particularly ripe for this kind of training system.

Allied Medical Fields

Health science is projected to rank first in the number of jobs added and second in growth rate through 2018. Entry-level positions require at least an associate's degree or postsecondary nondegree certification. Middle-skill jobs in health include those for personal care aides, home health aides, physical therapist assistants, dental hygienists, diagnostic medical sonographers, and veterinary technicians.[1] The highest growth rates will be concentrated among personal care and home health aides as well as physical- and occupational-therapy assistants. Veterinary technologists will not be far behind.

Approximately five million health care jobs (or 45 percent) are in middle-skill occupations.[2]

Health care jobs are distributed across the country, but since 2001 the fastest area of growth for community college–trained health care workers has been in Texas, Colorado, Arizona, and Arkansas.[3] These workers are well paid: nationally, the median income in these fields is about $17.01 an hour, and in some more specialized occupations in this category, such as nuclear medicine, technologists can earn more than twice this sum.[4]

Business and Finance

Almost a third of all workers in business and finance have only an associate's degree or some college education. They have jobs in bookkeeping, accounting, auditing, and sales, and these fields are booming. The business, finance, and sales industries anticipate an 11.1 percent growth rate in job openings from now until 2024.[5]

Jobs can be found in a variety of industries. Middle-skill workers are employed in the management of companies (4.5 percent of all jobs), physicians' offices (4.4 percent), and accounting, tax preparation, bookkeeping, and payroll services (4.2 percent). As the health care industries expand, they will represent one of the fastest-growing areas of opportunity for middle-skill business and finance jobs.[6]

The Skilled Trades

There is—and will continue to be—high demand for workers trained in the skilled trades, which comprise a wide range of occupations from carpentry, welding, and electrical work to plumbing, HVAC, and masonry. These workers are usually employed in the construction, manufacturing, and energy industries, and these are jobs that cannot be outsourced. Twenty percent of middle-skill jobs in the skilled trades are with electrical and other wiring installation contractors. Machine shops (6 percent) and metalworking machinery manufacturing (3 percent) are the next most common fields for people in the skilled trades. Among the fastest-growing sectors is the oil and gas industry.[7]

A 2012 survey by the ManpowerGroup, one of the nation's largest employment agencies, of over thirteen hundred American employers indicated that the hardest jobs to fill are in these skilled trades. The dearth of trained carpenters, plumbers, electricians, and "other tool wielding professionals" is making it difficult for these companies to fulfill their contracts.[8]

Construction—a big employer of skilled tradespeople—has bounced back from the housing bust and recession of 2008–9 and has grown by 5 percent since 2010.[9] In New York City, the construction industry accounted for nearly 115,000 jobs and $30 billion in spending in 2012 alone.[10] Between 2010 and 2020, about 14,200 additional workers will be added to the payroll in construction-related industries in the Big Apple. These workers are raking in high salaries: the majority of them earned over $50 an hour, or an average salary of $75,000 per year. In some trades, the salary figures are double that amount. These wages place construction workers well up into the American middle class.

Welding is a trade that is in particular demand, yet it is a field in which the majority of skilled practitioners are nearing retirement. By 2024 we will need more than 400,000 welders as well as thousands more workers who need welding skills, like pipe fitters, plumbers, and boilermakers.[11] The Bureau of Labor Statistics pegs the average wage at $36,300 a year, but anecdotal evidence suggests that this is the low end of the scale, with some firms paying as much as $75,000 to $100,000. In Texas and North Dakota, where the gas and oil industries are growing like wildfire, the industry needs more than just petroleum workers. Trained electricians, pipe fitters, carpenters, and other middle-skill workers are essential to building the infrastructure necessary to deliver the product. In Texas and Appalachia, welders in the shale industry can earn as much as $7,000 a week.[12]

Leisure and Hospitality

The service industry is another source of middle-skill jobs. Workers without a college degree represent 80 percent of total employment in travel.[13] In 2012, in New York City alone, there were 363,050 hospitality and leisure jobs, a 27.4 percent increase since 2006.[14] The leisure and hospitality sector is expected to produce 3.3 million jobs between 2010 and 2023.[15]

Information Technology

While IT has a much larger share of workers with advanced degrees (66 percent) than workers with an associate's degrees or some college/training (28 percent),[16] there are a number of IT occupations—including for network and computer system administrators and information security analysts—for which less than four years of postsecondary education is acceptable.

"Available tech jobs aren't just for people with bachelor's degrees," said Hagos Mehreteab, head of talent acquisition of AppNexus. "New York City's technology sector also desperately needs people that have specialized skills training and the motivation and passion for learning new things."[17]

New York City's technology sector comprises nearly sixty-six thousand jobs and is expected to grow by 15 percent over the next five years. Middle-skill jobs within this sector accounted for 16 percent of all middle-skill jobs in the city in 2014, or what amounts to a little more than eighty-one hundred jobs. Notably, the demand for IT jobs is high in the finance and insurance sectors, at two times greater than national demand.

In ten middle-skill technology occupations, which include those for information security analysts and help desk or entry-level computer support, median hourly salaries range from $26 to $56. These jobs are in high demand in New York City, ranging from twenty-five hundred postings for information security analysts to more than fifty-one hundred postings for computer user support specialists. Entry-level IT support roles, such as help desk or entry-level computer support, account for over half (57 percent) of middle-skill IT jobs in New York. Upward roles such as network support, help desk manager, and advanced computer support require more technical IT skills.[18]

Transportation

Career opportunities in transportation are growing across a range of occupations. Employment in this industry sector, as a whole, increased 6.1 percent nationally in just three years, from 2010 to 2013. Workers whose jobs involve handling the logistics of transportation have seen a 3 percent rise and a median hourly wage of $35. The demand for bus drivers is growing and jobs for service technicians and mechanics have grown as well.[19] We even have more need for truck drivers. In 2014 alone, more than fifteen thousand jobs were added in this field.[20]

Automotive service technicians and mechanics are also in increasing demand as, in recent years, cars have become increasingly complex machines. Diagnosing their problems and undertaking repairs require specialized training in electronics and computer systems. Unlike the past, when young men learned how to do car repair in the family garage, today's mechanic needs more sophisticated training. But because that training is hard to find, we are seeing a shortage of auto mechanics all over the country. We will need 17 percent more of them over the period 2010–2020, adding 124,800 jobs for a total of 848,200. In 2012, auto technicians overall earned an average of $36,000, but 10 percent earned more than $60,000. Master mechanics, however, can earn a lot more—about $100,000 a year.

STEM

We hear a great deal about STEM occupations, the science, technology, engineering, and mathematical fields that are often cited as drivers of innovation and national economic competitiveness. The US workforce lost STEM jobs during the Great Recession and currently has a small proportion of STEM jobs overall. But that state of affairs will not last for long since jobs in this field are expected to grow by 17 percent between now and 2018, while non-STEM jobs will increase more slowly.

Most of these jobs will require at least a bachelor's degree, but there are two STEM occupations (electrical and electronic engineering technicians and surveying and mapping technicians) in which students with either some college (including postsecondary certificate holders) or associate degrees will earn more on average than workers who hold bachelor's degrees, although the differences are rather small.[21]

Notes

Epigraph

1. Jeffrey Goldberg, "A Matter of Black Lives," *Atlantic*, September 2015, http://www
.theatlantic.com/magazine/archive/2015/09/a-matter-of-black-lives/399386/.

Introduction

1. Andrea Cheng, "Record Number of Manufacturing Jobs Returning to the US,"
Marketwatch, May 1, 2015, http://www.marketwatch.com/story/us-flips-the-script
-on-jobs-reshoring-finally-outpaced-offshoring-in-2014-2015-05-01.
2. Megan Woolhouse, "Some Offshored Manufacturing Jobs Return to US," *Boston
Globe*, July 26, 2015.
3. Harold L. Sirkin, Michael Zinser, and Douglas Hohner, "Made in America, Again:
Why Manufacturing Will Return to the U.S.," Boston Consulting Group (August
2011), https://www.bcg.com/documents/file84471.pdf.
4. EMSI, *Middle-skill Spotlight: An Analysis of Four In-demand Sectors with a Community College Focus* (Moscow, ID: EMSI, 2014), http://www.economicmodeling.com
/cc-report2014/.
5. Darren Dahl, "A Sea of Job-Seekers, but Some Companies Aren't Getting Any
Bites," *New York Times*, June 27, 2012, http://www.nytimes.com/2012/06/28
/business/smallbusiness/even-with-high-unemployment-some-small-businesses
-struggle-to-fill-positions.html.
6. Tom Morrison et al., "Boiling Point? The Skills Gap in U.S. Manufacturing," Deloitte
and the Manufacturing Institute (2011), http://www.themanufacturinginstitute.org
/~/media/A07730B2A798437D98501E798C2E13AA.ashx.

7. EMSI, *Middle-skill Spotlight.*

8. Mark Memmott, "2 Million 'Open Jobs'? Yes, But U.S. Has a Skills Mismatch," National Public Radio, June 15, 2011, http://www.npr.org/sections/thetwo-way/2011 /06/15/137203549/two-million-open-jobs-yes-but-u-s-has-a-skills-mismatch.

9. "Occupational Projections for Direct-Care Workers 2010–2020," PHI (February 2013), http://phinational.org/sites/phinational.org/files/phi_factsheet1update _singles_2.pdf.

10. William C. Symonds, Robert Schwartz, and Ronald F. Ferguson, *Pathways to Prosperity: Meeting the Challenge of Preparing Young Americans for the 21st Century* (Cambridge, MA: Pathways to Prosperity Project, Harvard University Graduate School of Education, 2011).

11. Pamela M. Prah, "Has U.S. Manufacturing's Comeback Stalled?," *USA Today*, July 30, 2013, http://www.usatoday.com/story/news/ation/2013/07/30/us-manufactur ing-comeback-stalling/2599059/.

12. Indeed, less than 40 percent of manufacturing employees produce objects. Nearly one-third of all the employees counted as "manufacturing workers" are managers and professionals. Another large group are in sales, design, logistics, and information technology. Marc Levinson, "Job Creation in the Manufacturing Revival," Congressional Research Service, 7-5700 (July 2, 2015), 4, https://www.fas.org/sgp/crs /misc/R41898.pdf.

13. Furthermore, as it happens, Germany isn't blameless. It shares a currency with its neighbors, greatly benefiting German exporters, who get to price their goods in a weak euro instead of what would surely have been a soaring deutsche mark. Yet Germany has failed to deliver on its side of the bargain: To avoid a European depression, it needed to spend more as its neighbors were forced to spend less, and it hasn't done that. Paul Krugman, "Those Depressing Germans," *New York Times*, November 3, 2013, http://www.nytimes.com/2013/11/04/opinion/krugman-those -depressing-germans.html?_r=0.

14. The quote comes from the National Educational Policy Center's citation for the 2014 annual Bunkum Awards. See National Educational Policy Center, "2014 Bunkum Honorees," http://nepc.colorado.edu/think-tank/bunkum-awards/2014.

15. Executive Office of the President, *Increasing College Opportunity for Low-Income Students: Promising Models and a Call to Action* (Washington, DC: White House, January 2014), https://www.whitehouse.gov/sites/default/files/docs/white _house_report_on_increasing_college_opportunity_for_low-income_students .pdf.

16. White House Office of the Press Secretary, "FACT SHEET: The President and First Lady's Call to Action on College Opportunity," White House, January 16, 2014, https://www.whitehouse.gov/the-press-office/2014/01/16/fact-sheet-president-and -first-lady-s-call-action-college-opportunity.

17. National Skills Coalition, "Middle-Skill Jobs: United States" (Washington, DC: National Skills Coalition, 2014), http://www.nationalskillscoalition.org/resources /publications/file/middle-skill-fact-sheets-2014/NSC-United-States-MiddleSkillFS -2014.pdf.

18. Ibid.

19. Tamar Jacoby, "Vocational Education 2.0: Employers Hold the Key to Better Career Training," *Civic Report* 83 (November) (New York: Manhattan Institute, 2013).

20. Anthony P. Carnevale et al., *Career Clusters: Forecasting Demand for High School Through College Jobs, 2008–2018* (Washington, DC: Georgetown University Cen-

ter on Education and the Workforce, 2011), http://www.nrccte.org/sites/default/files/uploads/clusters-complete-update1.pdf.

21. D. Hendricks, "That Shop Class Could Be Valuable," *My San Antonio*, March 15, 2013, http://www.mysanantonio.com/business/business_columnists/david_hend ricks/article/That-shop-class-could-be-valuable-4358516.php.

22. MaryJo Webster, "Where the Jobs Are: The New Blue Collar," *USA Today*, September 30, 2014, http://www.usatoday.com/story/news/nation/2014/09/30/job-economy-middle-skill-growth-wage-blue-collar/14797413/.

23. National Skills Coalition, "State FactSheets" (Washington, DC: National Skills Coalition, 2014), www.nationalskillscoalition.org/state-policy/fact-sheets/.

24. Achieve, Inc., *The Future of the U.S. Workforce: Middle Skills Jobs and the Growing Importance of Postsecondary Education* (Washington, DC: Achieve, Inc.), 12, http://www.achieve.org/files/MiddleSkillsJobs.pdf.

25. ManpowerGroup, "ManpowerGroup Annual Survey Reveals U.S. Talent Shortages Persist in Skilled Trades, Engineers and IT Staff," ManpowerGroup (press release, May 29, 2012), http://press.manpower.com/press/2012/talent-shortage/.

26. Of course, matching people to jobs is not just a question of skills. People can often make more money with the same skills if they are willing to move or work in a different part of the country or even a different part of the state than where they live. However, moving is not always possible, due to family ties and obligations, not to mention the fact that depressed housing prices in certain regions can make it hard to sell one's home and relocate to a more expensive area. Also, a lack of transportation options can make commuting to an area with better wages difficult. For example, in Milwaukee, three-quarters of the jobs are in the suburbs, but for people who don't own a car there are few public transportation options to get to them even if they have the qualifications to compete for them.

27. These figures come from a 2013 study by the Century Foundation. Thirty percent of community college funding comes from state government, while 40 percent comes from the federal government, mostly through the Pell Grant program. Century Foundation Task Force on Preventing Community Colleges from Becoming Separate and Unequal, *Bridging the Higher Education Divide: Strengthening Community Colleges and Restoring the American Dream* (Washington, DC: Century Foundation Press, 2013), https://collegesdorecrd.ed.gov/.

28. While the attention to workforce development in gubernatorial races is encouraging, there are indications that some Republican governors championing workforce training may make job training a mandatory requirement for recipients of public benefits. In the past, such proposals have used mandatory training as a way to move large numbers of people off of essential safety net programs as opposed to helping to move them to self-sufficiency. Governor Walker has indicated that he wants to tie receipt of public benefits in Wisconsin to drug tests and mandatory job training. Governors Brownback (Kansas) and Mead (Wyoming) have indicated that they would like to tie Medicaid expansion to "workforce development" requirements. In addition, some governors appear to be in support of imposing work requirements for certain federal benefits, despite eligibility for waivers that would allow recipients of these benefits to participate in employment-focused adult basic education and job-training programs.

Rachel Unruh, "Analysis: What the 2014 Elections Mean for Skills," National Skills Coalition, November 12, 2014, http://www.nationalskillscoalition.org/news/blog/analysis-what-the-2014-elections-mean-for-skills.

29. "Between 1998 and 2008, the U.S. spent about 0.5 percent of GDP on labor force policies. . . . Most of the money, around 70 percent, went toward what are called 'passive' programs, which support people who have lost their jobs—unemployment insurance is the main example of this kind of program. Only 30 percent of the money went toward 'active' programs, which intervene to help the unemployed find work." Jun Nie and Ethan Struby, "Would Active Labor Market Policies Help Combat High U.S. Unemployment?," *Economic Review* 96, no. 3 (2011): 35–69, https://www.kansascityfed.org/publicat/econrev/pdf/11q3Nie-Struby.pdf.

30. Timothy Williams, "Seeking New Start, Finding Steep Cost Workforce Investment Act Leaves Many Jobless and in Debt," *New York Times*, August 18, 2014, http://www.nytimes.com/2014/08/18/us/workforce-investment-act-leaves-many-jobless-and-in-debt.html.

1. The Limits of the "College Solution"

1. The term "the talented tenth," though indelibly linked to Du Bois, was first coined by Henry Lyman Morehouse, a white liberal for whom Morehouse College was named. Seven years before Du Bois used the phrase, Morehouse wrote an essay in the *Independent* magazine in which he described the role of elites in leadership: "In the discussion concerning Negro education," he wrote, "we should not forget the talented tenth man. An ordinary education may answer for the nine men of mediocrity; if this is all we offer the talented tenth man, we make a prodigious mistake. . . . The tenth man, with superior natural endowments, symmetrically trained and highly developed, may become a mightier influence, a greater inspiration to others than all the other nine, or nine times nine like them." Quoted by Henry Louis Gates in his essay "Who Really Invented the 'Talented Tenth'?," *The Root*, February 18, 2013, http://www.theroot.com/articles/history/2013/02/talented_tenth_theory_web_du_bois_did_not_really_invent_it.html.

2. W. E. B. Du Bois, "The Talented Tenth," from *The Negro Problem: A Series of Articles by Representative American Negroes of Today* (New York: J. Pott, 1903).

3. Gates, "Who Invented the 'Talented Tenth'?"

4. Ibid.

5. Data come from the US Census Bureau October Current Population survey. Richard Fry, "U.S. High School Dropout Rate Reaches Record Low, Driven by Improvements Among Hispanics, Blacks," *FactTank*, October 2, 2014 (Washington, DC: Pew Research Center), http://www.pewresearch.org/fact-tank/2014/10/02/u-s-high-school-dropout-rate-reaches-record-low-driven-by-improvements-among-hispanics-blacks/.

6. See Susan Aud, Sidney Wilkinson-Flicker, Thomas Nachazel, and Allison Dziuba, *The Condition of Education 2013*, National Center for Education Statistics, 2013-037 (Washington, DC: US Department of Education, 2013). See also Alexandria Walton Radford, Lutz Berkner, Sara Wheeless, and Bryan Shepherd, *Persistence and Attainment of 2003–04 Beginning Postsecondary Students: After 6 Years, First Look*, National Center for Education Statistics 2011-151 (Washington, DC: US Department of Education, December 2010), http://nces.ed.gov/pubs2011/2011151.pdf.

7. "Digest of Education Statistics," US Department of Education, Institute of Education Sciences, National Center for Education Statistics (2014), https://nces.ed.gov/programs/digest/d14/tables/dt14_104.20.asp.

8. Anna M. Phillips and Robert Gebeloff, "In Data, 'A' Schools Leave Many Not Ready

for CUNY," *New York Times*, June 21, 2011, http://www.nytimes.com/2011/06/22 /nyregion/many-from-a-rated-nyc-schools-need-help-at-cuny.html.

9. Jennifer Wine, Natasha Janson, Sara Wheeless, and Tracy Hunt-White, *2004/09 Beginning Postsecondary Students Longitudinal Study (BPS:04/09): Full-scale Methodology Report*, US Department of Education, Center for Education Statistics, 2012-246 (November 2011), http://nces.ed.gov/pubs2012/2012246_1.pdf.

10. "Like so many other community colleges, particularly those serving low-income students in urban areas, CUNY's six community colleges have long struggled to improve their graduation rates. CUNY's colleges have a track record of innovation and experimentation reaching back decades. They introduced summer immersion workshops in the mid-1980s and learning communities in the 1990s and 2000s. The College Now program, offered through both the community and the senior colleges, has long been a mainstay of the University's collaboration with the New York City public schools aimed at better preparing high school students for college. CUNY is also home to LaGuardia's path-breaking use of e-Portfolios, and to experiments with remedial instruction that have included acceleration and contextualized instruction. Yet despite its best intentions and its proven willingness to innovate, the University must confront a stubborn fact: Graduation rates have not improved. Since the early 1990s, the six-year degree completion rate for freshmen entering associate programs has oscillated within a range of 25% to 28%. Recently, one-year retention rates have begun to rise, signaling hope for improvement in graduation rates not too far in the future. But even if higher graduation rates do materialize, they are not likely to match the high aspirations of our students and the best intentions of faculty and administrators." CUNY Office of Academic Affairs, *Proposals to Improve Success Rates for Students in Developmental Education at CUNY*, Report of the Working Group on Remediation, CUNY Office of Academic Affairs (August 2011), http://www.cuny.edu/about/administration/offices/ue /cue/ReportoftheRemediationWorkingGroup8-11.pdf.

11. Paul Attewell and David Lavin, *Passing the Torch: Does Higher Education for the Disadvantaged Pay Off Across the Generations?* (New York: Russell Sage Foundation Press, 2007).

12. Even more important, perhaps, is Attewell and Lavin's finding that the adult children of first-time college-going students experience significant income and occupational mobility as a consequence of their mother's education. Ibid.

13. According to the US Government Accountability Office, the annual median family income in 2008 of for-profit college students was $22,932; that of private, nonprofit college students was $61,827; that of public colleges was $44,878. Veterans and their families also make up a significant percentage of the for-profit student demographic. In 2011, black and Hispanic students made up 28 percent of undergraduate students nationwide, but they represented nearly half of all students in the for-profit college sector, which includes large online schools such as the University of Phoenix, Kaplan University, and smaller, privately owned trade schools. For-profit students also tend to be female and single parents. Institute for Higher Education Policy, "Portraits: Initial College Attendance of Low-Income Young Adults" (Washington, DC: Institute for Higher Education Policy, June 2011), http://www .ihep.org/research/publications/portraits-initial-college-attendance-low-income -young-adults.

14. Ibid.

15. Representation of low-income students grew from 15 percent to 19 percent in the

for-profits and dropped from 20 percent to 15 percent in public four-year institutions. Ibid.

16. John Lauerman, "Pell Grant Cuts Hurt For-Profit Colleges After 8-Fold Rise," *Bloomberg Business*, April 15, 2011, http://www.bloomberg.com/news/articles/2011 -04-15/pell-grant-cuts-hurt-for-profit-college-after-8-fold-increase.

17. *HuffPost College*, "Pell Grants and For-Profit Colleges: Where the Money Goes (PHOTOS)," July 28, 2010 [updated May 25, 2011], http://www.huffingtonpost.com /2010/07/28/pell-grants-and-for-profi_n_661826.html.

18. This analysis was conducted by the Federal Reserve Bank of New York. Meta Brown, Andrew Haughwout, Donghoon Lee, Maricar Mabutas, and Wilbert van der Klaauw, "Grading Student Loans," *Liberty Street Economics*, March 5, 2012 (Federal Reserve Bank of New York), http://libertystreeteconomics.newyorkfed.org/2012 /03/grading-student-loans.html?.

19. Adrienne Lu, "States Crack Down on For-Profit Colleges, Student Loan Industry," *Stateline*, April 14, 2014 (The Pew Charitable Trusts), http://www.pewtrusts.org/en /research-and-analysis/blogs/stateline/2014/04/14/states-crack-down-on-forprofit -colleges-student-loan-industry.

20. Massie Ritsch, "Fact: Too Many Career-Training Programs Lead to Low Wages, High Debt," Homeroom, The Official Blog of the U.S. Department of Education, April 2014, http://www.ed.gov/blog/2014/04/fact-too-many-career-training -programs-lead-to-low-wages-high-debt/.

21. The 72 percent statistic, which came from Arne Duncan and the Department of Education, used Current Population Survey data to put the median high-school dropout's annual wage at $22,860. The Labor Department, which put the median annual wage about $4,000 lower than the DOE, found that only 49 percent of these programs produced graduates who earned less, on average, than high-school dropouts. The same article noted that officials also confirmed that graduates of 57 percent of private institutions (a range that included Harvard's dental school and child-care training programs) earn less than high school dropouts. The argument here is that, in trying to make a point, the DOE compared apples to oranges. See Glenn Kessler, "Do 72 Percent of For-Profit Programs Have Graduates Making Less Than High School Dropouts?," *Washington Post*, April 11, 2014, http://www.washingtonpost .com/blogs/fact-checker/wp/2014/04/11/the-obama-administrations-claim-that-72 -percent-of-for-profits-programs-have-graduates-making-less-than-high-school -dropouts/.

22. Education Secretary Arne Duncan, news conference at the White House, March 14, 2014. "Obama Administration Takes Action to Protect Americans from Predatory, Poor-Performing Career Colleges," press release, March 14, 2014, US Department of Education, http://www.ed.gov/news/press-releases/obama-administration-takes -action-protect-americans-predatory-poor-performing-career-colleges.

23. "Benefitting Whom? For-Profit Education Companies and the Growth of Military Educational Benefits," US Senate, Health, Education, Labor and Pensions Committee, Tom Harkin, chairman, December 8, 2010, http://www.nacacnet.org/issues -action/LegislativeNews/Documents/HELPMilEdReport.PDF.

24. Frank Donoghue, "Who Goes to For-Profit Colleges?," *Chronicle of Higher Education*, June 27, 2011, http://chronicle.com/blogs/innovations/who-goes-to-for-profit -colleges/29725.

25. As James Rosenbaum has pointed out, underneath this average lie huge disparities between BA recipients who were at the bottom of the high school performance dis-

tribution and those who emerged from high school with stronger records. The lowest-earning BA holders earned only $3,000 more over thirty years than the average BA holder. James E. Rosenbaum, *Beyond College for All: Career Paths for the Forgotten Half* (New York: Russell Sage Foundation, 2001).

26. US Department of Education, College Scorecard, https://collegescorecard.ed.gov/.

27. Austin Clemens and Marshall Steinbaum, "The cruel game of musical chairs in the US labor market," http://equitablegrowth.org/research/cruel-game-musical-chairs-u-s-labor-market/ Posted September 2, 2015 at 8:15 a.m.

28. Jaison R. Abel, Richard Deitz, and Yaqin Sin, "Are Recent College Graduates Finding Good Jobs?," *Current Issues in Economics and Finance* 20, no. 1 (Federal Reserve Bank of New York, 2014), http://www.newyorkfed.org/research/current_issues/ci20-1.pdf.

29. Abel and colleagues reported the underemployment rate from 1990 to 2012 for two different groups: all college graduates and recent college graduates. For college graduates as a whole, the underemployment rate has held steady at around 33 percent over the past two decades—meaning that about one in three college-educated workers typically holds a job that does not require a degree. The fact that the rate has remained fairly uniform at different points in the business cycle suggests that it is not unusual for a significant share of college graduates to work in jobs that do not require a degree.

"For recent college graduates, the picture looks quite different. First, in all years, the underemployment rate is higher for recent college graduates than for college graduates as a whole, indicating that underemployment is consistently more widespread for this group. Second, the underemployment rate for new college graduates has not held steady. The rate rose to 46 percent during the 1990–91 recession, then fell significantly during the economic expansion of the 1990s. By 2001, the rate had dropped to 34 percent. During the first decade of the 2000s, the underemployment rate rose somewhat sharply after both the 2001 and 2007–09 recessions and, in each case, only partially retreated, resulting in an increase to roughly 44 percent by 2012. Thus, it appears that the underemployment rate has, in fact, been rising for recent college graduates since 2001. Nevertheless, the high rate over the past few years is not unprecedented; rather, it represents a return to the level that prevailed in the early 1990s. . . . This pattern suggests that recent graduates do, in fact, tend to have relatively high levels of underemployment upon graduation, but that underemployment declines as these graduates spend time in the labor market. However, the age-underemployment profile we estimate for 2009–2011 is somewhat higher than the profile for 1990, and significantly higher than the profile seen in 2000."

30. David H. Autor, "Skills, Education, and the Rise of Earnings Inequality Among the 'Other 99 Percent,'" *Science* 344, no. 6186 (May 23, 2014): 843–51, http://www.sciencemag.org/content/344/6186/843.

31. Mary Beth Marklein, "Study Examines Vocational Certificates' Big Rewards," *USA Today*, June 5, 2012, http://usatoday30.usatoday.com/news/education/story/2012-06-06/vocational-education-degrees-pay/55410846/1.

32. Ibid.

2. A History of Ambivalence

1. The names of students in this chapter are pseudonyms.

2. Inside Schools, "Sheepshead Bay High School," http://insideschools.org/component/schools/school/937.

3. Ibid. Today, Sheepshead Bay High School does have some rigorous preprofessional programs in health sciences, law, and math and finance, and most of the students in these programs do go to college (of 2005 graduates, 76 percent went to college, with nearly two-thirds of college-bound graduates headed to four-year schools). However, it is unclear whether these programs existed when Melissa was a student there.

4. According to the US Census, one in four high school students work. Carrie Coppernoll, "1 in 4 High School Students Work, U.S. Census Finds, Including Many in Oklahoma to Support Families," *NewsOK*, January 25, 2013, http://newsok.com /1-in-4-high-school-students-work-u.s.-census-finds-including-many-in-oklahoma -to-support-families/article/3748886.

5. N. Deterding, "Defining American Vocationalism: A Person-Centered Approach to Modeling High School Work Orientation and Post-Secondary Outcomes," paper presented at Innovative Approaches for Using Publicly Available Data for Social Policy Research, Institute for Quantitative Social Sciences, Harvard University, December 2010.

   Using a model-based clustering technique and data from the National Longitudinal Survey of Youth 1997 (NYSY97), Deterding defined a four-category typology to represent high school "workforce orientation," using information about students' course-taking, employment, and school-to-work behaviors. She used this typology to examine two central questions in the tracking literature in the sociology of education: 1) Is there observable demographic sorting of high school students into groups with different workforce orientation? 2) What are the postsecondary education and labor market outcomes for students taking different paths? Results indicate that while academic students are substantially more advantaged than their peers, students in the three nonacademic groups are quite demographically similar, allaying fears that the most disadvantaged students are shunted into early workforce preparation. When compared to the other nonacademic students, work-oriented students display more positive early labor market outcomes. The data indicate that unfocused students, whose experiences prepare them for neither further education nor the workforce, faced the most substantial challenges after high school.

6. The average work-oriented student spent 84 percent of his or her time in work or in school, greater than the 79 percent spent by Mid Mixers and similar to the amount of time academic students were occupied between ages eighteen and twenty-two (Model 1b).

7. Andrew J. Hawkins, "Vocational Students Graduate at Higher Rates," *Crain's New York Business*, February 24, 2014, http://www.crainsnewyork.com/article/20140224 /BLOGS04/140229933/vocational-students-graduate-at-higher-rates.

8. The New York State Education Department applied for, and was granted, a waiver allowing the New York City Department of Education greater flexibility in the provision of No Child Left Behind programs.

9. Ursulina Ramirez and Edith Anne Sharp, *Path to the Future: Strengthening Career and Technical Education to Prepare Today's Students for the Jobs of Tomorrow*, Report by the Office of Bill de Blasio, Public Advocate for the City of New York, January 2012, http://archive.advocate.nyc.gov/cte.

10. Harry J. Holzer, Dane Linn, and Wanda Monthey, "The Promise of High-Quality Career and Technical Education: Improving Outcomes for Students, Firms, and the Economy," the College Board and Georgetown Center on Poverty, Inequality, and

Public Policy (October 2013), http://www.careertechnj.org/wp-content/uploads/2013/11/Georgetown.BR_.CB-CTE-report-11.2013.pdf.

11. Colonial Williamsburg Foundation, "Q & A: Colonial Apprenticeships," http://www.history.org/history/teaching/enewsletter/volume4/november05/apprenticeship.cfm.

12. Melvin L. Barlow, "200 Years of Vocational Education, 1776–1976: The Vocational Education Age Emerges, 1876–1926," *American Vocational Journal* 51, no. 5 (May 1976): 45–58, eric.ed.gov?id-EJB9040.

13. Ibid.

14. Herbert M. Kliebard, *The Struggle for the American Curriculum: 1893–1953* (New York: Routledge & Kegan Paul, 1987).

15. Annual Report of the Bureau of Industries for the Province of Ontario, January 1, 1894, p. 86.

16. Ibid.

17. Kliebard draws this conclusion based on an exhaustive history of American curricular reform from the 1870s to 1950. Ibid.

18. Charles H. Ham, *The Co-Education Mind and Hand*, Monograph prepared for the New York College for the Training of Teachers, vol. 3, no. 4 (July) (New York: T. Laurie, 1890).

19. Stephen F. Hamilton, *Apprenticeship for Adulthood: Preparing Youth for the Future* (New York: Free Press, 1990), 92.

20. Claudia Goldin and Lawrence F. Katz, "Mass Secondary Schooling and the State: The Role of State Compulsion in the High School Movement," in *Understanding Long-Run Economic Growth: Geography, Institutions, and the Knowledge Economy*, ed. Dora L. Costa and Naomi Lamoreaux, National Bureau of Economic Research (Chicago: University of Chicago Press, 2011).

21. W. Norton Grubb and Marvin Lazerson, "Community Colleges Need to Build on Their Strengths," *Chronicle of Higher Education*, Community Colleges, Special Supplement, October 29, 2004, http://web.monroecc.edu/Manila/webfiles/MCCMiddleStates/CommCollBuildStrength.pdf.

22. Aviation High School in New York was founded in 1925. In 1957, the School of Aviation Trades moved into a new $9 million facility in Long Island City, Queens, and became the new Aviation High School. For a short history of the school, see Aviation High School, "School History," Aviation High School, last modified February 11, 2012, http://www.aviationhs.net/site_res_view_template.aspx?id=a057d48e-a5d4-4049-86df-12ff765a9577.

23. Harlow G. Unger, "Federal Committee on Apprentice Training," *Encyclopedia of American Education,* 3rd ed. (New York: Facts on File, 2007). American History Online, Facts on File, Inc.

24. Rutgers School of Management and Labor Relations, "History of Labor Education at Rutgers University," Carey Library, Rutgers University, http://smlr.rutgers.edu/smlr/smlr/smlr/carey-library/exhibits-and-collections-at-the-carey-library/history-of-labor-education.

25. M. L. Wolfe, "The Vocational Education Act of 1963, as Amended: A Background Paper" (Washington, DC: Congressional Research Service, Library of Congress, 1978).

26. Lawrence Mishel, "Unions, Inequality, and Faltering Middle-Class Wages" (Economic Policy Institute, August 29, 2012).

27. Robert D. Atkinson, Luke A. Stewart, Scott M. Andes, and Stephen J. Ezell, *Worse*

Than the Great Depression: What Experts Are Missing About American Manufacturing Decline (Information Technology & Innovation Foundation, March 2012), http://www2.itif.org/2012-american-manufacturing-decline.pdf.

28. See Mary Brinton's book *Lost in Transition*, which describes the enormous difficulty of Japanese youth in today's labor market, now that the financial bubble has burst. Mary Brinton, *Lost in Transition: Youth, Work, and Instability in Postindustrial Japan* (Cambridge, UK: Cambridge University Press, 2011).

29. Specialization required taking four or more courses in a single occupational program with at least two of those courses beyond the introductory level. (Vocational education is defined as family and consumer sciences education [home economics, child development, food and nutrition, clothing], general labor market preparation [typing, word processing, career exploration], and specific labor market preparation [which consists of ten areas: agriculture, business, marketing, communications, trade and industry, health care, child care and education, protective services, food service and hospitality, and personal and other services].) Karen Levesque, Doug Lauen, Peter Teitelbaum, Martha Alt, and Sally Librera, *Vocational Education in the United States: Toward the Year 2000. Statistical Analysis Report*, National Center for Education Statistics, 2000-02 (Washington, DC: US Department of Education, 2000), http://files.eric.ed.gov/fulltext/ED437583.pdf.

30. Thomas Bailey and Katherine Hughes, *Employer Involvement in Work-Based Learning Programs* (Berkeley: University of California, Berkeley, National Center for Research in Vocational Education, 1999), http://files.eric.ed.gov/fulltext/ED436641.pdf.

31. Robert I. Lerman, "Can the United States Expand Apprenticeship? Lessons from Experience," IZA Policy Paper, No. 46 (Bonn: Forschungsinstitut zur Zukunft der Arbeit, 2012), https://www.econstor.eu/dspace/bitstream/10419/91788/1/pp46.pdf.

32. Richard Kazis, *Pennsylvania Youth Apprenticeship Program: An Historical Account from Its Origins to September 1991* (Cambridge, MA: Jobs for the Future, 1991), 23, about a youth apprenticeship program in Pennsylvania.

33. Mary Agnes Hamilton and Stephen F. Hamilton, "Toward a Youth Apprenticeship System: A Progress Report from the Youth Apprenticeship Demonstration Project in Broome County, New York" (Ithaca, NY: College of Human Ecology at Cornell University, 1993), http://files.eric.ed.gov/fulltext/ED393970.pdf.

34. Jobs for the Future, *Voices from School and Home: Wisconsin Parents and Students Focus on Youth Apprenticeship* (Cambridge, MA: Jobs for the Future, 1991), 23.

35. Beyond these concerns, it seems American employers have long been less concerned about "hard skill," assuming they will provide it on the job, and more concerned about "soft skills," which are often less developed among young people.

In a 1995 paper on encouraging employer involvement in youth apprenticeship programs, Christine Bremer, a researcher at the University of Minnesota's Institute on Community Integration, and Svetlana Madzar, senior lecturer in strategic management and organization at the University of Minnesota, cite a 1991 *Harvard Business Review* article (viii) that reported that while many employers complain about the quality of job applicants, only 5 percent of employers expected education and skill requirements to rise. Further, only 15 percent of employers reported that they had difficulty finding appropriately skilled workers. These employers were primarily in craft-apprentice trades and traditionally female-dominated occupations such as nursing and secretarial work. "The skills more than 80 percent of employers worried about were not academic but social—a good work ethic, a pleasant demeanor, reliability" (p. 52). Discussions of high-skill workplaces tend to center around technical and problem-solving skills, not social skills. Few employers are likely to have much interest in attempting to teach social skills to young people. Similarly, employers do not wish to raise expectations about the availability of jobs by providing technical training unless there is a clear need for additional employees. Christine D. Bremer and Svetlana Madzar, "Encouraging Employer Involvement in Youth Apprenticeship and Other Work-Based Learning Experiences for High School Students," *Journal of Vocational and Technical Education* 12, no. 1 (Fall 1995), http://scholar.lib.vt.edu/ejournals/JVTE/v12n1/bremer.html#Stone3.

36. Ramirez and Sharp, *Path to the Future.*

37. "O Brave New World," *Economist* (London), no. 7854 (March 12, 1994): 19–20, 26.

38. For a more extensive timeline on this program, see "Youth Apprenticeship History," State of Wisconsin, Department of Workforce Development, http://dwd.wisconsin .gov/youthapprenticeship/history.htm.

39. Harvey Kantor and David B. Tyack, eds., *Work, Youth, and Schooling: Historical Perspectives on Vocationalism in American Education* (Palo Alto, CA: Stanford University Press, 1982).

40. Torben Iversen, of the Institute for Quantitative Social Science at Harvard, and Marius Busemeyer, professor of political science at the University of Konstanz, argue that "as important as it is to focus on the supply side, this is still insufficient from a comparative perspective because wages in many countries are not determined simply by demand and supply, but rather by agreements reached through collective bargaining. If unions and business associations set wages, the supply of newly skilled workers only matters for the dispersion of wages if already skilled workers adjust their wages downward. Employers in fluid and nonunionized labor markets that rely on general-skill workers will be able to replace older and better-paid skilled workers in response to rising supply. In contrast, when workers have acquired firm- or industry-specific skills or high institutional barriers against replacing workers exist, there is (often a large) cost involved in skilled labor turnover. This cost can be used by unions to block the downward adjustment of wages." Marius R. Busemeyer and Torben Iversen, "Collective Skill Systems, Wage Bargaining, and Labor Market Stratification," in *The Political Economy of Collective Skill Formation*, ed. Marius R. Busemeyer and Torben Iversen (New York: Oxford University Press, 2012), 205–33.

41. Margarita Estevez-Abe, Torben Iversen, and David Soskice, "Social Protection and the Formation of Skills: A Reinterpretation of the Welfare State," in *Varieties of Capitalism: The Institutional Foundations of Comparative Advantage*, ed. Peter A. Hall and David Soskice (New York: Oxford University Press, 2001).

3. The New Vocational Turn in American High Schools

1. In addition to this, there are also what is known as career academies, or schools within schools that focus on career areas such as health sciences, law, business, and finance; while these schools do offer some form of work-based learning, unlike vocational high schools, they are not generally intended to lead directly to a job after graduation.

2. Paul Barnwell, "Will the Common Core Derail True College and Career Readiness?," *Education Week, Teacher,* June 25, 2013, http://www.edweek.org/tm/articles /2013/06/25/fp_barnwell_career.html.

3. Meredith Goldstein, Globe Staff, "MCAS Goals Upgraded," *Boston Globe*, September 28, 2003, http://www.boston.com/news/local/articles/2003/09/28/mcas_goals_upgraded/.

4. Ibid.

5. Alison Fraser and William Donovan, "Hands-On Achievement: Why Massachusetts Vocational Technical Schools Have Low Dropout Rates," Pioneer Institute White Paper, no. 96 (January 2013), www.shawssheentech.org/pdf/Voc-Tech%20wp%20FINAL.pdf.

6. These services help to link the school to the wider community, which may not have a direct impact on specific training but keeps the community aware of what goes on at the school and also brings the kids into contact with the public in a way that fosters "soft" skills.

7. Leslie Garisto Pfaff, "Tech Time: New Jersey's Vocational Schools," *New Jersey Monthly*, August 28, 2014, old.njmonthly.com/articles/towns-schools/tech-time-new-jerseys-vocational-schools/html.

8. But then again, all of these young women were going on to college and this may make a big difference. They don't feel like they can't hack it.

9. Students who score at level 3 or 4 have met or exceeded state learning standards. Students who score at level 1 or 2 have not met standards and may not be promoted to the next grade level.

10. Eliza Shapiro, "Brooklyn Principal Insists Her School Is Improving, Slowly," *Politico New York*, March 18, 2015, http://www.capitalnewyork.com/article/city-hall/2015/03/8564239/brooklyn-principal-insists-her-school-improving-slowly.

11. John Hildebrand, "Regents: High School Students Can Seek Waiver of One History Exam," *Newsday*, January 12, 2015, http://www.newsday.com/long-island/regents-high-school-students-can-seek-waiver-of-one-history-exam-1.9800090.

4. What Industry Needs

1. Joleen Kirschenman and Kathryn M Neckerman, "'We'd Love to Hire Them, But . . .': The Meaning of Race for Employers," *Urban Underclass* 203 (Washington, DC: Brookings Institution, 1991), 203–32.

2. Deirdre Royster, *Race and the Invisible Hand: How White Networks Exclude Black Men from Blue-Collar Jobs* (Berkeley: University of California Press, 2003).

3. Rosenbaum, *Beyond College for All*, 136.

4. Despite the bad name that standardized tests have garnered, especially for bias of various kinds, in employment it has been shown that firms making use of tests are fairer in their hiring decisions than those that rely on interviews. Data are superior to subjective judgments, even if the data have its problems. "There is evidence that shifts in the demand for labor are disadvantaging young black men. To help explain this change, we analyze a set of quantitative measures derived from face-to-face interviews of employers in Detroit and Los Angeles. The measures encompass employer skill demands, hiring procedures, and racial attitudes, with racial representation (relative to the key outcome variable). Among other results, we find lower black representation (relative to area population) in firms with a literacy or numeracy requirement and firms that rely on the personnel interview as their primary screening device."

Christopher Tilly, "Skills and Race in Hiring: Quantitative Findings from Face-to-face Interviews" (with Philip Moss), *Eastern Economic Journal* 21, no. 3 (1995): 357–74.

5. Deirdre Royster's work shows that even when black and white students are trained in the same vocational programs, the homegrown, kinship, and neighborhood-based networks of whites advantage them in job seeking. This is why institutions need to step in and cultivate employer connections. Royster, *Race and the Invisible Hand*.

6. John H. Bishop and Ferran Mañe, "The Impact of School-Business Partnerships," in *The School-to-Work Movement: Origins and Destinations*, ed. William J. Stull and Nicholas Sanders (Westport, CT: Praeger, 2003), 189–202.

7. The report touted public-private partnerships as a way of creating new schools that would be better aligned with opportunities in the job market and set forth a list of broad and vague recommendations for improvement, including: defining core competencies all students need to succeed; expanding beyond core competencies to skills and knowledge needed for successful postsecondary transitions; empowering industry to define sector-specific skills; creating innovative courses and programs of study; and putting more students on a path to success. The report also advocated altering funding so that schools offering CTE classes would get more money and developing alternative, non-Regents-based assessments of their students. Mayoral Task Force on Career and Technical Education Innovation, *Next-Generation Career and Technical Education in New York City*, Final Report and Recommendations (July 2008), http://schools.nyc.gov/NR/rdonlyres/91B215BF-21F8-4E11-9676 -8AFCFBB170E0/0/NYC_CTE_728_lowres.pdf.

8. In Massachusetts, all vocational teachers must be certified by the Massachusetts Department of Elementary and Secondary Education (DESE) and have specific education credentials. They also have to have six years of work experience in the field in which they are licensed (this requirement can be reduced to four years if they have gone through some sort of degree program in their field, for example, an RN degree). For certain fields, program instructors are required to have Massachusetts and/or federal government– or industry-issued licenses or certifications. Vocational teachers also have to pass written and performance subject area tests, and anyone seeking to teach in a VT program is required to pass either the standard MTEL Communication and Literacy Skills Test or the Vocational and Technical Literacy Skills Test (all of the academic teachers at VT schools are required to hold state academic licenses in their fields of instruction). In addition, every five years VT teachers have to recertify by amassing 150 professional development points, half of which have to be specific to the trade in which they teach. Massachusetts Department of Elementary and Secondary Education, "Chapter 74 Guide for Professional Vocational Technical Educator License Renewal," Office of Educator Licensure, (n.d.), http://www.mass.gov/edu/docs/ese/educator-effectiveness/licensing/vte-chapter -74-guide-professional-license-renewal.pdf.

9. According to a report by the US Department of Education for the school year 2010–11, the estimated national four-year adjusted cohort graduation rate for public high school students was 79 percent and for the school year 2011–12 it was 80 percent. This indicates that nearly 4 out of 5 students receive a regular high school diploma within four years. Marie C. Stetser and Robert Stillwell, "Public High School Four-Year On-Time Graduation Rates and Event Dropout Rates: School Years 2010–11 and 2011–12: First Look," National Center for Education Statistics, 2014-391 (Washington, DC: US Department of Education, 2014), http://nces.ed.gov/pubs2014 /2014391.pdf.

10. According to the US Census Bureau, educational and health services added the most jobs to the county between 2007 and 2012. The jobs doing the most hiring

in 2011–12 were accommodation and food services and the retail trade, most of which can be attributed to the high concentration of seasonal resorts in the area. "Key Industries in Cape May County, NJ," Office of Research and Information, Data for Decision Making Series (May 2013), http://capemaycountynj.gov /DocumentCenter/Home/View/436.

11. Project Lead the Way is a nonprofit provider of STEM curricula and professional development nationwide, and in the South Carolina high schools it is considered an honors program for college-bound students.

12. This is a pseudonym.

5. The Community College Connection

1. In 2004, the majority of postsecondary students were pursing vocational fields: 81 percent of students in certificate programs, 64 percent of students in associate's degree programs, and 60 percent of students in bachelor's degree programs. Karen Levesque et al., *Career and Technical Education in the United States: 1990–2005: Statistical Analysis Report,* National Center for Education Statistics, 2008-035 (Washington, DC: US Department of Education, 2008), https://nces.ed.gov/pubs2008 /2008035.pdf.

2. American Association of Community Colleges, "2015 Fact Sheet" (Washington, DC: American Association of Community Colleges, 2015), http://www.aacc.nche.edu /AboutCC/Documents/FactSheet2015_grey.pdf.

3. Scholars have debated whether community colleges divert students away from four-year institutions or whether they serve students who otherwise would not have attended college. On the one hand, community colleges have allowed state universities to become more selective. See Kevin Dougherty, *The Contradictory College: The Conflicting Origins, Impacts, and Futures of the Community College* (Albany: State University of New York Press, 1994). On the other hand, more than half of community college students are nontraditional students who probably would not have attended four-year institutions.

    See Thomas J. Kane and Cecilia Elena Rouse, "The Community College: Educating Students at the Margin Between College and Work," *Journal of Economic Perspectives* 13, no. 1 (1999): 63–84.

4. Ten percent of students at public four-year institutions were African American and 9 percent were Hispanic. Laura Horn and Stephanie Nevill, *Profile of Undergraduates in U.S. Postsecondary Institutions: 2003–04: Statistical Analysis Report*, National Center for Education Statistics, 2006-184 (Washington, DC: US Department of Education, 2006), http://nces.ed.gov/pubs2006/2006184_rev.pdf. See also "Background Information on Community Colleges" (National Center on Education and the Economy, May 2013), http://www.ncee.org/wp-content/uploads/2013 /05/Community-College-Background-Reportjcc1.pdf.

5. In 2013 median age of community college students was twenty-four, compared to twenty-one years old at public four-year institutions. Thirty-five percent of community-college students were thirty years old or older (compared with 13 percent at public four-year institutions), 18 percent were between twenty-four and twenty-nine years old (compared to 16 percent), and 38 percent were between nineteen and twenty-three years old (compared with 60 percent at public four-year institutions). "2015 Community College Fast Fact," American Association of Community Colleges (January 2015), http://www.aacc.nche.edu/AboutCC/Pages/fastfactsfactsheet .aspx.

6. In 2011–12, 17 percent of community college students were single parents. "2014 Fact Sheet," American Association of Community Colleges (January 2014), http://www.aacc.nche.edu/AboutCC/Documents/Facts14_Data_R3.pdf.

7. Mina Dadgar and Madeline Joy Trimble, "Labor Market Returns to Sub-Baccalaureate Credentials: How Much Does a Community College Degree or Certificate Pay?," *Educational Evaluation and Policy Analysis* (2014): 1–20 DOI: 10.3102/0162373714553814.

8. Forty-three percent reported seeking an associate's degree, 17 percent reported seeking a certificate, 42 percent reported seeking job skills, and 46 percent reported enrolling for personal interest. Burton R. Clark, "The 'Cooling-out' Function in Higher Education," *American Journal of Sociology* 65, no. 6 (May 1960): 569–76.

9. Ibid.

10. Doug Shapiro, Afet Dundar, Xin Yuan, Autumn T. Harrell, and Phoebe Khasiala Wakhungu, *Completing College: A National View of Student Attainment Rates—Fall 2008 Cohort*, Signature Report No. 8 (Herndon, VA: National Student Clearing-house Research Center, November 2014), http://nscresearchcenter.org/wp-content/uploads/SignatureReport8.pdf.

11. Ibid.

12. This is especially worrisome with respect to underrepresented minorities. Data from the Beginning Post Secondary Students (BPS) Longitudinal Study (2003–2009) found that only 17.1 percent of black and 15.4 percent of Latino men who enter the community college will have earned a certificate, degree, or transferred to a four-year college or university within 150 percent of normal time (three years). In contrast, 27 percent of white men will have attained their goals in this same time frame.

    BPS (2009). *Three year attainment rates for community college students, by male, by race/ethnicity.* Computed using PowerStats. Washington, DC: National Center for Education Statistics.

    Also see Thomas Bailey, Davis Jenkins, and D. Timothy Leinbach, "What We Know about Community College Low-Income and Minority Student Outcomes: Descriptive Statistics from National Surveys" (Community College Research Center, Teachers College, Columbia University, 2005), http://ccrc.tc.columbia.edu/publications/low-income-minority-student-outcomes.html.

    Thomas R. Bailey, Shanna Smith Jaggers, and David Jenkins. *Redesigning America's Community Colleges: A Clearer Path to Student Success.* Cambridge, MA: Harvard University Press, April 2015.

13. Quoted in Steven Brint and Jerome Karabel, *The Diverted Dream: Community Colleges and the Promise of Educational Opportunity in America, 1900–1985* (New York: Oxford University Press, 1989), 35.

14. Ibid., xliii.

15. Ibid., 84.

16. A 2009 study by the Center for American Progress on the existing state of collaboration between community colleges and apprenticeship programs stated that "just over half the sponsors report using a community college or a public technical college for the related instruction. Since programs differ significantly in terms of the number of apprentices, most apprentices still might not use community colleges. Only about one-third of all apprentices obtain their academic instruction from community or technical colleges." Brian Pusser and John Levin, "Re-imagining

Community Colleges in the 21st Century: A Student-Centered Approach to Higher Education" (Center for American Progress, December 2009), https://cdn.americanprogress.org/wp-content/uploads/issues/2009/12/pdf/community_colleges_reimagined.pdf.

17. Brint and Karabel, *Diverted Dream.*

18. Kane and Rouse, "Community College."

19. Dougherty, *Contradictory College,* 191. For additional material on this topic see Community College Research Center, "Senior Research Associates: Kevin Dougherty," Teachers College, http://ccrc.tc.columbia.edu/person/kevin-dougherty.html?other=publications. There is a lot there on funding.

20. In 2010, about 21 percent of community college students majored in the health professions, followed by business and marketing (16 percent), engineering (7 percent), and security/protective services and computer/information services (each 4 percent). Demand for these occupations is robust and community college students are well informed about the prospects. "Background on Community Colleges" (National Center for Education and the Economy, May 2013), http://www.ncee.org/wp-content/uploads/2013/05/Community-College-Background-Reportjcc1.pdf.

21. Sarah Bohn, Belinda Reyes, and Hans Johnson, "The Impact of Budget Cuts on California's Community Colleges" (Public Policy Institute of California, March 2013), http://www.ppic.org/content/pubs/report/R_313SBR.pdf.

22. David Moltz, "Vying for Limited Slots," *Inside Higher Ed,* July 21, 2010, https://www.insidehighered.com/news/2010/07/21/nursing#sthash.NwQC1W75.dpbs.

23. Libby Nelson, "More Students and Not Enough Space: Rural Community Colleges Discuss Challenges," *Chronicle of Higher Education,* February 24, 2010, http://chronicle.com/article/More-StudentsNot-Enough/64365/.

24. Office of the Press Secretary, "FACT SHEET: A Blueprint to Train Two Million Workers for High-Demand Industries Through a Community College to Career Fund" (White House, Office of the Press Secretary, February 13, 2012), https://www.whitehouse.gov/the-press-office/2012/02/13/fact-sheet-blueprint-train-two-million-workers-high-demand-industries-th.

25. Keith Button, "5 Pros and Cons of Obama's Free Community College Plan," *Education Dive,* January 26, 2015, http://www.educationdive.com/news/5-pros-and-cons-of-obamas-free-community-college-plan/356289/.

26. See Dougherty, *Contradictory College.* In addition, there are higher returns to employment related to the field of study and higher returns for women than men. W. Norton Grubb, "Learning and Earning in the Middle, Part I: National Studies of Pre-baccalaureate Education," *Economics of Education Review* 21, no. 4 (August 2002): 299–321.

27. Kane and Rouse, "Community College"; Grubb, "Learning and Earning."

28. Rosenbaum, *Beyond College for All.*

29. Grubb, "Learning and Earning."

30. Dougherty, *Contradictory College.*

31. Joint union-management apprenticeship programs in the construction industry are less likely than the average program to use community-technical colleges, but outside construction, joint programs are equally likely to assign their apprentices to community-technical colleges.

32. This figure is similar to the share of sponsors supporting the instruction provided by other organizations such as public technical colleges and proprietary trade schools. Robert I. Lerman, "Training Tomorrow's Workforce: Community College

and Apprenticeship as Collaborative Routes to Rewarding Careers" (Center for American Progress, December 2009), https://cdn.americanprogress.org/wp-content/uploads/issues/2009/12/pdf/comm_colleges_apprenticeships.pdf.

33. Michelle Van Noy and James Jacobs, "The Outlook for Noncredit Workforce Education," *New Directions for Community Colleges* 146 (Summer 2009): 87–94.

6. What Vocational Education Could Be: The German Model

1. All of the names in this chapter are pseudonyms (except Hermann Nehls), though the names of the firms are real.

2. MIT political scientist Kathleen Thelen has explored the relationship between collective bargaining and training and how it impacts labor market stratification. She has found that the weakening of collective constraints on individual firm behavior not only decreases the involvement of firms in collective training schemes but also disables built-in protection mechanisms against the potentially deleterious consequences of firm involvement. She has linked labor market stratification in Germany over the last decade to the erosion of the German collective wage-bargaining system. Bruno Palier and Kathleen Thelen, "Institutionalizing Dualism: Complementarities and Change in France and Germany," *Politics and Society* 38, no. 1 (March 2010): 119–48.

3. "When bargaining centralization is high, firm involvement in training has a strongly negative impact on levels of youth unemployment. This negative impact weakens when bargaining is less centralized. Hence, encompassing bargaining institutions are needed as 'beneficial constraints' in order to overcome the problem of rationing training places, a problem representing the flip side of high levels of firm involvement. What is more, public investments in vocational training are not as effective in lowering youth unemployment as are high levels of firm involvement, but they have a negative effect when wage bargaining is highly centralized. This finding resonates well with the sociological literature on labor market transitions." Wolfgang Streeck, "Successful Adjustment to Turbulent Markets: The Automobile Industry," in *Industry and Politics in West Germany: Toward the Third Republic*, ed. Peter J. Katzenstein (Ithaca, NY: Cornell University Press, 1989), 113–56; Wolfgang Streeck, "Beneficial Constraints: On the Economic Limits of Rational Voluntarism," in *Contemporary Capitalism: The Embeddedness of Institutions*, ed. J. Rogers Hollingsworth and Robert Boyer (Cambridge, UK: Cambridge University Press, 1997), 197–219. Wolfgang Streeck, *Social Institutions and Economic Performance: Studies of Industrial Relations in Advanced Capitalist Economies* (London: Sage, 1992), 1–40. See also Jutta Allmendinger, "Educational Systems and Labor Market Outcomes," *European Sociological Review* 5, no. 3 (1989): 231–50; Walter Müller and Markus Gangl, eds., *Transitions from Education to Work in Europe: The Integration of Youth into EU Labour Markets* (New York: Oxford University Press, 2003).

4. While his principal responsibilities were domestic, with the advent of the EU there was a push on to harmonize training policy across the member states. This is particularly important for the southern European countries where youth unemployment remains a crushing burden, boosted up toward 50 percent in Spain, Greece, Italy, and Portugal. Hermann traveled constantly to these regions, spreading the gospel of dual-education systems typical of Germany, Austria, and Luxembourg.

5. German American Chambers of Commerce, "German American Business Outlook 2015: The Annual Survey Among German Firms in the U.S." (German American

Chambers of Commerce, 2015), 7, http://www.gaccmidwest.org/fileadmin/ahk _chicago/GABO/GABO_brochure_2015_final.pdf. Brochure printed by the German American Chambers of Commerce.

6. Michael Axmann, "Apprenticeship System Finance," Graphic Demonstration and Transcript, December 6, 2013, https://prezi.com/su4am9ojtg-q/apprenticeship -system-finance/.

7. *National Assessment of Career and Technical Education: Interim Report* (Washington, DC: US Department of Education, Office of Planning, Evaluation and Policy Development, Policy and Program Studies Service, 2013), https://www2.ed.gov /rschstat/eval/sectech/nacte/career-technical-education/interim-report.pdf.

8. Royster, *Race and the Invisible Hand.*

9. Sandra Susan Smith, *Lone Pursuit: Distrust and Defensive Individualism Among the Black Poor* (New York: Russell Sage Foundation, 2010).

10. "Two Unamalgamated Worlds," *Economist* (London), April 3, 2008, http://www .economist.com/node/10958534.

11. Hermann Nehls, personal communication.

12. Karin Schuller, "Ethnic Inequality in Vocational Education and Training in Germany: The Role of Educational Policy," poster presented at Education Systems: Inequalities, Labour Markets and Civic Engagement Conference, Amsterdam Centre for Inequality Studies, February 13, 2014.

13. Organisation for Economic Co-Operation and Development, *Equal Opportunities?: The Labour Market Integration of the Children of Immigrants* (Paris: OECD Publishing, 2010), http://www.nbbmuseum.be/doc/seminar2010/nl/bibliografie/kansen groepen/ocde2010.pdf.

14. A March 2014 article noted low immigrant participation in the dual apprenticeship system. According to this article, while less than 25 percent of all German companies offer vocational training, only 14 percent of companies run by immigrants do (this is based on numbers from the Federal Institute of Vocational Training). There is a vocational training program for immigrants called KAUSA, which is federally funded and is a part of the Jobstarter program. According to the article, "KAUSA was established with the aim of winning over more companies with immigrant roots to offer training and more young people from immigrant families to pursue vocational training. Since its launch, the program has acquired nearly 9,000 training positions, the majority of them with businesses that have agreed to offer training for the first time." Matilda Jordanova-Duda, "Immigrants Discover Germany's Dual Training System," *DW News*, January 3, 2014 (Deutsche Welle), http://www .dw.com/en/immigrants-discover-germanys-dual-training-system/a-17337959.

15. In its efforts to allow workers' representation in a multinational corporation, Volkswagen's workers' representatives responded to a call from unions like the metalworkers' union IG Metall by agreeing with the company to found a world works council. Volkswagen has now been joined by five other corporations (machine tool manufacturer SKF, Danone, the former Daimler-Chrysler, Renault, and Lego) that have also founded a world works council, accepted by management as being a serious partner for debate. Another example involves cooperation, since 1984, between the German works councils at Mercedes-Benz and the Trade Union Works Commission at Mercedes do Brasil. In 2002, the Brazilians downed tools for half an hour in support of their German colleagues at Daimler-Chrysler in Düsseldorf. In October 2003, three workers were dismissed from MAHLE, a supplier in São Bernardo, for producing substandard goods. The management of that company

refused to negotiate with the Trade Union Works Commission and the entire staff went on strike. After eight days, the company went to court and had the strike declared illegal. It dismissed the six members of the Works Commission.

On December 5, 2003, there was another demonstration at the plant. The union members at Daimler-Chrysler and VW in Germany then threatened to refuse to use any parts manufactured by MAHLE in their assembly lines, because their two companies had signed a social charter in which they pledged to use parts produced only by firms that respect fundamental rights. The secretary-general of the International Metalworkers' Federation submitted a letter of protest; union stewards and colleagues in Germany also signed a declaration demanding that the dismissed workers be reinstated. The outcome of these protests was successful. Source: "Workers' Representation, Commitment to Decent Work," Decent Work Worldwide (Düsseldorf: DGB Bildungswerk), http://www.decent-work-worldwide .org/index.php?option=com_content&task=blogcategory&id=53&Itemid=76.

16. Audit ("correspondence") studies in Germany that send out identical résumés to real job openings using names that are clearly German, Turkish, and other immigrant minorities find that it is considerably more difficult for immigrants and children of immigrants to land job interviews. See Frauke Lüpke-Narberhaus, "Vornamen-Diskriminierung: 'Keiner will einen Ali im Team haben,'" *Der Spiegel Online*, March 26, 2014, http://www.spiegel.de/schulspiegel/wissen/auslaendische -vornamen-migranten-diskriminierung-durch-firmen-bestaetigt-a-960855.html.

17. For more on the German dual system see Nancy Hoffman, *Schooling in the Workplace: How Six of the World's Best Vocational Education Systems Prepare Young People for Jobs and Life* (Cambridge, MA: Harvard Education Press, 2011).

7. The Math Puzzle

1. Andrew Hacker, "Is Algebra Necessary?," *New York Times*, July 29, 2012, www .nytimes.com/2012/07/29/opinion/sunday/is-algebra-necessary.html.

2. Joseph P. Williams, "Who Is Fighting for the Common Core?," *US News & World Report*, February 27, 2014, http://www.usnews.com/news/special-reports/a-guide-to -common-core/articles/2014/02/27/who-is-fighting-for-common-core.

3. Allison Fuller and Lorna Unwin, *Contemporary Apprenticeship: International Perspectives on an Evolving Model of Learning* (London: Routledge, 2012), p. 115.

4. Judith Summerfield, Paul Arcadia, Crys Benedict, David Crooks, Phyllis Curtis-Tweed, Erin Martineau, and Timothy Stevens, "CUNY Task Force on Retention: Creating the Conditions for Students to Succeed" (New York: City University of New York, Office of Academic Affairs, Office for Undergraduate Education, February 2006), http://www.hunter.cuny.edu/middle-states/repository/files/standard-8 /CUNY%20RetentionReportFINAL.pdf.

5. John P. Smith III, "Tracking the Mathematics of Automobile Production: Are Schools Failing to Prepare Students for Work?," *American Educational Research Journal* 36, no. 4 (1999): 835–78.

6. The growth of personal medical monitoring and fitness-related instruments (like FitBit) may reduce the need for many kinds of routine tests and data gathering by medical assistants. For now, this remains one of their main responsibilities.

7. Smith, "Tracking the Mathematics of Automobile Production."

8. Celia Hoyles and Richard Noss, "The Visibility of Meanings: Modelling the Mathematics of Banking," *International Journal of Computers for Mathematical Learning* 1, no. 1 (1996): 3–31.

9. Quoted in Rudolf Straesser, "Mathematical Means and Models from Vocational Contexts: A German Perspective," in *Education for Mathematics in the Workplace*, ed. Annie Bessot and Jim Ridgway (New York: Kluwer, 2000).

10. Ibid.

11. Ibid., 74.

12. Ibid., 76.

13. Donna Pearson, George Richardson, and Jennifer Sawyer, "The Oregon Applied Academics Project: Final Report," National Research Center for Career and Technical Education (Louisville, KY: University of Louisville, December 2013).

14. Elizabeth Often, "Crosswalks and Quality: Linking Math Language and CTE Standards," *Techniques: Connecting Education and Careers* 86, no. 3 (March 2011): 52–55, http://files.eric.ed.gov/fulltext/EJ926079.pdf.

15. CTEA Architecture students can receive a national certification aligned with industry standards.

8. Bringing the Dual System to the United States

1. German American Chambers of Commerce, "German American Business Outlook 2015," 7.

2. The consortiums are responsible for: establishing local boundaries and/or governance structure for the program (e.g., part of a larger school-to-work partnership or operating independently); selecting the program areas (i.e., printing, finance, etc.) and designing the local program; submitting applications for funding; hiring and/or arranging for a local youth apprenticeship coordinator; recruiting local businesses to hire youth apprentices; developing a marketing strategy to inform parents, students, employers, and the community about the program; developing recruitment and selection procedures for students applying for the program; developing local policies and procedures for the program; monitoring the program to ensure compliance with state and local requirements; ensuring that school services (counseling, health, etc.) are accessible to youth apprentices; developing linkages with other programs in the community as appropriate to assist with referrals and operation; complying with the Youth Apprenticeship Program Assurances in the state of Wisconsin Department of Workforce Development–approved application; and fiscal management of grant funds. Students are instructed by qualified teachers and skilled worksite mentors.

3. Specifically, participants have included the City of Wausau Public Works Department; Olson Tire and Auto Service, Wausau; POWER Engineers, Inc., Plover; Valley Communities Credit Union, Mosinee; Valley Communities Credit Union, Mosinee; Divine Savior Healthcare Extended Care, Portage; Hammer Chiropractic, LLC, Milton; A to Z Machine Company, Appleton; USEMCO, Inc., Tomah; Midwest Engineering Consultants, Glendale; Colby Metal, Colby. "Employer Testimonials," Youth Apprenticeship, State of Wisconsin, Department of Workforce Development, http://dwd.wisconsin.gov/youthapprenticeship/testimonial-employer.htm.

4. "Employer Testimonials," https://dwd.wisconsin.gov/youthapprenticeship/testimonial-employer.htm.

5. "Youth Apprenticeship Program," Georgia Department of Education, http://www.gadoe.org/Curriculum-Instruction-and-Assessment/CTAE/Pages/Youth-Apprenticeship-Program.aspx.

6. Harry J. Holzer and Robert I. Lerman, "Work-Based Learning to Expand Jobs and

Occupational Qualifications for Youth," Center on Budget and Policy Priorities, April 2, 2014, http://www.pathtofullemployment.org/wp-content/uploads/2014/04/holzerlerman.pdf.

7. J. C. Reindl, "Experts: Apprenticeship Degree Can Land In-Demand Job," *Detroit Free Press*, October 6, 2014, http://www.freep.com/story/money/business/michigan/2014/10/06/middle-skill-jobs-michigan-college-degree/16785777/.

8. "A Chattanooga Milestone: The Volkswagen Academy Opens," *Chattanooga Times Free Press*, March 31, 2010, http://chatterchattanooga.com/news/2010/mar/31/chattanooga-milestone-volkswagen-academy-opens/.

9. Ibid.

10. Alexander C. Kaufman, "Volkswagen Might Have Found a Fix for America's Youth Unemployment Problem," *Huffington Post*, February 16, 2015, http://www.huffingtonpost.com/2015/02/13/volkswagen-apprenticeship_n_6679084.html.

11. Chris Bryant, "A German Model Goes Global," *Financial Times*, May 21, 2012, http://www.ft.com/intl/cms/s/0/4f43b5c4-a32b-11e1-8f34-00144feabdc0.html#axzz3k3vjeWqc.

12. Paul Davidson, "More High Schools Teach Manufacturing Skills," *USA Today*, November 12, 2014, http://www.usatoday.com/story/money/business/2014/11/12/high-schools-teach-manufacturing-skills/17805483/.

13. Julie Bird, "A Big Investment in Charlotte Youth," *Charlotte Business Journal*, June 17, 2011, http://www.bizjournals.com/charlotte/print-edition/2011/06/17/a-big-investment-in-youth.html.

14. Ibid.

15. "What Is 5S?," Graphics Products, http://www.graphicproducts.com/tutorials/five-s/#ixzz3KUjurFmz.

16. A registered apprenticeship program is sponsored by an individual business or an employer association and may be partnered with a labor organization through a collective bargaining agreement. Upon finishing the training program, an apprentice earns a "Completion of Registered Apprenticeship" certificate, an industry-issued, nationally recognized credential that validates proficiency in an apprenticeable occupation.

17. Smith, *Lone Pursuit*.

18. The United Services Military Apprenticeship Program (USMAP) is a formal military training program executed by the Center for Personal and Professional Development that provides active duty U.S. Coast Guard, Marine Corps, and Navy service members the opportunity to improve their job skills and to complete their civilian apprenticeship requirements while they are on active duty.

19. This figure includes federal, state, and local funds directed at community college students. Robert I. Lerman, "Proposal 7: Expanding Apprenticeship Opportunities in the United States," The Hamilton Project, Brookings Institution, (June 19, 2014), http://www.brookings.edu/~/media/research/files/papers/2014/06/19_hamilton_policies_addressing_poverty/expand_apprenticeships_united_states_lerman.pdf.

20. See Lerman, "Can the United States Expand Apprenticeship?," 6.

21. Robert Lerman, Lauren Eyster, and Kate Chambers, *The Benefits and Challenges of Registered Apprenticeship: The Sponsors' Perspective*, Center on Labor, Human Services, and Population (Washington, DC: Urban Institute, March 2009), http://www.urban.org/research/publication/benefits-and-challenges-registered-apprenticeship-sponsors-perspective/view/full_report.

22. "Apprenticeship: An Important Avenue for Building a Skilled Workforce in South Carolina," South Carolina Chamber of Commerce (May 2002).

23. "Apprenticeships Provide Boost for SC Skilled-Worker Pool," Alliance Pickens, October 1, 2014, http://www.alliancepickens.com/cms/One.aspx?portalId=10351 &pageId=106503.

24. Nonetheless, in July 2014, the UAW announced that it was forming a new local union for VW employees based on the "works council" model. However, as of October 2014, VW still did not have a works council at the Chattanooga factory. Indeed, that month, Labor Secretary Thomas Perez traveled to Germany to meet with VW officials to learn more about how such a works council would function at the Tennessee plant. "U.S. Secretary of Labor Thomas Perez Visits Wolfsburg to Learn About Dual Vocational Training and Co-Determination at Volkswagen," *Volkswagen News*, October 28, 2014, http://www.vwvortex.com/news/volkswagen-news /u-s-secretary-labor-perez-visits-wolfsburg-learn-dual-vocational-training-co -determination-volkswagen/.

25. Steven Greenhouse, "VW to Allow Labor Groups to Represent Workers at Chattanooga Plant," *New York Times*, November 12, 2014, http://www.nytimes.com/2014 /11/13/business/vw-to-allow-labor-groups-to-represent-workers-at-chattanooga -plant.html.

9. Where Do We Go from Here?

1. Thomas Bailey, "Can Youth Apprenticeship Thrive in the United States?," *Educational Researcher* 22, no. 3 (April 1993): 4–10.

2. American Apprenticeship Grants, United States Department of Labor, http://www .dol.gov/apprenticeship/grants.htm.

3. "Carl D. Perkins Career and Technical Education Act of 2006," Laws & Guidance, Vocational Education, US Department of Education, last modified: March 3, 2007, http://www2.ed.gov/policy/sectech/leg/perkins/index.html.

4. States can match up to 5 percent of the state administrative funding provided through Perkins, and the balance of the 5 percent is returned to the state's formula funding. If states choose to match only 1 percent of state administrative funding, for example, the remaining 4 percent would not be provided for state administrative needs but would be returned to the state's formula funding for local schools and programs. Beyond this match, the amount of funding contributed by each state varies significantly. "A Look Inside: A Synopsis of CTE Trends," CareerTech, National Association of State Directors of Career Technical Education (February 2013), http://careertech.org/sites/default/files/SynopsisofCTETrends-Funding-2012.pdf.

5. "Ready to Work: Job-Driven Training and American Opportunity," Office of the White House (Washington, DC: July 2014), https://www.whitehouse.gov/sites /default/files/docs/skills_report.pdf.

6. Scott Paul, "No More Detroits," *Huffington Post*, July 19, 2013, http://www .huffingtonpost.com/scott-paul/detroit-manufacturing-jobs_b_3624937.html.

7. Zeke J. Miller, "Gov. Rick Snyder Explains How Detroit Was Saved," *Time*, December 11, 2014, http://time.com/3630172/gov-rick-snyder-explains-how-detroit-was -saved/.

8. "Oh-Penn Manufacturing," Oh-Penn Interstate Region, http://www.ohpenn.com /manufacturing/.

9. "Skills for Chicagoland's Future," http://www.skillsforchicagolandsfuture.com /about-us/.

10. Nelson D. Schwartz, "A New Look at Apprenticeships as a Path to the Middle Class," *New York Times*, July 13, 2015, http://www.nytimes.com/2015/07/14/business /economy/a-new-look-at-apprenticeships-as-a-path-to-the-middle-class.html?_r=0 4/6.

Appendix: What's Growing?

1. The entry education level for registered nurses is an associate's degree, but hospitals are increasingly requiring a four-year degree, and often experience or a specialty focus. As of 2010–2011, 55 percent of nurses held at least a bachelor's degree. See "The U.S. Nursing Workforce: Trends in Supply and Education," Health Resources and Services Administration, Bureau of Health Professions, National Center for Health Workforce Analysis (April 2013), http://bhpr.hrsa.gov /healthworkforce/reports/nursingworkforce/nursingworkforcefullreport.pdf.
2. Economic Modeling Specialists Intl., "Middle-Skill Spotlights: An Analysis of Four In-Demand Sectors with a Community College Focus" (2014), http://www .economicmodeling.com/cc-report2014/.
3. Health care occupations defined as middle-skill have seen particularly high growth rates in McAllen-Edinburg-Mission, Texas (74 percent). Fort Collins, Colorado, and Provo, Utah, have also seen considerable growth (both 57 percent), along with Phoenix and Fayetteville, Arkansas (both 55 percent). Ibid.
4. Ibid.
5. "Occupation Report: Middle Skills Jobs Outlook," Office of Institutional Effectiveness, Planning, and Research, College of Lake County (Fall 2014), http://dept .clcillinois.edu/res/misc/Middle%20Skill%20Job%20Outlook%20for%20CLC _FINAL%2020140910%20%28with%20cover%29.pdf.
6. Economic Modeling Specialists, "Middle-Skill Spotlights."
7. Ibid.
8. "Manpower Group Annual Survey Reveals U.S. Talent Shortages Persist in Skilled Trades, Engineers and IT Staff," ManpowerGroup, May 29, 2012, http://press .manpower.com/press/2012/talent-shortage/.
9. Economic Modeling Specialists, "Middle-Skill Spotlights."
10. Esther R. Fuchs, Dorian Warren, and Kimberly Bayer, *Expanding Opportunity for Middle Class Jobs in New York City: Minority Youth Employment in the Building and Construction Trades—Case Study: Edward J. Malloy Construction Skills Pre-Apprenticeship Program*. Case Study Series in Global Public Policy: 2014, Volume 2, Case 1 (New York: Columbia University School of International and Public Affairs, March 2014).
11. Tamar Jacoby, "This Way Up: Mobility in America," *Wall Street Journal*, July 22, 2014, http://www.wsj.com/articles/this-way-up-mobility-in-america-1405710779.
12. Ibid.
13. "Travel Means Jobs," U.S. Travel Association (2012), https://www.ustravel.org /sites/default/files/page/2012/08/e-Travel_Means_Jobs-2012.pdf.
14. An average of 13,033 tourism jobs were added each of those six years, totaling 78,200 jobs over the period. "NYC & Company Releases First-Ever Comprehensive New York City Tourism Industry Overview," NYC & Co. (July 8, 2013), http://www.nycandcompany.org/communications/nyc-company-releases-first-ever -comprehensive-new-york-city-tourism-industr.
15. JPMorgan Chase & Co., "Report Reveals Solutions to Fill Vital Healthcare and Technology Jobs in New York City," (October 30, 2014), http://www.jpmorganchase .com/corporate/Corporate-Responsibility/pr-new-skills-gap.htm.

16. Economic Modeling Specialists, "Middle-Skill Spotlights."
17. JPMorgan Chase, "Report Reveals Solutions."
18. Ibid.
19. Sean Kilcarr, "Trucking Job Growth: A Bellwether for Better Times?," *Fleet Owner*, May 24, 2014, http://fleetowner.com/blog/trucking-job-growth-bellwether-better -economic-times.
20. Ibid.
21. US STEM workers who haven't attained a bachelor's degree earn about 10 percent higher, or an average salary of $53,000, than non-STEM employees with the same educational background. Chevron, "The Jobs of Today," http://www.theatlantic .com/sponsored/chevron-stem-education/the-jobs-of-today/196/. Additionally, workers with some college will earn higher wages on average than associate degree holders in eight STEM occupations by 2018. See Achieve, Inc., "The Future of the U.S. Workforce: Middle Skills Jobs and the Growing Importance of Postsecondary Education" (September 2012), http://www.achieve.org/files/MiddleSkillsJobs.pdf.

and the steel towns of Gary, Indiana, the same relentless destruction of American industry gathered force in the '70s and '80s. By 2010, when Katherine moved to Baltimore, there was virtually nothing left of what had once been a mighty industrial city. In its place lay acres of burned-out, abandoned housing, a thriving drug trade, and shocking murder rates. This twisted history was chronicled in *The Wire*, a five-season chronicle of life in a hollowed-out city, wracked by corruption, poverty, and deadly violence. There is nothing so tragic as to see thousands of young people, especially young black men, with so few options for a family wage. Not only do they suffer when there are such meager alternatives; their families do as well. Would-be breadwinners were ending up in prison by the millions, having succumbed to the drug trade where nothing else was growing.

Reskilling America: Learning to Labor in the Twenty-First Century was conceived as an effort to imagine what kinds of changes in the preparation of young people for the labor market might make a difference in cities like Baltimore. As industry began to filter back to the United States, the search for the "next economy" was attracting the attention of think tanks like Brookings, urban mayors, state development officials hoping to revive the tax base, and even university presidents worried about whether public safety problems would deter parents from sending their children to schools like Johns Hopkins or Yale. Whatever prospects there might be for giving birth to a new industrial renaissance in cities such as Detroit were contingent not only on making the case to the private sector that the time (and price) was right to reinvest in those abandoned factory sites, but that the skilled labor would be there to make it worth their while.

Answering that question is the mission of this book. The core insights that inform it came initially from a set of interviews conducted during Katherine's time as a faculty member at Princeton University. With the support of the Woodrow Wilson School Faculty Research fund, and the assistance of Dr. Alexandra Murphy, then a doctoral candidate in sociology and now an assistant professor at the University of Michigan, a sample of graduates from New York's low-performing high schools was interviewed ten years after their graduation. All sixty of them had attended schools with poor track records on the Regents examinations. We were interested in what had become of them in the labor market. Among the most successful of these people—by that time in their late twenties—were former students of New York's remaining vocational schools. They had risen quickly into the ranks of stable, decently paid jobs. Not all of them had gone into the trades for which they had trained as teenagers. Some had gone an entirely different route, finding their way to college and in some instances into doctoral programs. What they had in common, especially compared to New Yorkers who attended "zone" or "neighborhood schools" without a vocational curriculum, was a positive experience of education. Despite their (undeserved) reputation as dumping grounds, the work-focused schools like Aviation High School turned out to be serious institutions, with dedicated teachers and committed students, many of whom commuted many hours to get to school in the first place.

It was these interviews that first led us to be interested in the rich possibilities of vocational education. Joanne Wang Golann, another Princeton sociology doctoral student, contributed a long memo on the history of vocational education in the twentieth century, with a special emphasis on community colleges. Noting the similarity of intention (linking school to work), Katherine enlisted the interest of Harvard sociologist Mary Brinton, an expert on education and inequality in Japan. Brinton made us aware of the extraordinary success of the Japanese system of job placement through vocational schools that prevailed before the "bubble burst" and the country began the long period of economic stagnation from which it still has not recovered. Kathleen Thelen at MIT and Claus Offe at the Hertie School in Berlin have done a great deal to explain the historical origins of the German dual-education system and conversations with both have been very helpful.

Looking for models of robust training for high-performance manufacturing, the German example was an obvious model to emulate. We learned much of what we know about it from Professor Thomas Bals, an expert on the German dual-education system at the University of Osnabrück. Bals was visiting Columbia University's Teachers College in 2012 and was kind enough not only to spend many hours talking about the complex structure of dual education, but organized an opportunity to visit a number of German companies—from the large steel mills in Osnabrück and the mammoth Volkswagen plant in Wolfsburg to small

244 | Acknowledgments and a Note on Research

family firms in the HVAC installation business—for Katherine to see in
the summer of 2013. Bals and his marvelous research colleagues, Janika
Grunau and Sibylle Drexler, traveled across the western part of the country, from Osnabrück to Berlin, translating where necessary, to ensure
that we would make the most of the opportunity to interview firm leaders, managers, and apprentices themselves. Many people took time out
from their busy workdays to educate us about the German apprenticeship model, from hiring managers at GMH and training directors at ZF,
to the company leadership in family-owned firms like Hermann Mohle
and Amazone.

This exposure confirmed the wisdom of the German approach, while
making it clear that their dual-education system required levels of coordination and common cause among institutions that are often rivalrous
in the United States: labor unions, firms, and educational institutions.
Hermann Nehls, then responsible for the union contribution to dual
education in his role at the High Council of the German Trade Unions,
devoted an afternoon in Berlin to explaining not only how the policy
process supported this remarkable achievement but what the prospects
were for its spread throughout the European Union.

Nicola Michels, the vice president of the German American Chamber of Commerce, first introduced us to the notion that this remarkable
system of labor market preparation had a future in the United States. In
collaboration with the German embassy, thousands of German subsidiaries in the United States were planning to import their own methods of
training, creating new collaborations to train American workers to fuel
the increasing demand for new workers in a reviving manufacturing
industry. Much of that action is unfolding in the Sunbelt right-to-work
states of the Southeast. To understand firsthand what it would mean to
transfer the German approach to American soil, and what dedicated American enthusiasts of vocational training were achieving on their own, we
turned to many generous people, including: Carla Whitlock, apprenticeship
consultant, South Carolina Technical College System; Brad Neese, director
of Apprenticeship Carolina; Patrick Lark, design engineer at Cornell Dubilier, Greenville, South Carolina; Mike Bryan, training specialist at the
Bosch Rexroth Fountain Inn Manufacturing Facility; Warren Sneed
Cooper, human resource manager, Cooper Standard Automotive, Spar-

tanburg, South Carolina; and Ken Hitchcock, director of the Pickens County Career and Technology Center, Pickens County, South Carolina.

Although the Southeast seems to be farthest ahead in adapting German approaches to training, in conjunction with German firms, signs of revival in vocational education are also evident in the Northeast. We learned much of what there was to know, especially on the educational side of this equation, from Steve Wynn, assistant principal at the High School for Construction Trades, Engineering and Architecture in Ozone Park, Queens; Jean Mallon, principal of Tri-County Regional Vocational High School in Franklin, Massachusetts; Mary-Ellen MacLeod, director of cooperative education at Tri-County Regional Vocational High School in Franklin, Massachusetts; Mike Adams, principal of Cape May County Technical High School, Cape May Court House, New Jersey; Caterina Lafergola, principal of Automotive High School, Greenpoint, Brooklyn, New York; and Deno Charalambous, principal of Aviation High School in Long Island City, New York. Their students welcomed us into their shop classes and patiently explained what they were learning and why it mattered to them. Their names have all been changed, as promised, but we thank them for giving us insight into the beginning of their work lives.

Nigeria Williams (real name) came to New York City to accept the high honor of being named the 2014 "trainee of the year" by the German American Chamber of Commerce for the work she does at MTU. Katherine serves every year on the jury for this prize and was pleased to interview Nigeria, and the director of Human Resources at MTU, Arjonetta Gaillard, who is responsible for developing the German-certified apprenticeship program in their company. At seventeen years old, this African American student can look forward to a high wage in a skilled trade. That means a lot to Nigeria, who lives in a community where most of the alternatives do not pay a living wage.

The results of all of this fieldwork were hundreds of pages of notes, compiled over a number of years. Translating them into this book required time and resources. We are grateful to Johns Hopkins University, where Katherine was supported by faculty research funds provided to her as the dean of arts and sciences. President Ronald Daniels generously enabled her to continue her own vocation as a social scientist and enabled the support for Hella Winston's postdoctoral position there. Chancellor

Index

About the Authors

KATHERINE S. NEWMAN is the author of twelve books on topics ranging from urban poverty to middle-class economic insecurity to school violence. Her *No Shame in My Game: The Working Poor in the Inner City* received the Robert F. Kennedy Book Award and the Sidney Hillman Foundation Book Award. Newman, who has held senior teaching and administrative positions at Johns Hopkins, Harvard, and Princeton, is currently Provost and Torrey Little Professor of Sociology at the University of Massachusetts, Amherst.

HELLA WINSTON, a sociologist and investigative journalist, is the author of *Unchosen: The Hidden Lives of Hasidic Rebels*. She has held postdoctoral fellowships in sociology at Princeton and Johns Hopkins and is currently a senior fellow at the Schuster Institute for Investigative Journalism at Brandeis University. She lives in New York City.